The Art of Short Selling

The Art of Short Selling

Kathryn F. Staley

JOHN WILEY & SONS, INC.

New York • Chichester • Brisbane • Toronto • Singapore • Weinheim

The MetaStock™ charts in this book are used by permission of Equis International, Inc., 3950 South 700 East, Suite 100, Salt Lake City, UT 84107, 1-800-882-3040 or 801-265-8886, Fax 801-265-3999, http://www.equis.com.

This text is printed on acid-free paper.

Published by John Wiley & Sons, Inc.

Library of Congress Cataloging-in Publication Data

Staley, Kathryn F.
The art of short selling / Kathryn F. Staley.
p. cm.
Includes index
ISBN 0-471-14632-3 (cloth : alk. paper)
1. Short selling. 2. Speculation. 3. Stocks. I. Title.
HG6041.S728 1997
332.63'228—dc20 96-30153

Printed in the United States of America

10 9 8 7 6 5 4 3 2

Bears can make money only if the bulls push up stocks to where they are overpriced and unsound.

Bulls always have been more popular than bears in this country because optimism is so strong a part of our heritage. Still, over-optimism is capable of doing more damage than pessimism since caution tends to be thrown aside.

To enjoy the advantages of a free market, one must have both buyers and sellers, both bulls and bears. A market without bears would be like a nation without a free press. There would be no one to criticize and restrain the false optimism that always leads to disaster.

Bernard Baruch

Preface

In the 1980s, short selling was a discipline practiced by a cadre of smart investors who made returns in excess of the market in good years and bad. The analytical methods of those investors were characterized by prodigious analysis attentive to the quality of earnings, quality of assets, and quality of management. They believed that the market, inefficient in the short run, would eventually recognize a bad business run by incompetent managers and that inflated stock prices would settle to levels consistent with the earnings power of the bad businesses they had uncovered.

The years 1991 to 1993 decimated the population of short sellers and the net worth of anyone that persisted in believing that the truth of financial statements would win out. Those years saw the ascendancy of mutual funds, of momentum investing, and of the short squeeze as an accepted investment philosophy. What happened was that companies with questionable financial statements had a heyday of stock-price appreciation. What also happened was that short sellers got killed.

In 1994, the problem companies, one by one, began to give up the ghost, and short selling worked again for a year. Snapple, Cott, Scoreboard, Bell Sports—reading their financials mattered, and the flaws within the company structure again affected the price.

By 1996, the concept of shorting for profit was thought by the smart circles of Wall Street to be extinct or the province of fools. Nobody would admit publicly that they did it.

Then came the setback of the summer, and short sellers once again got respect—and made money.

In recent months, the massacre of the most visible short targets (Iomega, Diana Corp., Presstek) suggests that perhaps we can get back to reading financial statements and doing analytical work and forget about on-line stock touts, short squeezes, and thundering mutual fund purchases.

Those bull-market years taught all of us who continued to practice the arcane art of short selling to beware of manias, and they taught us fear. But, even in the worst of times, the curiosity and pleasure of detecting the truth kept some of us idly punching our calculators, watching inventories and cash flow, reading an occasional prospectus.

"What's the point?" we were asked, particularly by the money managers who had sworn off shorting. The point is that the toughest call for investors—even in a bull market—is when to sell. The best managers either sell stocks soon with a small loss, realizing a mistake, or sell stocks later, noting a change in prospect after gains, when prices begin to drop. Short-selling skills teach us the discipline of anxiety, of when to be scared. The analytical wisdom shows us when the numbers start to turn bad in a sacred-cow holding or which stocks not to buy at all. The simplest techniques work year in and year out. Rising inventories predicted the decline of U.S. Surgical and Royal Appliance and Scoreboard and Snapple and Bell Sports, even in our dumb years. Selling shareholders alerted us to Autotote and Michaels Stores.

I have used classic examples to illustrate the analytical methodology of short sellers, examples of how to find the rotten apples before they drop. Accompanying these examples are tables showing short interest, balance sheets, income statements, and so on. There are also figures showing short interest and graphs of stock prices. Chapter 3 starts with the simplest short sale: the bubble companies complete with new issue prospectus and products that might not exist at all. Chapter 4 talks about fads and franchises and shows how to uncover nonrecurring revenues, how to track insider transactions, and how to evaluate business plans. Chapter 5 follows several full-blown growth companies and suggests ways to determine when they stop growing. Chapter 6 attempts to detail more complicated accounting tricks that companies use to obscure the truth about the health of their business. Chapter 7 is about tracking cash flow and financing needs in companies that suck money from the financial markets without paying stockholders in earnings. Chapter 8 tells the stories of companies that resort to selling out when access to money fails (via earnings or financing streams). Chapter 9 is about leveraged companies and cyclical business downturns.

As the company complexity increases, so do the analytical skills: A no-product company is easier to analyze than a one-product company, one store easier than a franchise system. Each case should show you the detecting exercise for at least one of the quality problems. Chapter 10 brings them all together—quality of earnings, quality of assets, and quality of management—in a classic short story.

When I first started selling short, only one book, written in 1932, detailed the practice. The veritable demise of short selling during the great bull market has silenced the few talkative short sellers who remain. These collected case studies should remind all of us how to sell stocks or how to sell them short—particularly when the market turns flat or down and investors are not as forgiving of bad business plans and bungled earnings efforts. Short selling or merely selling might be fun or profitable again as it has been off and on for centuries. And for a certain group of cynics with a penchant for quality, the sound of a stock crashing nicely will evoke a knowing and whimsical smile.

KATHRYN F. STALEY

New York, New York
November 1996

Acknowledgments

My particular thanks to the short sellers whose ideas and analytical methods appear in this book, as well as to the money managers who shared their thoughts on short selling.

In collecting data on case studies, I was assisted by Jim Chanos, Scott Bessent, Charles Hobbs, Andrea Lerner, Bill McGarr, Caroline Ford, Sue Hardiman, Deborah Lamb, Amanda Macklowe, and Jeff Perry. The stock price charts and short-interest data following many of the case studies were compiled from public information.

K. F. S.

Contents

Part One

Facts and Practitioners

1
Overview: Wealth with Risk

When Media Vision finally went belly up, when Scoreboard matched its spectacular ascent with an equally spectacular descent, when Bank of New England took major bites from its equity capital with real estate write-offs, a small group of people on Wall Street benefited. This is a book about the people who profit from collapse and who specialize in detecting disaster and about the methods those people use to track the demise of companies, like equity seismographers watching for the first tremors of an earthquake.

Short sellers unearth facts from financial statements and from observation to ascertain that a stock is overpriced. They act with conventional wisdom—they buy low and sell high, but they sell before they buy. When the stock of Crazy Eddie, a retail electronics chain, expanded like a balloon gone berserk, short sellers studied the company and saw that inventories were growing faster than sales, that management made more money than the stockholders, and that competition was brutal in retail electronics in New York City. Wall Street continued to puff up the Crazy Eddie balloon in a frenzy of enthusiasm, so the short sellers sold at a high price—$40 a share—stock they did not own. When the stock collapsed and Crazy Eddie Antar himself (founder and ex-corporate chief) disappeared, the short sellers bought the stock for $2 a share to close the trade and to make a profit of $38 a share in less than a year.

◆ *Who Sells Short?*

Selling short is selling a security that the seller does not own but promises to deliver by borrowing it from someone else, in order to profit from the subsequent price drop. *Selling long*, the opposite, is selling a security that the seller does own and that is, thus, long in the account of the seller. Like sellers of stock who own it before selling it, short sellers expect the price appreciation to be limited. They also bet that the price will go down after the stock is sold.

Specialists on the exchanges, market makers, and block traders all sell short to provide market liquidity. When a large order causes temporary trading imbalances that would result in volatile prices, trading professionals create supply by selling short.

Arbitrageurs also buy one security and sell another one short to realize profits on temporary price disparities in markets or like securities.

Institutions, money managers, and individuals sell short to speculate on price declines. Short sellers who sell in anticipation of price declines are generally *information-based traders*—traders whose valuation studies show that a security is overpriced and who trade on that information. Their bets contribute to pricing efficiencies in the market.

Portfolio managers also sell short to hedge another holding. If the outlook for the airline industry is mixed, the managers might sell one airline stock and buy another to hedge the outlook on the industry while profiting from individual security characteristics.

Bernard Baruch, Joseph Kennedy, and many other financial titans of the first decades of the twentieth century were adept at selling short; in fact, they used the technique as casually as buying and selling stocks and bonds. Before 1983, no solely short funds existed, and short selling was primarily the venue of hedge-fund managers and sophisticated individuals. Short selling—fundamental, information-based, non-computer-motivated short selling—is practiced as a full-time profession by only 10 or 15 people in the United States. From 1988 to 1992, additional short sellers expanded the ranks after the 1990 market correction. The ensuing bull-market years have served to reduce the number of full-time short sellers to a handful. The mystery that surrounds the group is increased by an occasional ground swell from executives who malign both the practice and its cabal of disciples as unpatriotic, destructive, and self-serving.

Short selling is perceived by professionals, as well as by casual investors, as risky and speculative. A frequent criticism of short selling as an investment alternative states that stocks can go only to zero on the way down, but to infinity on the way up. Short sellers respond that they have seen a lot more stocks at zero than at infinity. Because they take greater risks than other investors, short sellers must be confident that their conclusions are correct, and they must have strong evidence to support cases for price declines. Because reverses are terrifying and sudden, the burden of evidence rests on a solid, careful analysis completed before the stock is shorted.

Short sellers are usually hard-working, creative people who enjoy going against the grain and competing with the mind of Wall Street (represented by the prices of stocks). They enjoy solving puzzles that other people find frustrating, confusing, or unsolvable.

◆ *Why Opportunities for Short Selling Exist*

Money managers and individuals alike find that it is tough to make consistent profits in the financial markets. Why, then, do short sellers always find broad gaps in stock valuation that can lead to dramatic price drops?

Clearly, short selling is a niche, and a small one relative to the stock market as a whole, and that situation creates inefficiencies in stock pricing. Several studies in security-price behavior suggest that there is theoretical justification for short selling. Brokerage houses add to pricing discrepancies with buy-side vigor and with reliance on computer analytical models.

Edward M. Miller, professor of financial economics at the University of New Orleans, proposed an amendment to the efficient market theory when he suggested that "prices are bounded by limits set by the buying and short-selling of informed investors."[1] The upper limits of securities prices are set by short sellers who will stop the ascent of the price if the potential return is great enough to augment the costs of being short. The short seller's ability to sell becomes the critical variable in the upper-price boundary. Because, Miller argued, there are many restrictions on short selling (institutional prohibitions, transaction costs, borrowable shares), stocks trade not at one efficient price but within a band of prices. The dynamics of Miller's theory of the bounded efficient market suggest that portfolio managers are well advised to look for mispriced stocks to sell because more overpriced than undervalued stocks can be identified.

Paul Asquith and Lisa Meulbroek went several steps further in "An Empirical Investigation of Short Interest." In a study that tracked stock prices on high short-interest stocks from 1976 to 1990, they found that there was a strong negative correlation between stock price and high short interest and that abnormal excess returns of 120 percent (or 5.5 percent a year) could have been earned by shorting stocks with *high short interest* (defined as "short interest greater than 5 percent of shares outstanding") from 1976 to 1990. They commented that this study "provides a foundation for the view that stock prices reflect positive information more efficiently than negative information."[2] Large short-interest ratios, therefore, appear to be more bearish than the common wisdom predicts.

Research studies by Henry Latane, Charles Jones, and Richard Rendleman, Jr., provide evidence that negative-earnings surprises affect stock prices to a greater degree than positive-earnings surprises and that the effect persists over time.[3] The common wisdom that there is no such thing as one bad quarter has a statistical basis. Robert Hagin coined the phrase "torpedo stocks" to describe the effect on a port-folio of a negative earnings surprise. "Stocks become torpedos when very high earnings expectations give way to earnings disappointments. . . . The higher one's expectation for earnings growth, the deeper the disappointment if the expectation is not realized."[4]

Academic research on speculative bubbles shows what short sellers have known for centuries: Evidence exists that bubbles form and then collapse. Cohn Camerer reviewed the research, both theoretical and experimental, on bubbles in an article for the *Journal of Economic Surveys*.[5] Economists are attempting to discover why prices vary from intrinsic value. One theory suggests that fads linger in the security market because institutional investors are too averse to risk and too aware of short-term relative performance to bet against the fad and sell.

A bias against selling that exists in the market allows pricing disparities to remain; brokerage houses add to that bias. Most brokerage stock recommendations range from *buy* to *hold*, with few analysts willing to rank stocks as *sells*. Analysts are constrained by corporate finance relationships or by their need to maintain communication channels with company executives.

Donald Trump's March 1990 attack on analyst Marvin Roffman and Roffman's subsequent firing by Janney Montgomery Scott, Inc., gave credence to an analyst's fear of honesty. Company executives have gotten more aggressive in defending their stocks against adverse sentiment, and lawsuits have proliferated in response to the occasional Wall Street analyst's frank statement of negative opinion. Sy Jacobs at Mabon, Nugent & Company was placed in "investor relations Siberia" because of his sale recommendation on Household International, Inc.[6] Charles Peabody at Kidder, Peabody & Co., Inc., was cut off by Valley National Bank and NCNB after offering negative opinions. David Korus at Kidder Peabody raised the ire of executives at Dell Computer with his sale recommendation. Some executives apparently feel an open market should not provide a forum for discussion or dissent, so the quality of analysis and information declines with the restrictions on speech.

Brokerage-house estimates also tend to be over optimistic, thereby providing potential for negative surprises with greater regularity than positive surprises. The concentration on optimism makes for more inefficiency in short-term stock prices and gives prices a positive bias.

◆ *Analytical Techniques: How to Detect the First Tremors of the Quake*

Terminal short sellers (as they are called to distinguish them from technical or computer-model short sellers) spend their days identifying publicly traded companies with flaws that might cause bankruptcy or major income reversals, companies that are overvalued relative to the present value of their potential stream of income. Securities sold short in their portfolios are sometimes not bought back for years—until the prices in the market reflect the perceived condition of the company or the flaw becomes apparent to Wall Street.

How do short sellers work? What signs do they look for so they can capture the price anomalies? How do they then analyze the securities and where do they find the data?

Short-sale candidates cluster in three broad categories:

1. Companies in which management lies to investors and obscures events that will affect earnings.
2. Companies that have tremendously inflated stock prices—prices that suggest a speculative bubble in company valuation.
3. Companies that will be affected in a significant way by changing external events.

Short sellers are always alert to publicly traded corporations that fall into these three categories. No computer screen or set of screens and no consistent mechanical method can capture this universe. And that is what makes short selling lucrative: It takes too much work for most people to fool with it.

So how do short sellers find the stocks? They read hundreds of financial statements. They talk to everybody about everything: to baby-sitters about tennis shoe trends, to children about toy purchases, to doctors about new equipment or drugs. They talk to brokers, money managers, and company executives about competitors and suppliers. They read newspapers, business journals, and trade papers like the *Poultry Times* and *Gaming and Wagering Business*. They listen for stocks about which people are excited and pay attention to trends in regional real estate and retail purchases.

When they find an industry that appears to be overvalued, they begin to look for more specific company evidence. Clues that something is amiss in a corporation are the starting point of a short seller's quest. These trail signs are grouped around several characteristics:

- Accounting gimmickry: clues that the financial statements do not reflect the true state of corporate health.
- Insider sleaze: signs that insiders consider the company a personal bank or think the stock should be sold.
- Fad or bubble stock pricing: usually marked by a stellar price rise over a short period.
- A gluttonous corporate appetite for cash.
- Overvalued assets or an ugly balance sheet.

If one or more of those characteristics is apparent in a company, short sellers proceed in the quest for comprehensive information. To piece together the story of a corporation, short sellers do labor-intensive work. A framework for stock analysis follows this rough outline:

1. Short sale analysis is dependent on financial analysis—cash-flow pro formas, balance-sheet strength, and the quality of earnings. Start with at least two years of company financials and analyze the numbers by using the fundamentals of financial analysis: balance-sheet and rate-of-return ratios, income-statement analysis, cash-flow breakouts. Overlay traditional analysis with an especially tough look at quality of assets and earnings. Work from the 10Qs and 10Ks because these versions of the quarterly and annual reports that are filed with the Securities and Exchange Commission (SEC) have more data and less puff.
2. Use the proxy and the SEC insider filings to track management's salary, stock activity, and attitude toward the company and its stockholders.
3. Check in the marketplace to see what the execution of the business strategy looks like—look at the products, the competitors, the suppliers of production inputs.

4. Follow the trading patterns, the short interest, and the ownership by watching price and volume, 13D filings (investor filings with the SEC when the investor attains a 5 percent or greater position), and institutional ownership.
5. Read anything in the media—magazines, newspapers—and the Wall Street research pool to determine consensus.
6. Watch everything about the company over time to see what happens, how earnings and price progress, what changes.

The main precept of short-selling analysis is bulk. Short sellers accumulate volumes of disparate facts and observations, then they make an intuitive leap based on the information at hand. Frequently, the signs point to large problems that will not be revealed in total until after the collapse. Crazy Eddie had slowing inventory turnover. Short sellers did not find out until after the stock collapsed that the building inventory was bogus. So short sellers have to be able to make a logical leap without complete information. They have to trust their experience and judgment. They have to know where to look for signs and what the impact of those signs might be.

Where does the material come from? The financial documents and proxy can come from the company, from a service that microfiches SEC documents, or from a library that subscribes to a microfiche service.

Insider transactions and 13Ds are also reported to the SEC. *Barron's* and the *Wall Street Journal* print the largest of them. Several newsletters, such as *Vickers* and the *Insider Chronicle*, copy all of them from the SEC and have on-line computer subscriptions as well as weekly or monthly hard-copy subscriptions.

Short interest is disclosed in the *Wall Street Journal* and *Barron's* around the 20th of the month for the New York Stock Exchange (NYSE) and the American Stock Exchange (AMEX) and around the 25th for the National Association of Securities Dealers Automated Quotation System (NASDAQ). The exchanges report this information as of stock-transaction settlement day, the 15th. These lists do not include all short positions—just positions over a certain arbitrary cutoff point, currently greater than 250,000 shares short. Standard and Poor's *Daily*

Stock Price Record and the *Quarterly History Tape* also provide short-interest data.

Brokerage reports, the least useful information on the list, can be obtained from the brokerage houses (sometimes) or from the company. Some business-library databases also include brokerage reports on-line.

Any major public library has tremendous research resources, including computerized searching by company name for article citations and summaries, industry information, and price history. Dow Jones and Dialog on-line computer services also can search for articles and price histories through a large pool of business publications.

The accounting-based analysis is not difficult to do, but it takes time, patience, and a suspension of belief. A Wall Street pundit recently commented that this level of fine-toothed work is too costly for brokerage analysts or institutional managers to perform because of the time and skill required. The lack of attention by other professional investors to these financial details provides the inefficiency in information dissemination that is so central to the short seller's art.

Insider information is never a problem with short sellers because management rarely talks to known vociferous critics. Typically, short sellers have an adversarial relationship with corporate insiders. One of the maxims of short analysis is that public information should provide all an analyst needs to know: Careful reading of SEC-filed documents and observation of the execution of the corporate business plan in the marketplace should tell the story of the company.

There is a certain measure of the moralist in short sellers. As detectives on Wall Street, they enjoy revealing the emperor without his clothes and relish the collapse of an overvalued empire. Some short-seller targets in recent years have been highly touted corporate giants with well-developed personal-selling skills, secure in their ability to finance shaky businesses with public funds. Charles Keating, Jr., of American Continental (see Chapter 9), the Zises brothers of Integrated Resources (see Chapter 7), Morley Thompson of Baldwin United (see Chapter 2), Fred Carr of First Executive (see Chapter 7), Gene Phillips of Southmark (see Chapter 13), and Frank Lorenzo of Texas Air (see Chapter 8) were all the gratifying quarry of short sellers.

Short sellers normally disagree with Wall Street and enjoy beating highly paid, highly visible Wall Street analysts. The conflict of interest inherent in the job description of a Wall Street analyst strikes short sellers as a consistent reason for flawed information. Analysts are paid to follow stocks, yet many rarely read financial documents with care. Short sellers are contemptuous of analytical skills that primarily regurgitate the management line.

◆ *Who Can Benefit from the Wisdom of Short Sellers?*

Any student of the markets should find the analytical techniques of short sellers interesting, particularly during a period when fundamental analysis is supplanted by computers and technicians and when research departments are understaffed and overrun by investment bankers.

Anyone who buys stocks, loans money to corporations, or runs a company can benefit from the collective wisdom of short sellers. Identifying the tragic flaw in a business long before the company's demise is a timely skill in any economy and an irreplaceable one in a recession.

Institutional managers should find the discipline enticing on several levels: as an analytical methodology, as a means of enhancing returns through avoidance of torpedoes, and as a hedging technique. As a methodology, short-sale analysis is not significantly different from classic fundamental work. It places heavier emphasis on cash-flow dissection and on the reality underlying reported earnings. It attempts to identify the long death rattle of a company in decline. In security analysis, managers are rarely trained by using examples of poorly run companies. Yet it is easier to identify trouble spots if education includes examples of corporate mistakes. Short selling is, therefore, another tool in a tradesman's bag.

In his essay, "The Loser's Game," Charles Ellis wrote, "Almost all of the really big trouble that you're going to experience in the next year is in your portfolio right now; if you could reduce some of those really big problems, you might come out the winner in the Loser's Game."[7] As an equity research skill, short selling gives analysts the ability to avert disaster in good times as well as in bad. And it gives them the ability to enjoy the joke when a sham is discovered because the fun might not be at their expense. The art of short selling trains analysts to avoid torpedo stocks or to profit from them.

Short sales should be considered by portfolio managers who want to hedge or to decrease the volatility of total returns by setting the market sensitivity of their portfolios with more precision. Because short positions have a negative correlation with a stock portfolio, a balanced portfolio of shorts and longs can even out the market effect, reduce risk, and afford returns based purely on stock selection.

Individuals can employ the analytical techniques of short selling to avoid owning stocks that will explode otherwise well-conceived portfolios and to escape the new-issue frenzy of rabid retail brokers. Knowledge of professional methods of short selling saves money in the long run.

The main weakness of professional short sellers—an inability to judge the timing of collapses—is a strong argument for attention to short selling by any entity that owns stocks. Short sellers are consistently years too early when they sell stocks. Stockholders are always slow to sell even when the evidence is irrefutable and the future for profit bleak. The years of irrational price behavior in a deteriorating company provide stock owners with years to sell a problem stock. Portfolio managers or individuals who attempt to educate themselves about the reasons for escalating short interest in stock holdings can radically improve the returns by avoiding torpedo hits—they can use the weakness of the discipline as a strength.

◆ *Mechanics and Risks*

Short sellers of common stocks borrow stock from a brokerage house to sell in the organized markets. They must put up 50 percent of the short-sale price to satisfy the current Federal Reserve requirement. The broker, in turn, gets the to-be-borrowed stock from customer margin accounts or from another broker dealer.

If the short sale is made on the NYSE, the AMEX, or NASDAQ, the trade can be executed only on an uptick or on a zero-plus tick—the stock price must move up before a short sale can be made.

After the short sale is made, the brokerage house uses the closing security prices to compute a daily or weekly gain or loss on the positions. If the price has moved down, the seller has use of the funds for security purchases, short sales, or money market purchases. If the price moves up, the seller must put up more collateral (see Table 1.1).

Although most brokerage houses do not pay interest on the short-sale proceeds, a few do pay interest at a negotiated percentage of the broker call rate. Most managed short funds or hedge funds receive 60 to 90 percent of the broker call rate on short credit balances. The borrower is also charged by the broker for all cash and stock dividend payments on the short positions.

To close a position, the seller must buy the stock and deliver the shares to the broker, who then returns them to the original owner. (The Appendix has a detailed explanation of the brokerage and margin requirements.)

The short seller of common stocks runs two risks:

1. The price moves up after the stock is sold, thereby requiring more cash infusions into the account.
2. Or the lender demands the return of the stock.

The brokerage house can ask for the return of the stock if the client who owns the stock sells it or wants physical delivery or if the lending broker requires it for similar reasons. At that time, if the broker cannot find another position to loan to the short seller, the customer will be forced to buy it at the current market price (a buy-in).

Short sellers fear most a sustained rally in a stock followed by a forced buy-in of their position, resulting in a loss out of their control. For that reason, short sellers tend to be secretive about positions in stocks with *small floats* (shares available for purchase, or outstand-

Table 1.1 A Simplified Example of a Short Sale

A client sells short 100 shares of XYZ @ $100:

Sell 100 shares × $100	=	$10,000	
Reg T* requirement 50%	=	+ 5,000	client deposit-equity
		$15,000	credit balance

If the stock declines to $80 per share:

$15,000	credit balance
– 8,000	current market value
$ 7,000	equity

If the client chooses to cover the stock by buying it at $80 per share and to close out the margin account, the client would make a $2,000 profit plus the return of the initial investment of $5,000, for a total of $7,000, excluding commissions:

$7,000	equity
–5,000	initial deposit
$2,000	profit

If the stock increases to $120 per share:

$15,000	credit balance
–12,000	current market value
$ 3,000	equity

If the client chooses to cover at $120, the client would incur a loss of $2,000.

*See Appendix.

ing shares minus insider and 5-percent positions), particularly in companies with floats below 10 million shares. Despite popular fears that short sellers band together to pound small companies into the ground, the reality is that a good idea is closely held by its originator. Any action that forces owners to sell can create a shortage of stock to borrow if the new owner takes delivery of the position. When short sellers go public with a stock-sale idea by communicating the story to the press and the stock has fewer than 10 million shares outstanding, they are betting on an immediate collapse to give them the opportunity to cover the borrowed shares at lower prices. Generally, however, publicity accompanied by only a slight downturn in price can create more problems for short sellers than it solves because the limelight might trigger buy-ins.

To avoid the risk of buy-ins, some short sellers short only *large cap stocks* (stocks whose market price times the number of shares outstanding is greater than $500 million), and some never discuss positions or talk to reporters. The published short-interest columns are the only public sources of information about short sellers' activities.

◆ *Current Market Statistics and Growth Prospects*

Short selling is a small percentage of the overall market. *Short interest* (defined as "the total of all shares sold short and not covered as of a given date") as a percentage of NYSE shares outstanding for December 1995 was 1.30 percent, up from 0.07 percent in December 1960. Figure 1.1 shows short interest as a percentage of outstanding shares

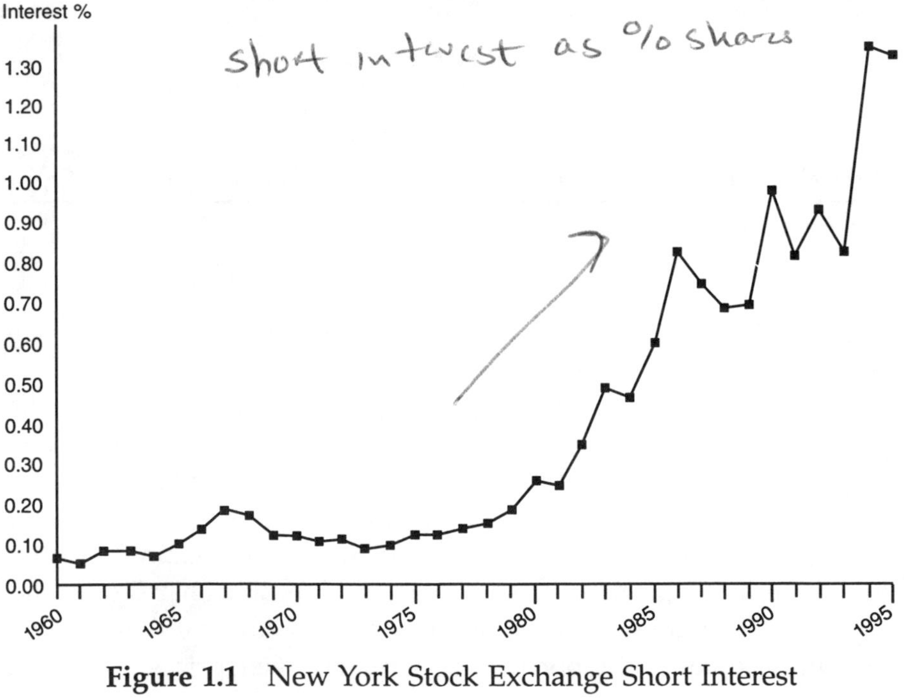

Figure 1.1 New York Stock Exchange Short Interest

on the NYSE. In December 1960, the NYSE had an aggregate of 6.15 billion shares listed, versus 4.4 million short. In 1995, those figures were 154.8 billion, versus 2.05 billion short.

The AMEX short interest went from 0.06 percent in 1960 to 1.07 percent in December 1995 (see Figure 1.2), with 10.49 billion shares outstanding and 112.4 million short in December 1995.

Short-interest statistics were not available for NASDAQ until December 1986: Short interest was 0.6 percent in December 1986 and 1.46 percent in December 1995, when short interest was 921.23 million, versus total shares of 62.95 billion.

Analysts have said that a high short-interest number is bullish because short sellers must cover and prices rise as the short sellers rush to cover shares. The short indicator as a market predictor has been under attack in recent years, however, because of the use of short sales in arbitrage positions and by institutions to hedge portfolio risk, as well as by brokerage houses to hedge put trans-actions by insiders locking in stock profits. Some analysts feel that this new

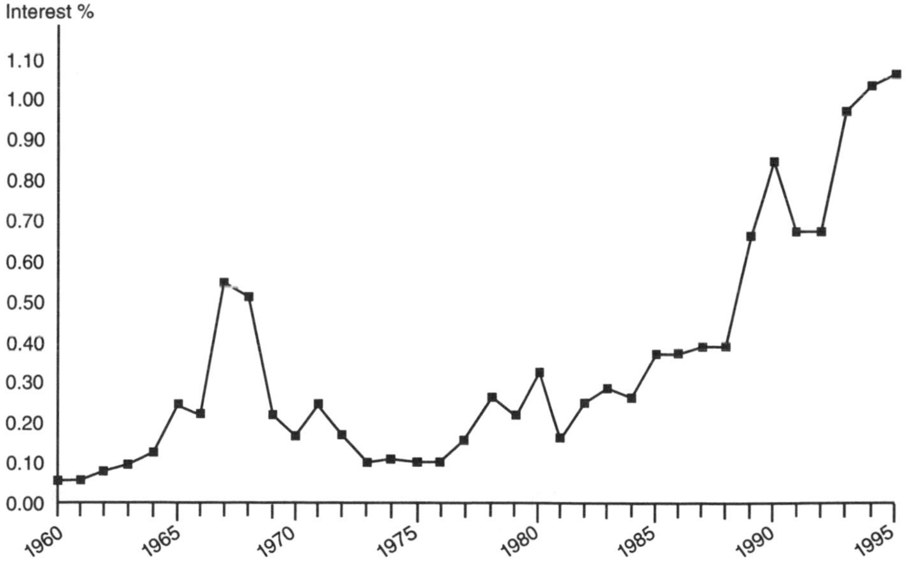

Figure 1.2 American Stock Exchange Short Interest

dimension has skewed the historical relationships. Short interest is also higher in December as a result of year-end tax strategies.

Managed funds dedicated to short selling totaled roughly $1 billion at the end of 1989. After a spike upward in 1991 to as high as $2 billion, the total had dropped well below the $1 billion mark by 1996 due to disastrous performance years in 1991, 1992, and 1995. Most of the growth in short interest has come from sources other than dedicated short management. Stock funds managed for mutual funds alone were $1.37 trillion in February 1996, so short selling continues to be a tiny niche in the investment world.

The size of short positions is expected to grow for three reasons: (1) the protracted bull market, (2) the interest of institutions in hedging or capturing market inefficiencies in portfolio returns, and (3) the growth of the *fund of funds* concept (diversified use of limited partnership funds with different investment styles).

A private-letter ruling allowing a pension fund to participate in short sales was handed down in 1988. A private-letter ruling applies only to the entity that asks for it, but it does establish a precedent. Two issues previously kept pension funds out of the short market: unrelated debt financed income and unrelated business taxable income.

The "unrelated debt financed income" question meant that tax-exempt funds could not borrow money without jeopardizing their tax-free status. If borrowing stocks was construed as "acquisition indebtedness," pension funds could not short. But the Internal Revenue Service (IRS) ruled that the short sale in an arbitrage transaction did not give rise to acquisition indebtedness if the trade was collateralized by cash or Treasury securities excluding the credit balance from the sale. If the manager did not short an amount in excess of the cash in the account, the short sale would not be considered a form of leverage.

The "unrelated business taxable income" issue questioned whether any income arising from short sales could be considered unrelated business taxable income. Interest on credit balances is generally thought to be excluded from this category. The recent rulings seem to put both issues to rest, therefore allowing pension funds access to another asset class.

The IRS issued Rev. Rul. 95-8 on December 30, 1994, which further clarified the issue. It said that a tax-exempt organization would not be subject to tax on unrelated business taxable income on short-sale gains, even when leverage is involved, or on the rebate fee. It failed to specify, however, whether short sales collateralized with stock or Treasuries would give rise to the tax.

The protracted bull market of the 1980s and 1990s, together with the increasing volatility of price swings, turned the interest of portfolio managers toward short sales. The advent of computer screens also made short selling easier as managers discovered that the firm's normal earnings momentum or value screens could be inverted for short sales.

The institutional quest for inefficient sectors of the market supports the growing curiosity toward short portfolios. Computer models that once generated equity portfolios are now spitting out short and long portfolios with zero betas and maximum alphas, portfolios that attempt to capture incremental company return without market risk. The growth of the futures and index options market, no doubt, has changed conservative investment thinking. For example, exposure to portfolio insurance and to hedging programs has increased manager and client comfort levels with more diverse asset classes and quantitatively driven strategies. It is part of this trend that short sales are no longer considered radical.

The growth in computer-driven short management for institutional investors is expected to exceed the growth in fundamental short management by a fair percentage. Some observers estimate current funds under management at close to $1 billion already. The implication for fundamental short sellers is that, although stocks might become harder to borrow, these programs also readily lend long positions for rebates.

◆ *Caveats*

Short selling is not for the faint of heart or for the inexperienced investor. If a stock moves against the position holder, the effect on a portfolio and net worth can be devastating. Short selling for the amateur can be as hazardous as selling uncovered puts or calls. Investors need to understand both the impact on their accounts and the consequences of getting bought-in before they indulge in short selling.

Simple selling, however, is a discipline for even the faint of heart, and the skills are the same. How to make money by shorting and how not to lose money by selling are different sides of the same coin.

There is a certain sense of power, of being in control, of being, somehow, smarter or more independent that comes with successful short selling. The discipline gives the truly addicted stock gamesperson the ability to play and to win in any economic environment: Muddled corporate strategic plans are always evident, bubbles of hope exist even when the market is undervalued, and villains are always somewhere nearby. Short selling is a game of wits, with the odds in favor of the analysts who do hard work and think for themselves, who turn jaundiced eyes on what passes for Wall Street wisdom.

Notes

1. Edward M. Miller, "Bounded Efficient Markets: A New Wrinkle to the EMH," *Journal of Portfolio Management* 13 (Summer 1987):4.
2. Paul Asquith and Lisa Meulbroek, "An Empirical Investigation of Short Interest," MIT paper in progress.
3. Charles P. Jones, Richard J. Rendleman, Jr., and Henry A. Latane, "Stock Returns and SUEs during the 1970s," *Journal of Portfolio Management* 10 (Winter 1984):18.
4. Robert L. Hagin, "The Subtle Risk of High Expected Growth: How to Avoid Torpedo Stocks," Kidder, Peabody & Co., research, 30 March 1984, 1.
5. Colin Camerer, "Bubbles and Fads in Asset Prices," *Journal of Economic Surveys* 3 (1989): 3.

6. Sy Jacobs quoted in Eric Berg, "Risks for the Analysts Who Dare to Say Sell," *New York Times*, 15 May 1990, C1.
7. Charles D. Ellis, "The Loser's Game," in *Classics: An Investor's Anthology*, ed. Charles D. Ellis (Homewood, IL: Dow Jones-Irwin, 1989), 535.

2
Short Sellers

Historically, significant money has been made selling short, but nobody talks about it much. In the past 20 years, *hedge funds* (limited partnerships composed of accredited investors that have few restrictions on strategy or investment instruments) have consistently used short sales to augment returns. Robert Wilson, whom John Train profiles in *The Money Masters,* is the acknowledged grandfather of the short-selling hedge-fund managers. Other great fund managers—George Soros, Michael Steinhardt, and Julian Robertson—are as comfortable with either side of the market as an ambidextrous person.

Hedge Funds and Investment Advisors

Julian Robertson of Tiger Funds[1]

Detailed company analysis is practiced by most of the top-performing hedge funds. Julian Robertson of Tiger Funds has been shorting stocks for over 30 years. He uses the same fundamental approach to the short side as to the long—prodigious research, a bottom-up analytical methodology, and a long-term time horizon. The generic drug stocks are an example of his thought process. The public perceived that the stocks were enormous growth vehicles and moved the prices up to earnings multiples of 30 or 40 times and 10 times sales and book value. In reality, the companies had no franchise and no sales force and produced commodity products. The product pricing and concomitant gross margins could not support the stock valuations with the built-in euphoria for earnings increases.

Robertson feels valuation bets on price alone make bad short sales: There must be either a fundamental change in the outlook for the company or a major misconception by the stock-buying public. He is known for his ability to match a long position in a good company with a short position in a deteriorating one—short Texas Air, long American Airlines, for example. He is equally adept at unhedged industry stock selection bets—long United, short Zenith Labs. Because Robertson declines to predict the market, his funds have always been short, with no specific weighting and no maximum percentage allocation.

Alex Porter of Porter, Felleman[2]

Alex Porter at Porter, Felleman, is another hedge-fund manager who has been shorting stocks for several decades. He shorts to reduce the risk in the overall portfolio, as an insurance policy against a protracted decline. The trick, he says, is to be short the stocks you can stay short without pain or expense, particularly the stocks where financial legerdemain denotes something is seriously wrong. His analytical work is company-based; therefore, his shorts are predominantly companies where management does not own much stock, where management is not realistic and forthright about their business, and where the company itself is leveraged or has a fatal balance-sheet flaw. Porter also feels that the long side of the market is more aggressive and persistent about hyping stocks than the short side and that the lemminglike agreement on Wall Street is greater on the rise than on the fall of a stock price.

Joe DiMenna of Zweig Funds[3]

Joe DiMenna, general partner and portfolio manager of the Zweig Group of Funds, is another experienced fundamental player on both the short and the long side. Total short exposure at Zweig is dictated by two variables: the number of attractive short-sale candidates their research uncovers and the net exposure to the market that their battery of indicators suggests (monetary policy, supply and demand of stocks, and so on). Fundamental analysis accounts for at least 75 percent of the decision.

DiMenna shorts five types of situations: frauds, earnings disappointments, hyped stocks where he can shoot holes in Wall Street's consensus expectations, industry themes where macroforces are negative, and deteriorating balance sheets. He reassesses short positions continually and, before he shorts, tries to determine the catalyst that will cause a stock to fall. He generally will not short stocks with strong relative strength and earnings momentum solely on the basis of overvaluation. Typically, he waits for these stocks to break before getting involved. He avoids short candidates in a crowded field unless the company is terminal.

◆ *Short Sellers—The Alter Ego of Wall Street*

From 1983 to 1989, a number of funds were founded that specialized in short selling. The Feshbach Brothers of California and one shy curmudgeon called McBear were the first two managers dedicated to short selling in 1981 and 1983. Jim Chanos came on the scene in 1985, followed by a covey of others in late 1988 and 1989. The dedicated short sellers were different in two respects: First, their performance belied common wisdom—they were up in up markets, as well as up in down markets (see Table 2.1); second, they did thorough fundamental analytical work, not the mainline Wall Street-style earnings-projection model.

Short sellers are odd people. Most of them are ambitious, driven, antisocial, and singleminded. As individuals, they are not very likely to own a Rolex watch or a Presidential springer spaniel or any other symbolic trapping of success; they are likely to have a wry, slightly twisted sense of humor. As a group, short sellers like to disagree, and they like to win against big odds. Typically, they have an axe to grind, a chip on the shoulder. As in the general population, some of them are

Table 2.1 Short Seller Investment Results

Year	*Rockbridge Short Sellers Index*	*S&P 500 Index (with dividends)*
1984	6.79%	6.27%
1985	12.04	32.16
1986	32.33	18.47
1987	45.82	5.23
1988	12.08	16.81
1989	26.82	31.69
1990	45.58	–3.1
1991	–31.66	30.47
1992	–3.7	7.62
1993	0.25	10.08
1994	13.54	1.32
1995	–15.53	+37.47

Data courtesy of Michael R. Long, Rockbridge Partners.

cretins and some are not, but they are all smarter (most of them, in fact, are intellectual snobs) and more independent than most people. Contrary to popular wisdom, they do not form a cabal and bash stocks senseless. They normally are secretive and slightly paranoid. And they are frequently irreverent in their regard for business leaders and icons of Wall Street. Dana L. Thomas summed up the breed in this statement:

> *Professional short sellers usually have a zestfully unbiased attitude toward men and affairs. They are often men of biting humor. After all, their stock in trade is an ironic transubstantiation of values—a satiric commentary on the standards of men.*

The Feshbachs: Stock Patrol on NASDAQ[4]

The most famous short sellers in recent years were the Feshbach Brothers—Kurt, twins Joe and Matt, and non-Feshbach Tom Barton. Feshbach Brothers, founded in 1982, was the first group formed to concentrate on short selling. At the height of their funds, they managed more money by a significant factor than any competitor—$600 million in 1990, individual, institutional, and pension fund money. They made their mark early as small cap, stock police with a specialty in investigative frauds. In more recent years, the portfolios under their management have been more traditionally balanced with long-equity holdings as well as some shorts.

The Feshbachs looked for terminal shorts with these four characteristics:

1. Stock prices overvalued by at least two times Feshbach-perceived valuation.
2. A fundamental problem at the company.
3. A weak financial condition—working-capital problems or high long-term debt, for example.
4. Weak or crooked management.

The Brothers perceived themselves as hype detectors serving an important watchdog function for the public. They enjoyed the chase and the challenge of short selling and the camaraderie of being four against the world. Conversely, they also consistently reap the wrath of bear baiters like the *OTC Review*'s editor, Bob Flaherty.

Their first short was Universal Energy, a stock the Feshbachs thought was manipulated by an insider/owner, a stock that crashed quickly and created a model for subsequent ideas. The Feshbachs' keystone is intense work and, sometimes, informational overkill. They start with fundamental methods of analysis and overlay that process with information gathering from a wide range of sources.

The Feshbachs do not short a stock unless they expect it to decline in price by 50 percent, because they believe that the risk of short selling is too great for marginal plays. "We short stocks where the negatives so overwhelm the positives that, over time, the market can't just shrug off the bad news—eventually the stock price will reflect it," Joe says.

"Everybody has the same balance sheet and income statement

that we do. The only thing we're looking for in an income statement or balance sheet is a story that appears to defy basic economic laws—a company that is spending more than it's making, for example. Those kinds of things are obvious, not subtle points at all," Feshbach continued. Kirschner Medical is an example of this principle. Any analyst could figure out that the company had over 400 days of inventory, but the Feshbachs developed sources that said Kirschner had over $10 million in obsolete inventory. Overkill, perhaps, but the Feshbachs feel that detailed masses of information are part of their success. "The reason we put so much emphasis on phone calls to competitors, suppliers, and customers is that's where we get our edge—in discovering what drives the numbers. Everybody knows what the numbers are on a historical basis. If they don't, they're either illiterate or just lazy. Sometimes, they misinterpret them."

ZZZZ Best (Chapter 3) was their most publicized short, but Circle K is representative of the way their research proceeds. When a broker from Boston called the Feshbachs with the convenience store chain Circle K, they hired an industry consultant to tell them how much the chain was worth per store. The consultant came back with a number that precluded a short sale. Later, the consultant called to lower his evaluation because he had found that the sale/leasebacks of stores meant that Circle K did not really have much to sell. He also discovered that many top people were leaving. The stock was still around $14 a share, so the Feshbachs went to work.

What they found was a highly leveraged company with ugly operating fundamentals, a rising off-balance-sheet liability, and a declining industry. The balance sheet had $1 billion in debt—half in junk bonds, half in bank debt. All the assets had been sold to the company's largest shareholder, Carl Lindner. Same-store sales were declining, and operating income was no longer covering interest.

They also found that Circle K had understated the liability for gas-tank remediation. Ex-employees told them that Circle K bought locations sight unseen with no testing. So not only were the locations old and expensive to fix, but the transferred title meant that the new lender assumed the liability.

The Feshbachs developed a network of ex-employees, competitors, and suppliers who confirmed that operationally the company was failing. First, they found that CEO Karl Eller had developed a relationship with the Steve's Ice Cream owner, Richard Smith; he used Smith as an unpaid consultant to run the company's day-to-day operations. Smith made a crucial mistake: He thought customers were insensitive to price, so he raised prices across the board and attempted to negotiate suppliers' contracts lower in an effort to raise margins to 40 percent. The customers walked, and the suppliers told them to buy elsewhere. Same-store sales dropped, margins dropped, and customers were permanently alienated.

One other factor made the stock a great short. The industry trends were changing radically. When existing gas stations rebuilt convenience stores and could sell gas for less than Circle K could buy it, Circle K was in serious trouble. It was a national trend. Simultaneously, grocery stores started staying open 24 hours a day.

So, the company's internal environment and the industry external factors led the Feshbachs to short 1.4 million shares above $10. Then they shorted the convertible when it continued to trade at $70 (because of a 1991 put provision) after the stock crashed to $5. Circle K was institutionally owned and Wall Street covered. They bought in positions for around $1.

Because the Feshbachs have specific target prices, turnover is low. When they take a position, they typically add to it as more data come in, and they only cover because they made a mistake or because the stock hits the target price—not with a 20-percent decline for a quick profit.

The Feshbachs do not find company visits or Wall Street analysts productive ways to gather information. Talks with management are not fruitful: "The company didn't get to be a good short without management's help." Wall Street is no help: "That's the place to get the bull story, not the bear story. The bias negates their usefulness to us in a lot of incidents."

Some segments have been more lucrative than others. Banks and savings and loans have been money makers for years, not just six months: American Continental, Commonwealth Savings of Houston, Sunrise Savings and Loan, Sun State Savings and Loan, and Bank of

New England are companies that the Feshbachs have made good money shorting.

The buyout frenzy of the 1980s provided massive opportunities for the Feshbachs. Their stock analysis is similar to what investment bankers use to determine private market value, so their methodology kept them out of trouble. The Sony acquisition of Guber Peters caught them short, but Joe Feshbach likens that to a natural disaster—there was no way to anticipate the buyout at those ludicrous prices.

The most difficult part of short selling is timing, and the Feshbachs do not presume to have an answer to what determines the optimal trigger point. Joe uses the example of CopyTele: What is an appropriate indicator that the stock is finally ready to give up the ghost? (CopyTele has no earnings or revenues and only the promise of a product.) They believe that to sell short you have to be certain that you see an important factor that other people do not see. "But," Feshbach continues, "it's not enough to see it if it doesn't make a difference in the way the company is ultimately valued. You have to see those mechanics begin to impact the income statement and the balance sheet." You have to visualize how the change evolves through the health of the company. The Feshbachs feel that talking to competitors and suppliers reveals the climate and how long it might continue and gives insight into possible triggers. Joe Feshbach says, "You look for something that is obviously misperceived, obviously important, and obviously detrimental. At that point, if you're comfortable that it's already started to happen, that it's not discounted in the price, and that it is substantial enough to get you to the price target, then you ought to get started." He cautions that the first position is not necessarily the biggest because stocks go up and you want to be able to average up. But the time you really want to add to the position is when those factors become overwhelmingly apparent and the stock is still up.

As the often-accused pundit of the supposed group of stock-bashing bears, Joe Feshbach says that all investors share information and develop research relationships. He is not aware of a single incident where short sellers got together and "agreed to pummel a stock. We like to hear new ideas, but we don't view it as any different from a portfolio managers' dinner in New York where six guys get together and throw out their best ideas. If that's illegal, there won't be room in the jails for any criminals."

The Feshbachs feel the most important characteristic in a short seller or an investor is the ability to remain analytical when other people panic. They credit Dianetics for contributing that characteristic or set of responses to their management style. Joe Feshbach comments,

> We don't flip out when a stock goes up. The whole purpose of Dianetics is to eliminate reactive patterns whereby a person operates on a stimulus response basis and isn't being analytical. That's the starting point. Money managers make the same mistake over and over—that's part of whole reactive pattern. We try to get to the bottom of errors we make. We've developed a check list of good short criteria and a training manual based on successful and unsuccessful actions. We have learned by doing, and not everybody, just by doing it, learns it. We attribute that to Dianetics.

The Oldest Living Short-Fund Manager[5]

"McBear" launched his fund in mid-1983 at age 40. After earning a Stanford M.B.A., he worked as a special-situations analyst and as a director of research and managed money for wealthy individuals. As the oldest short-fund manager, McBear jokes that his age gives him greater experience with the credit cycle. Consequently, his signature short ideas are based on extensive credit work. His formative short was Caterpillar Tractor (Cat) in 1984. The financials read like a disaster. Cat's main customers were the Saudis, oil drillers, national mining companies, and the notorious South American countries—once flush, they all were now broke or cash short. In spite of the dismal reality, Wall Street analysts were estimating $4 in earnings per share. Caterpillar's stock was widely owned and frequently featured by strategic thinkers as a portfolio necessity. The Street missed by $9 a share that year—Cat lost $5. McBear identified kindred plays, and he then shorted drillers, mining companies, machine tools, and all the bets connected to the sinking Cat. The Street was predicting a cyclical turnaround. "Understanding Cat gave me the insight into understanding the structural problems at that time in the economy. Inflation-driven industries had huge capacity, and the Street felt the problems were cyclical, not structural, and expected a turn in late 1983 or 1984. But the economy missed a cycle."

In what he believed to be a turn in the credit cycle, McBear was particularly adept with the real estate, bank, and leveraged buyout (LBO) phenomena. He was first to short the New England banks, and, if a company levered up and made a large acquisition, he looked at it. The stub stocks Harcourt Brace Jovanovich; U.S. Gypsum; and Carter, Hawley, Hale—deals that did not work from day one, he says—were large portfolio shorts for his fund.

Ames is a good example of the work of McBear and his associate. They first got interested in Ames when the company bought Zayre in October 1988 and added substantial debt to the balance sheet. Because the purchase was made below book and Zayre had ugly margins, Wall Street simply added the revenues together, applied peak margins from Ames to the result, subtracted the new interest, and came up with $1.40 to $1.45 in earnings. When Ames bought Zayre, sales were $2.1 billion with operating margins of 2.2 percent in fiscal 1987. The balance sheet was clean. Zayre's sales were $2.9 billion, and the purchase price was $778 million. The discount retail environment was under pressure with Walmart's aggressive pricing and expansion plans, so McBear felt the margin history was the key to the company's health. "You get a window on a stock before the facts are announced when analysts can say anything they want—and they do. The institutions like to listen and believe because they've been in a bull market so long. An Ames analyst could say Zayre will work out, but sooner or later came the time of reckoning." So McBear and his associate started tracking the margins through time, quarter by quarter, from 1985—the peak year at 4.8 percent. Wall Street was using 3 percent and implying that number was conservative. "It was unbridled optimism that peaked on the convertible deal in October 1989 with the stock at $18," says McBear's associate.

The 1989 quarters supported the thesis that the debt was not serviceable with the company's margin history. The company lost money every quarter and showed negative comps at Zayre. The Street, with the exception of the Goldman, Sachs analyst, continued cheerful about the operating and financial leverage. Furthermore, Ames immediately had heavy cash drain from refurbishing seedy Zayre stores, closing overlap stores, and cleaning up inventories. All the depreciation and amortization appeared to be going to necessary capital expenditures, throwing off Street analysts' cash-flow projections. Also, Zayre customers were accustomed to heavy promotions, and Ames's policy was consistent low prices; so Zayre's regular revenue base disappeared. Murphy's Law worked in the bears' favor. The expected Christmas 1989 sales never materialized, vendors were not paid after Christmas, and the company filed for bankruptcy in April 1989, a victim of acquisition mania.

McBear understood the effect of the acquisition of Zayre and the potential impact on the equity of Ames, together with the dynamics of the problem and how the problem develops. "A problem takes more than three months to solve that took five years to evolve."

McBear keeps a low profile relative to his peers because he gathers important information by visiting companies. He feels Wall Street analysts are a poor conduit for company insights because they screen out relevant facts. A good listener asking thoughtful questions can learn critical facts about business trends. He uses the example of Cross and Trecker: The company was leading analysts to a $1.20 earnings estimate at one point, while the Street still estimated $4.00.

McBear is scorching in his contempt for Wall Street investment bankers who have shepherded their clients into breakneck acquisitions. He feels that part of the satisfaction of short selling is going against Wall Street. Corporate management is rarely the target, unless there is fraud. It is generally Wall Street that has engineered the ascent of the stock. "Many corporate managers are odd lotters," he comments. "They are under relentless pressure from investment bankers, and they are herded into mistakes. They do things when everybody else does them, like institutional money managers. If it's in vogue to buy oil companies or to make acquisitions, they all do it." He thinks Wall Street research has always been bad, but it is worse now because investment bankers are controlling the process. He implies that investment bankers have about the same value to society as drug dealers. In the summer of 1989, he thought it was clear when the credit cycle peaked because investment bankers could say anything and the analysts would complacently repeat it. Back in 1983, concept stocks—high-multiple, high-growth stocks—were hot; and you could, to some degree, understand the rationale of stock valuation even if you did not agree with it. "But the summer of '89 wasn't a concept market—the numbers just didn't add up. Investment bankers said one plus one equals three, and the prospectus put it in writing. It was the end of a cycle with extreme exaggeration, a truly speculative market."

The environment of Wall Street creates enough slippage for short sellers to make money. "The market is inefficient," he says, "because there is a bias to buy. There are six professional short sellers and twelve thousand investment advisors, a hundred buy reports for every sell, and, therefore, a natural upward bias to stocks. It's particularly true in a bull market. It's always somebody else's money. Like Texas Air, investors lost a lot. So what! It was a bunch of commissions. It creates pain for short sellers in the short run but a lot of opportunity."

Jim Chanos: Financial Puzzle Artist[6]

James S. Chanos of Kynikos Associates, Ltd., made an early showing when he called the Baldwin-United bankruptcy at age 24 when he was an analyst fresh out of Yale at Gilford Securities. He is doomed, as a result, even as he ages to the sobriquet of youth. He moved on to Deutsche Bank Capital Corporation in 1983 to specialize in sale recommendations and overpriced securities. When he left their employment in 1985, he started his own short fund and now manages around $200 million.

Chanos's specialty is solving complex financial puzzles. He shorts large-capitalization financial companies with a high probability of bankruptcy. His average holding period is nine months, but his longest holding was Integrated Resources at over five years. The median equity market cap of the stocks in his portfolio is $900 million. He does not short frauds with small floats because of size constraints. In contrast to some of his competitors, he has not had a problem with buy-ins because of his use of large-cap stocks. Chanos maintains a concentrated portfolio of about 30 stocks, with 10 positions accounting for more than 50 percent of his portfolio.

Typically, he likes to short stocks with secular problems where he can make a "reasonably strong argument, based on the valuation of the business (much like the private market players look for discount to value), that the equity value of the enterprise is $0. When the stock trades to its warrant value, our analysis shifts to the valuation of the warrant. If there's a lot of debt, the warrant value may be nothing, or we may cover at $2 or $3."

Chanos does not visit companies and seems to use Wall Street as a corporate emissary or interpreter. He comments that,

> In a one-time corporate visit, they're not going to tell you anything they're not already telling the street. And if they do, you probably shouldn't be hearing it anyway because it's probably non-public. You can get a very good sense of what the company story is by using First Call and analyzing five years of data. We also attend some corporate presentations when management comes to town, one of the advantages of being based in New York. We tend to focus on the numbers. We're not big on hiring detective agencies or talking to ex-employees. We think a lot of traditional money managers tend to get sloppy. It's easy to do. One common shortcoming is to rely on management or Wall Street analysts. When they both get blindsided, you're left holding the bag. So to that extent we'd rather not rely.

Analytically, Chanos says he does not do anything that is very different from other managers, but his use of return on invested capital as a key financial indicator is unique. "'Using this, we've been able to find companies that are not what they appeared to be." His calculation is: earnings before interest and taxes divided by average total capital (which is defined as total liabilities plus equity minus current liabilities plus short-term debt or, to say it another way, the return on all interest-bearing liabilities plus equity plus deferred taxes and short-term debt). "That ratio will reveal a lot of wormy companies and poor businesses. It's a tough number to screw around with."

Financial companies have been particularly lucrative for Chanos because of the potential for rampant earnings manipulation, which, he says, attracts its fair share of scoundrels. Chanos notes that the "leverage inherent in some of these companies is incredible. When the accounting gets murky, people tend to shy away from rigorous analysis and rely on management and just take earnings per share at face value. Therein lies the opportunity."

Chanos's analysis of Baldwin-United illustrates his persistence with puzzles and his ability to persevere in the face of marked hostility, both from the company and from peers. Baldwin was a high flyer with a large Wall Street following in the summer of 1982. Prudential Bache, Prescott Ball, Merrill Lynch, and Smith Barney all had Baldwin-United stock rated "a buy," with a euphoric perception of earnings momentum. Chanos took the time to read the annual convention statements, understand the tax accounting, and follow a complex trail of affiliated company financial transactions, all of which convinced him that the stock was next to worthless. The stock went from $20 to $50 with his sell recommendation in place—and then into bankruptcy, for the largest insurance-company scandal of the decade. The Street analysts at the time were concentrating on earnings momentum, Morley Thompson's publicity releases, and the perceived hot market for single-premium deferred annuities. Chanos did painstaking spread sheets on cash flow, never an easy task with subsidiaries moving assets.

The arguments on Baldwin revolved around Wall Street's belief that Thompson's superior strategies could create earnings from his convoluted financial stratagem. He convinced the analysts that his investment plan was newfangled corporate arbitrage—very sophisticated, very complex. The docile crowd of analysts regurgitated the information in buy recommendations and long reports. Everybody loved a winner, shuffling his companies like cards.

In the summer of 1982, part of the Street elation was the MGIC Investment Corporation acquisition. Merrill analyst Carol Neves was cheered by the "continuous source of taxable income" from MGIC, "so that BDW [Baldwin-United] can fully utilize the substantial tax credits being generated by its most successful product, SPDAs [single-premium deferred annuities]."[7] Robert Back at Prescott Ball & Turben had the stock "rated a very strong long-term purchase . . . at $62 per share, only 4.8 times our conservative 1983 estimate."[8]

Chanos wrote his first report in late August 1982. It was a sell recommendation based on the leverage, the cash flow, the quality of earnings, and the potential decline in revenues from rate declines and possible tax legislation. He stated the heretical opinion that Baldwin was losing money on its annuity business and that assets purchased by affiliates from MGIC were a serious liquidity problem for insurance portfolios, as well as a rate-of-return problem, because real assets were sold to purchase money-losing real estate—cash flow was the real issue, not reported earnings.

A brouhaha ensued. Chanos was excoriated publicly, threatened privately, and repudiated by management. Paul Mackay at Bache said to buy because short interest was over one million shares, "creating a unique trading opportunity."[9] And Baldwin believed that insurance assets could easily cover all SPDAs from current liquid investments.

Chanos persisted with another report in December 1982 after the stock had doubled. He pointed to declining fundamentals at MGIC, which would weaken cash flow and use of tax benefits. Then he went over cash flow again, in detail.

In March 1983, Baldwin announced it could not pay $900 million in short-term debt and subsequently filed for Chapter 11.

Chanos has continued to mine financial companies and complex financial statements for ideas and has made money from the stock collapses of the Zises of Integrated Resources, Gary Driggs of Western Savings and Loan, Charles Keating of American Continental, Fred Carr of First Executive, Frank Lorenzo of Texas Air, David Maniatis of Sun State Savings and Loan, as well as from Prime Motor Inns, Harcourt Brace Jovanovich, and Valley National.

Commenting on a variety of short-selling issues, Chanos laughs about frequent small-company criticism that a cabal of sellers exists. Any interchange with other sellers is no different from talking to friends about good ideas. He feels the Securities and Exchange Commission (SEC) is vigilant about stock-price manipulation and that it would certainly be aggressive about investigating collusion among the short community to drive share prices down. He notes that, because of the uptick rule, it is impossible for short selling to cause a stock to decline in price. Both the National Association of Securities Dealers (NASD) and the SEC view short sellers as another good source of information.

He feels the potential pension-fund entry into short selling is a looming issue, one that should shake up the business and make it tougher. Personally, Chanos prefers dealing with private clients who want to preserve capital, are farsighted, and add to the investment process. Chanos uses his partners' business experience and their contacts as part of the research process. "These people are interested in building wealth versus making a few extra basis points," he surmises.

Chanos thinks that he has a good relationship with the Street and that he talks to them more than any other short seller for two reasons: First, he shorts stocks that are covered by the Street, and, second, he runs money for the Street—principals at brokerage firms, as well as brokerage firms. He sees international short selling as the biggest new opportunity and made good money off Eurotunnel in 1994 and 1995. Although financial disclosures are semiannual, valuation more than makes up for the lack of quarterly disclosure because the stocks are conceptually, not analytically, priced. The proliferation of short funds managed by newsletter writers and traditional money managers does not bother Chanos over the long run. "Very few people have the stomach to take a fundamental short position. If a short position goes against most people, their first reaction is to cover, rather than sell more stock."

A Contracting List of Short Sellers

Dedicated short funds continued to spring up in the investment world well into 1991. The protracted bull market of 1991 to 1993 knocked most of the virgins back out of the business as fund-of-fund managers dropped short exposure and pension-fund participation failed to materialize. A new crop has sprung up to replace converted cynics, but dedicated short managers are a scarce breed again, even after a successful year in 1994 (funds under management are under a billion). The wizened veterans do not seem too concerned about competition or its demise. They apply their contrarian company attitudes to the business itself—less interest means more profit; the crowd is usually wrong.

Notes

1. Interview with Julian Robertson on 2 May 1990.
2. Interview with Alex Porter on 24 April 1990.
3. Interview with Joseph DiMenna on 6 June 1990.
4. Interviews with Joseph Feshbach on 1 and 14 June 1990.
5. Interview with "McBear" on 2 May 1990.
6. Interview with James S. Chanos on 2 May 1990.
7. Carol P. Neves, "Baldwin United," Merrill Lynch Pierce Fenner & Smith Securities, research division, 16 April 1982, 1.
8. Robert W. Back, "Baldwin-United Corporation," Prescott Ball & Turben, 11 June 1982, 4.
9. Paul A. Mackey, "Baldwin-United Corporation," Bache Halsey Stuart Shields Incorporated, institutional research, 25 August 1982, 2.

Part Two

CATEGORIES AND EXAMPLES

3
Bubble Stocks

A perfect short-sale candidate is a stock with a large float to allow ease of borrowing and no buy-ins, a high stock price for maximum return, and no business or assets to keep the risk nominal and the investment horizon short-term. Veterans of the bull market of the 1980s and 1990s will remember that a perfect short can cause terrible loss. Even a company with no revenues and no assets can produce the hope of future earnings. Many of these are technology or medical products companies with a purported new hot product in the pipeline. Shams are created by stockholders, brokerage houses, or corporate executives who relentlessly push the valuation higher without regard for the underlying financials, inflating the prices beyond expectation of future value. Management, in some cases, might believe in their ephemeral product and the public's bubble evaluation of it, or, as in the case of ZZZZ Best, they might be conning the public and the Securities and Exchange Commission (SEC).

Dirty Carpets: ZZZZ Best

The Feshbach Brothers were masters of the bubble company, as evidenced by their detective work on ZZZZ Best—the carpet cleaning company with no revenues. ZZZZ Best, whiz kid Barry Minkow's hot-growth company, had a market value of $200 million in the spring of

1987. Business was great for the company, and they announced a contract to clean two large buildings in Sacramento for $8 million. Carpet-cleaning competitors told Feshbach analysts that the two largest cleaning contracts to date (the MGM Grand and the Las Vegas Hilton) capped at a price of $3.5 million, so the Feshbachs smelled a skunk, started looking, and shorted aggressively. The stock price rallied despite rumors of false billing in late May of 1987. By July, ZZZZ Best was bankrupt. In March 1989, the amazing Minkow was sentenced to 25 years for fraud: no contracts, no revenues, and a money-laundering scheme. The Feshbachs, meanwhile, went home happy and richer.

Some professional short sellers feel this segment of the market is the natural preserve of individual investors. Because the stocks are frequently hard to borrow in sizes large enough to make a meaningful addition to portfolio returns, the stocks take more work in fighting for reliable information than they provide in returns. Individual investors, however, can show dramatic returns because they can borrow enough stock to impact a diversified short portfolio. The stocks are often inefficiently, even absurdly, overpriced.

◆ *Harrier: It Just Didn't Add Up*

Harrier, Inc., a new medical-products company, is a good illustration of how short analysis logically proceeds and of what short sellers look for in their framework of inverted value analysis. At first look in July 1988, Harrier, headquartered in Utah, appeared to be pure puffery—no assets, no sales, no products, and a $30 (presplit) stock price. With 2,808,000 shares outstanding, that represented a market capitalization (or public value) of $84 million.

The March 31, 1988, 10Q provided the balance sheet (Table 3.1), income statement (Table 3.2), and "unaudited condensed statements of changes in financial position," as it was called (Table 3.3). The top of the balance sheet provided some insight into the company—the date was wrong: Instead of 1988, the top of the column read 1987. Apparently, the document filed with the Securities and Exchange Commission (SEC) was produced so haphazardly that the dates were not proofread. The next point of note, again from the balance sheet, was that

Table 3.1 Harrier's Balance Sheet

	March 31, 1987	*June 30, 1987*
Assets		
Current Assets:		
Cash	$ 550,510	$104,758
Accounts receivable	359,325	—
Inventory	490,960	29,598
Interest receivable	9,221	—
Investment in marketable securities	104,095	—
Total Current Assets	1,514,111	134,356
Equipment, net	23,407	—
Other Assets:		
Product rights and technology, net	397,330	171,618
Other assets, net	14,311	1,918
Notes receivable from related parties	35,000	—
Receivable from related party	10,000	—
Certificate of deposit	500,000	—
Total Other Assets	956,641	173,536
	$2,494,159	$307,892
Liabilities and Stockholders' Equity		
Current Liabilities:		
Accounts payable and accrued expenses	$ 321,702	$ 15,451
Other Liabilities:		
Note payable	500,000	—
Total Liabilities	821,702	15,451
Stockholders' Equity:		
Preferred stock	—	—
Common stock	2,798	2,109
Capital in excess of par value	2,669,839	721,963
Accumulated earnings (deficit)	(1,000,180)	(431,631)
Total Stockholders' Equity	1,672,457	292,441
	$2,494,159	$307,892

The balance sheet at June 30, 1987, has been taken from the audited financial statements at that date and condensed.
Source: Harrier, Inc., Form 10Q (Alpine, Utah: Harrier, Inc., 31 March 1988).

Table 3.2 Harrier's Income Statement

	For the Three Months Ended March 31,		*For the Nine Months Ended March 31,*	
	1988	*1987*	*1988*	*1987*
Sales	$ 489,210	$ —	$ 540,797	$ —
Cost of Sales	352,865	—	380,899	—
Gross Profit	136,345	—	159,898	—
Expenses:				
Professional fees	15,953	767	41,277	31,536
General and administrative	125,635	4,251	310,636	9,690
Amortization and depreciation	12,324	72	29,170	216
Consulting and management compensation	173,104	107,921	541,288	144,556
Marketing	2,051	—	50,613	125,000
Research and development	48,731	—	48,731	—
Total Expenses	377,798	113,011	1,021,715	310,998
Income (Loss) from Operations	(241,453)	(113,011)	(861,817)	(310,998)
Other Income (Expense):				
Interest income	9,229	36	25,517	4,092
Interest expense	(13,096)	—	(13,132)	—
Gain on sale	—	—	15,523	—
Sale of license rights	250,000	—	250,000	—
Consulting income	15,360	—	15,360	—
Total Other Income (Expense)	261,493	36	293,268	4,092
Income (Loss) Before Tax Provision	20,040	(112,975)	(568,549)	(306,906)
Provision for Taxes (Benefit)	—	—	—	(42)
Net Income (Loss)	$ 20,040	$(112,975)	$(568,549)	$(306,864)
Earnings (loss) per Share	$ .01	$ (.06)	$ (.22)	$ (.26)

Source: Harrier, Inc., Form 10Q, 31 March 1987.

Table 3.3 Harrier's Statements of Changes in Financial Position

	For the Nine Months Ended March 31,	
	1988	*1987*
Working Capital Provided:		
Working Capital Provided (Used) by Operations	$ (539,379)	$ (306,648)
Issuance of common stock for cash 500,000		2,052,500
Issuance of common stock for cash in redemption of warrants	12,000	—
Issuance of common stock for assets	—	994
Issuance of long term debt	500,000	—
Total Working Capital Provided	2,025,121	194,346
Working Capital Used:		
Stock offering costs	115,935	3,737
Organization costs	—	—
Product technology costs	262,343	182,244
Patent	3,225	—
Note receivable from related parties	35,000	—
Addition to equipment	25,114	—
Receivable from related party	10,000	—
Addition to long term certificate of deposit	500,000	—
Total Working Capital Used	951,617	185,981
Total Increase in Working Capital	$1,073,504	$ 8,365

Source Harrier, Inc., Form 10Q 31 March 1988.

Harrier had assets of about $2.5 million on March 31, 1988, up from $307,892 in June 1987, and stockholders' equity of $1,672,457. In other words, the market valued $1.7 million of book value at $84 million. The opportunity existed, therefore, to sell $1.7 million worth of goods for a market cap or public value of $84 million.

The market, then, put the present value of Harrier's potential stream of revenues in excess of $82 million ($84 million less the $1.7 million book value). The next step for a short seller was to look at the income statement and see if the seeds of exponential earnings growth were visible in high-flying Harrier. The income statement (see Table 3.2) showed some revenues, with high proportionate expenses for general and administrative and for consulting and management and with low research and development costs. Someone was getting paid, although it was not the stockholders.

The big clue in the financials of Harrier was the Statement of Changes (see Table 3.3). The numbers literally did not add up. Never before have financials been seen—publicly filed financials—where the numbers did not add up. The total of working capital provided should have been ($27,379), not $2,025,121, in 1988 (just a small slip, about equal to their asset size) and $1,746,846, not $194,346, in 1987. Everybody had computers and spread sheets and calculators and accountants and bookkeepers, even in 1988, and the numbers still did not add up.

Prospectus: Going Public

After the verification of dramatic overvaluation, the next step in short-sale research is to backtrack through the past financial documents for evidence that either supports or contradicts the conclusion. Starting at the beginning, a careful reading of Harrier's initial-public-offering prospectus gave a history as compelling as a Charles Dickens subplot. The SEC-required prospectus is a favorite of short sellers for the detail and depth of company information; its existence in cases like Harrier is testimony to stockholders' preference for being led to slaughter blindfolded and smiling with misplaced hope.

Harrier was founded October 8, 1985, when a group of people assembled by Merlin Fish paid $21,500 for stock in a blind pool. The original owners were a former California client of Merlin; a real estate developer from Charleston, South Carolina; Merlin's brother, who owned a construction company in South Carolina; and a furniture company manufacturer's representative from Utah, who loaned them 200 square feet, apparently part of his home, for an office.

In May 1986, Harrier had its first public offering—25 million shares at $0.01. The prospectus was lurid in actual prospect; nowhere could one find the promise of the subsequent lofty price level. The proceeds were for "unspecified use."[1] No business had been identified for investment, and the management did not have the time, resources, or experience for analysis of such an opportunity. Of the proceeds, $170,000 would be available to invest. The funds probably would not be adequate and the competition was hot. The company slipped past the February 1986 Utah Securities Division Rule 11.1, which prohibited "blank check" offerings—public offerings of companies that existed without a stated business purpose. The new stockholders provided 92.08 percent of the capital for 69.93 percent of the stock. The underwriters got 19 percent of the new funds.

A New Life with New Products

In December 1986, on its way to respectability, Harrier had a 50-to-1 reverse split. In February 1987, new management and significant stockholders came on board to propel the shell to unprecedented heights. Jurg Kehrli and Armando Ulrich, two executives from a Swiss X-ray equipment manufacturer tried to merge their company, Kehrli AG, into Harrier. Both companies were disappointed to find that the Swiss company's financials would not meet reporting standards in the United States.

As a last resort, Kehrli and Ulrich exchanged a package (which included rights to market X-ray equipment, one of each model of the X-ray equipment, rights to the Bioptron Lamp, and rights to a Hungarian therapy process) for 994,000 shares of stock, or 58.3 percent of the shares outstanding. Harrier was satisfied that it had acquired valuable marketing rights, important technologies, and the skills of two pros to assist the company with still-undetermined products and strategies for the blind pool.

The Swiss brought three new technologies. The first was a Hungarian polarized light that appeared to have an effect on cell membranes. The result was the biostimulating effects of the Bioptron Lamp, which was supposed to improve the healing process in burns, other surface wounds, and, perhaps, wrinkles. It looked like a hand-held hair dryer and "stimulated cell renewal without stressing the skin or body."[2]

The second technology was biodynamics, acquired from the late Dr. Walter Ott of Zurich. Biodynamics had many potential new-product applications, including supersaturated water (ten times the oxygen in the water) and Diesel Cleaner.

Thymus compounds, "proprietary polypeptide fractions that serve to stimulate immunotherapeutic responses in the body to fight certain types of cancer," was the third and most expensive of the three technologies to develop. It would require large amounts of capital, presumably from joint ventures with pharmaceutical companies.[3] After spending an additional $125,000 on the marketing plan for the Kehrli X-ray equipment, Harrier dropped the product, and Kehrli returned $17,000 to the company. Kehrli and Ulrich stayed on, without their equipment but apparently with their wallets.

The June 30, 1987, 10K was a wonderful document. It revealed more specifics about the new-product rights and processes. The 10K on biodynamics stated, "This theory is based on discoveries in the use of centripetal force generated by eccentric motion to focus energy on an axis and to use that energy to accomplish certain phenomenon [*sic*] that may have commercial applications."[4] Huh? That included biodynamic water, whatever that is.

Kehrli and Ulrich consulted with Harrier for $27,000 a month and received annual rent of $5,000 for Swiss premises, for a total of $329,000 a year. No free rent there. The price of the stock, meanwhile, continued to sprint ahead, reaching a high of $7 in the June 1987 quarter, $15 by September. It was a race (soon to be resolved) to see whether insiders made more on fees than stockholders made on price appreciation.

By August 1987, Harrier had focused on the Bioptron Lamp, signed their first agreement, and sold 400,000 additional shares at $2.50 a share to a Liberian corporation. The first lamp agreement was announced with a flourish soon to be repeated many times: A Swiss corporation had the exclusive right to distribution in three countries and signed an initial purchase order of $2.4 million the first year, $2.8 million the next year, and $800,000 per quarter thereafter.

In September 1987, Harrier sold 200,000 shares at $3 a share to a new Swiss investor. By the March 31, 1988, 10Q, the shares outstanding were up to 2,808,000. March also brought another big contract from the Scandinavian countries, a minimum purchase of $6 million over three years with a minimum of $5 million in 1988.

Revenues for 1987 should have been a minimum of $2.4 million, with $7.8 million in 1988, if the previously announced contracts were added up.

A Little Help for Our Friends

Now that Harrier was a successful high-priced corporation, it began to help less fortunate friends. The March 1988 10Q noted that Harrier not only paid $448,000 to officers and directors, but also loaned $35,000 to several clients of its investment banker and bought $10,000 worth of stock in another investment banker client.

The most rousing recommendation of Harrier came from its investment banker, Merlin Group, in a 32-page report. The company's mission statement set the tone: "The goal is to produce quality environmental and health care products which will meet the challenges of our modern times to reduce human suffering from disease and pollution."[5] The Bioptron Lamp was touted first for its potential worldwide market of 525 million users for ulcers, burns, and tension headaches and then for use in sports medicine, plastic surgery, dermatology, neurology, gynecology, and dentistry—clearly, the most versatile medical discovery since aspirin. The Supersaturated Oxygen-Water and the Diesel Cleaner were also discussed in some detail as products with a wide range of applications—to save the world, a reader would surmise.

Partial Demise

On August 8, 1988, Alan Abelson at *Barron's* noticed Harrier and commented that even at $15, down from its postsplit high of $22 in July (see Figure 3.1), it seemed a mite overvalued. He noted the alliances with corporate artists—Henry Lorin, the "Abracadabra Man," for one. Abelson also cast some doubt on the two top products, the Bioptron Lamp and the Diesel Cleaner. He suggested that the light from the lamp was the wrong end of the color spectrum to cure burns. The Diesel Cleaner, he said, would require the addition of another tank on a truck, the size of the existing fuel tank.[6]

The next day, Harrier PR people came out with their best press release to date: "Harrier in Japan Distribution Pact."[7] Riding the wave of Japanomania, the company signed a $7.5 million contract. The stock failed to move with its usual bouncy step, but nobody who analyzes stocks expects press releases to be informational or relevant to actual earnings.

Simultaneously, Harrier gave the Kehrli-Ulrich team 600,000 more shares for rights to two new compounds, which supposedly strengthened the immune system and shrank tumors. The company also sold 157,500 shares for $1,050,000 to European interests.

The stock traded from $15 to $10 in the wake of Abelson's column—the insiders continued to sell.

In October 1988, prior to the release of the September 10Q, the

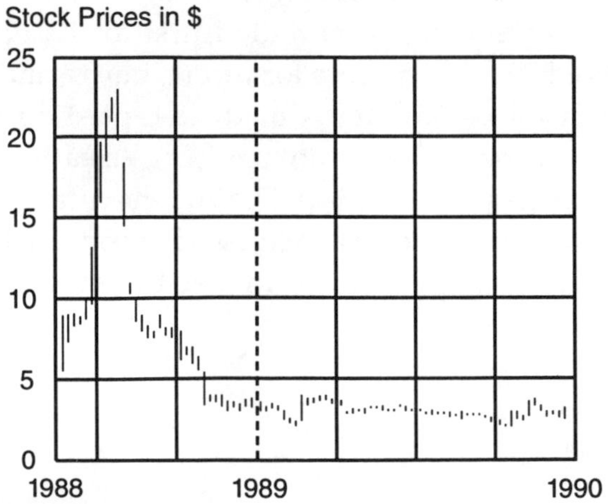

Figure 3.1 Harrier, Inc., May 1, 1988–December 31, 1989. Chart from MetaStock by Equis International, Inc.

price was still around $7. Harrier had continued to build its stock portfolio and showed marketable securities of $555,000 out of total assets of $5.3 million. Accounts receivable were the other pillar of the balance sheet with $1.8 million, up from $42,000 in June. The stock headed resolutely for $3, where it rested for the next great marketing push of the Harrier team.

A quick romp through the 1989 10K a year later suggested that sales were somewhat less than expected in the prior cheerful press releases: Fiscal 1988 revenues were $582,825; those for 1989 were $2.164 million. Previously announced contracts had totaled $7.8 million for sales anticipated in 1988. Some of the marketing agreements had been terminated because of their failure to perform. The Bioptron Lamp was then targeted for treatment of acne, rather than burns, and perhaps for biological sewage purification. The SEC has requested information from the company's accountants for a "matter under inquiry," and the stock still traded in fractions.

The main lesson of the Harrier frolic is: Always take a company seriously, even if its financials are knee-slapping, hoot-promoting drivel.

◆ *Second Derivation: Medstone*

One step removed from companies with no product are companies with a product accompanied by noteworthy claims by the investment banker or the company for proposed market share. Medstone International, Inc., a lithotripsy company that makes machines for noninvasive disintegration of kidney stones, was such an entity. Again, the prospectus of Medstone was the essential document. It alerted potential investors, or disinvestors, to critical product variables:

- The product was not patented.
- The competition was large and international with a significant installed base.
- The gross profit margins were 60 percent—maybe. (Revenues and expenses were not really matched in previous years, management said.)

The prospectus stated the usual caveats: limited operating history, deficit net worth, working capital deficit, dependence on two key executives, nonrepresentative earnings history, one-product company. Some of the money from the offering ($1.4 million out of $11.3 million) went to senior officers to pay for prior services (stock wasn't enough?).

The stock was priced at $13 in early summer 1988 and traded immediately to $19 and on to the high $20s, a perfect "doctor stock": Doctors are reputed to be the marginal suckers on new drug or medical-products companies for aggressive retail brokers. The doctors promote the stocks to peers and friends and enthusiastically inflate the market value, especially if the product is remotely associated with their area of expertise. Medstone peaked from this ebullient assault around $42 in August (see Figure 3.2).

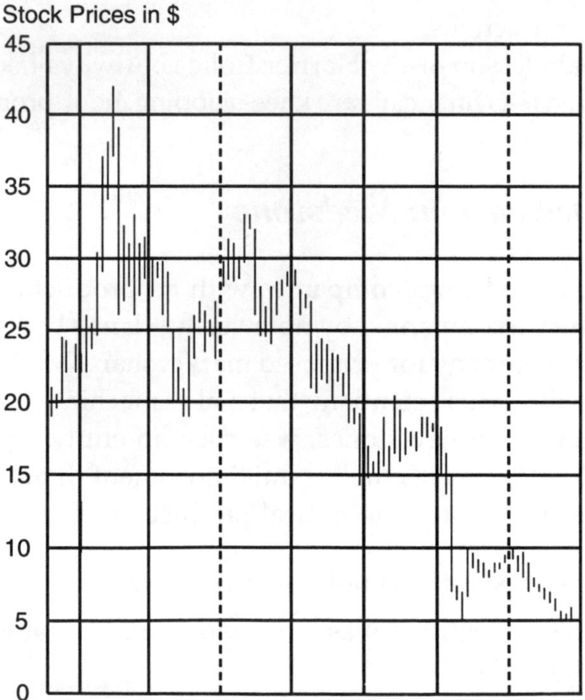

Figure 3.2 Medstone International Inc., June 1, 1988–March 31, 1990. Chart from MetaStock by Equis International, Inc.

The prospectus also mentioned, as it always does, that insiders could not sell for six months from the June 2, 1988, offering date without approval by the investment bankers. When key insider, founder, and president Richard Penfil sold 100,000 shares of stock in September before the deadline lapsed in December and Errol Payne, chairman of the board and founder, resigned, Medstone was a potential short. Jump-the-gun insiders should be more aware of product sales potential than Wall Street, after all.

Competitors Provide Comparison

Another company in a similar business (urology laser systems), Candela Laser Corporation, attempted to sell a secondary issue in October, after the Medstone initial public offering (IPO). Comparing prospectuses and business plans is a useful exercise with similar companies, particularly for the insight on valuation. The Candela story became particularly interesting when the offering was stopped because of an SEC inquiry about revenues: It appeared the company was too aggressive about when they booked sales of large machines.

Before the SEC problem, Candela was selling for $12.75 a share

Table 3.4 Medstone International, Inc., Short Interest

1988	*Number of Shares Short*	*1989*	*Number of Shares Short*
June	7,260	January	356,350
July	109,439	February	343,040
August	141,891	March	445,932
September	236,111	April	430,828
October	264,663	May	494,792
November	252,968	June	556,891
December	339,170	July	648,614
		August	726,047
		September	698,106
		October	685,504
		November	787,060
		December	754,556

with 3 million shares outstanding before the offering, or a market valuation of $38.25 million. Candela had 149 employees, a sales force, several products, four patents, and an operating history. Their kidney shock treatment was an alternative method to lithotripsy for kidney stones and one that was perceived by some to do less damage to the surrounding soft tissue than the machines of Medstone and Dornier (the largest player).

Medstone was by then trading for $29 with 4.5 million shares out, a market cap of $130 million. At the time of the offering five months earlier, the company had one product (nine sold), no patents, 33 employees, and no mention of a sales force.

The September 1988 quarter was strong: $0.52 versus $0.18 in earnings per share before extraordinary credit, and only 5 percent was from interest on the funds from the stock offering. Sales doubled.

Enthusiastic Support

The effusive puffery connected with Medstone came from one brokerage analyst in particular, who estimated earnings at $4.40 for 1989, up from $0.33 in 1987. This drove the price higher, as retail clients followed in their zeal to participate in a winning kidney play. Only six times this year's earnings! the analyst said, with the group trading at 15 to 20 times. Buy now! Participate in the only dual machine, effective on both kidney stones and gallstones (he perceived the gallstone market to be the growth engine).[8]

An agreement with General Electric (GE) Medical Systems was announced with fanfare in December 1988. GE would sell Medstone's machine in Europe and the Middle East, providing parts, installation, and maintenance.

The 10K from December 1988 made a couple of interesting points. Sales to a single stockholder, Dr. Gaines W. Hammond, and to his affiliated companies made up 13 percent of 1987 and 1988 revenues. The IPO document showed that he was an avid supporter of Medstone's work. He loaned the company $75,000 in November 1984. In connection with his first machine purchase in 1987, he "received a right of first refusal, exercisable until January 1989, to purchase and install any System for the treatment of kidney stones . . . within 100 miles of Spartanburg, South Carolina."[9] He also had the right to buy another machine at 80 percent of the price charged to third-party purchasers. He received $86,500 in consulting fees from Medstone in 1985 and an additional $123,000 at the close of the offering. It was a close relationship.

After a negative-earnings surprise in the June 1989 quarter (a loss of $0.04 a share versus $0.59 in the June 1988 quarter), the stock price moved down and then stabilized above $15 after repeated table poundings by the rabid analyst. The 10Q showed troublesome inventory levels—$5.5 million, versus $385,000 in June 1988. Sales were down, more of a problem for a hot new company than no earnings. Sales expenses were up significantly, no doubt the burden of new marketing costs.

In August 1989, Richard Penfil resigned, and the company reported "noncompliance regarding timely submission of required reports governing the X-ray imaging system used in its shockwave lithotripter."[10] The stock did not budge.

In October 1989, Medstone failed to get Food and Drug Administration (FDA) approval for its gallstone-shattering procedures, and the stock dived from $16 to $6, despite the untapped Japanese market for kidney-stone smashing. The third quarter was another disappointment—a loss of $0.34, the result of stopped shipments pending a corrective-action-plan filing to the FDA.

Earnings for 1989 were a loss of $0.45 per share with revenues of $13.6 million, down from $23.2 million in 1988. Another president was appointed in April 1990, the third in two years. Market valuation was a little more realistic at $20 million as of April 1990.

Financial analysis of Medstone was common sense. The stock was dramatically overvalued relative to a similar company. At $1 million per machine, how many machines must you sell to make the valuation realistic, and how many can you sell with a large experienced competitor—Dornier of Germany—ahead of you in the field with a patented product and most of the installed base, 250 machines? Part of the revenues were expected to come from servicing machines and selling disposable components. Yet how many hospitals will buy a $1 million machine that must be serviced by a company that has only placed nine machines when a dependable alternative exists?

The winning play was certainly a kidney straddle (or perhaps a kidney smash): Short Medstone and go long Candela Laser, which traded as low as $4 after the offering was dropped, whereas Medstone was still priced in the stratosphere. The lesson from Medstone? Consider shorting any stock with color pictures of organs in the prospectus, particularly if an enthusiastic analyst whips eager individuals into a stock-buying frenzy.

◆ *More on Prospectuses*

Most of the great bubble stocks are discovered in the first pages of new-issue prospectuses. Reading IPO documents is a quick and lucrative exercise both for short sellers searching for silly valuations and for growth investors looking to avoid disaster. The biotech and high-tech new-issue markets of the 1990s were heavy going for the nonscientist seeking a sure loser; consumer products and bad business plans were easier to analyze. Clinicorp and Happiness Express were two such companies.

Clinicorp, Inc.

The single most important section in a prospectus is the risk-factor section called "Investment Considerations." The company always tells you why it will fail. Clinicorp, Inc., a January 1992 IPO candidate, had a particularly attractive set of disclosures. Clinicorp—BACK was the stock symbol—was a chiropractic management company with no operating history and no assets. Clinicorp was acquiring another company, PMA, together with the services of its founder, Dr. Peter G. Fernandez. "PMA," the prospectus disclosed, "has incurred a substantial decline in its business operations and financial condition. . . . and it is expected that the decline will continue for the foreseeable future."[11]

BACK went on to tell the reader that there was litigation pending "regarding fee-splitting, franchise sales, and seller-assisted marketing plans. . . . including allegations of fraud, deceptive business practices, and breach of fiduciary duty."[12] Dr. Fernandez was named as a defendant as well.

And that was just for starters. The risk list continued through 14 items and 3 pages, including a financing program that lent to start-up chiropractors for working capital and equipment purchases and an underwriter with no experience. The prospectus told the reader that the business venture was fraught with peril—no previous history of success, adverse business trends, and litigation.

The deal was priced at $6.50 a share and was fortunately tough to borrow from the get-go. Despite the dire language of the IPO document, the stock moved up—to the teens, then twenties—with the help of Ray Dirks and his "ShortBuster Club." Lucky short sellers who watched were rewarded with a stock that became borrowable in the $20s, traded to $26, and then split 3 for 1. Press releases came out regularly announcing acquisitions, progress in the arena of a national chiropractic chain. It took close to a year for the stock price to crater back to $2. A reverse split and a company restructuring followed in time.

Happiness Express Inc.

The next level of complexity for short sellers seeking a perfect short is a company with revenues—revenues from a fad product already peaked in popularity. Happiness Express was one of the fastest descents among the toy fads; Coleco with Cabbage Patch dolls (Chapter 4) and Worlds of Wonder with the talking bear Teddy Ruxpin both took longer to die because of second products to engender second life. To own these stocks, the buyer must assume that the stock can be sold before the fad peaks or that the company will have a consistent flow of equally successful products. Alternatively, the seller or short seller must bet that the inflection point is here and that the revenues in subsequent quarters will drop off a cliff.

The Happiness Express Inc. secondary-offering prospectus of January 1995 was a favorite with bubble collectors. Not only was the stock symbol HAPY an attraction for curmudgeonal and ironic short sellers, but the company manufactured a bubblator bubble-blowing gun. The risk factors made the prospectus worth the read. Right there on page one of the risk factors, HAPY disclosed that 82 percent of sales came from Mighty Morphin Power Rangers—56 percent of sales from the Power Rangers sound-effect gloves alone. And Power Rangers were not at the beginning of the growth climb in January 1995: Anybody that knew a five-year-old boy knew that he knew and had known intimately the Power Rangers and was fully accessorized with Power Ranger gear by December 26, 1994.

So the percentage of sales made the reader flip to the business description to see what the company did before Power Ranger gloves. In the previous three fiscal years, lighting products with licensed character images had accounted for 68 percent, 51 percent, and 58 percent of sales, respectively. To add to the drama, the risk section stated that some of the licenses were nonexclusive.

A quick check of the financial statements showed the cash burn (obvious need for maximum funds) to be substantial—$10 million in the previous nine months—with a hefty buildup of inventory. The

Table 3.5 Happiness Express Inc., Short Interest

1995	*Number of Shares Short*
January	152,006
February	449,490
March	752,000
April	805,541
May	900,600
June	1,033,421
July	940,729
August	887,644
September	522,402
October	490,547
November	462,007
December	454,868

Source: Bloomberg Financial Markets.

inventory numbers were particularly interesting because the product was a kid's hot toy and the inventory date was December 31, 1994.

Two other details nailed the case: Insiders were selling half of their stock in the deal despite the prodigious cash burn, and the company was on the hook for minimum future royalty payments of $2 million and aggregate minimum annual executive compensation of $900,000. In other words, HAPY could not stop spending when the fad slowed. (More on this interesting phenomenon in Chapter 4 with Scoreboard.)

Valuation, however, did not signal a safe and secure short, a phenomenon frequently found in growth-stock disinvesting. Earnings for the March 1995 fiscal year were expected to be $1.10, up almost 50 percent from the previous year, with at least another 50 percent rise expected for fiscal 1996. That meant the stock was selling at less than nine times forward earnings.

HAPY finished the fiscal year in March 1995 in good repute—it made the estimates while burning another $4.5 million of cash with a substantial increase in inventory. It is a rare company that stiffs investments bankers the quarter after an offering (MediaVision in Chapter 5 is the exception), so short sellers were not surprised or even restive. The stock price hung around $12 to $14, except for a momentary fade in March to $9 (see Figure 3.3).

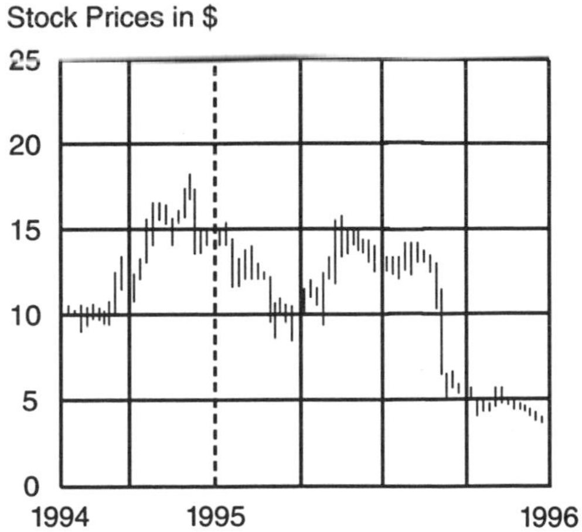

Figure 3.3 Happiness Express Inc., August 1, 1994–December 31, 1996. Chart from MetaStock by Equis International, Inc.

The June quarter was okay: sales up 139 percent, net income up 150 percent with inventories up again, cash flow still negative, and deal money disappearing—(only $4.9 million left in the coffers). The bulls said the stock was a bargain with the company's spectacular growth rate.

Finally, in September 1995, the stumble came. Management announced that earnings for the second quarter would not meet street expectations, and the stock traded to $5. In subsequent quarters, management wrote down uncollectible receivables and liquidated obsolete inventory with no sign of the next new fad in sight.

Bubble stocks, the purest and easiest form of short selling, whet the appetite for a more perilous bull-market game—high multiple-growth stocks. The simple skills of Harrier and Clinicorp, of Medstone and Happiness Express train short sellers for the next level of tracking fads that go to the moon.

◆ *Notes*

1. Harrier, Inc., Prospectus, 22 May 1986, 3.
2. The Merlin Group, "Harrier Inc.," May 1988, 11.
3. Ibid., 6.
4. Harrier, Inc., Form 10K, 30 June 1987, 4.
5. The Merlin Group, 7.
6. Alan Abelson, "Up and Down Wall Street," *Barron's*, 8 August 1988, 91–92.
7. Harrier, Inc., press release, 9 August 1988.
8. David H. Talbot, "Medstone International, Inc.," Arnhold & S. Bleichroeder, Inc., 21 December 1988, 1.
9. Medstone International, Inc., Prospectus, 2 June 1988, 28.
10. Medstone International, Inc., press release, 15 August 1989, 1.
11. Clinicorp, Inc., Prospectus, 13 January 1992, 6.
12. Ibid.

4

High-Multiple Growth Stocks, Part 1: High Risk, Low Return

Sometimes Wall Street's favorites—growth stocks—mimic the ascent and overvaluation of their more humble siblings—the bubble companies. Every bull market has its new-concept, high-multiple growth stocks. The simplest form comes from a company with a fad product that is perceived to have a long life—Coleco and Scoreboard, for example. The next level of financial complexity is a concept or theme stock from companies that sell a product or service to fill a newly perceived need—J. Bildners with its yuppy grocery stores and Jiffy Lube with quick oil changes, for example. In the 1960s, they were called one-decision stocks: Investors bought them and never sold them—thus, one decision, to buy.

By taking a cynical look at business plans, the investor can determine which of the numerous innovators might succeed and can then take advantage of brokerage hysteria and enthusiastic price inflation to sell the stock. The odds are with the short sellers: New-business statistics show failure rates far in excess of success. The Wall Street game, however, is a little more complex. Wall Street awards preliminary kudos to companies just for trying or just for hiring the right investment banker or public relations agent. And that is what makes shorting concept stocks chilling, palm-sweating, white-knuckle hard work.

From the short point of view, the most important decision on a concept stock is: Does this work—is the prospective return worth the risk for the stockholder? The second question is: How soon will the new company run out of money? Shorts almost always judge correctly if the business is dying. On the timing of the demise, they are seldom right. Someone is usually available to buy stock, loan money, offer short-term bank debt long after the company financials are in nearly terminal condition. Add two years to a short's best projection, and you might only have a couple more years to wait.

◆ *Computers and Cabbage Patch Dolls: Coleco*

In short-seller history books, Coleco Industries certainly deserves an honorable mention as a concept stock with terrible short timing. One of the megagrowth candidates of the early 1980s, the company was propelled to stellar stock heights with Street enthusiasm for a home computer in every pot. The stock moved from \$19 to \$65 from mid-1982 to 1983 with the excitement of a new idea (see Figure 4.1). Coleco's

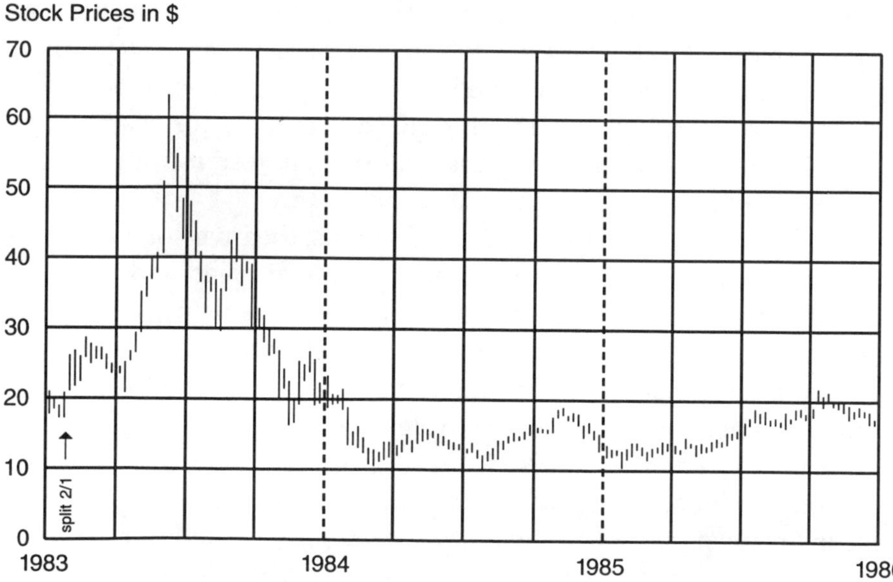

Figure 4.1 Coleco Industries, Inc., January 1, 1983–December 31, 1986

Adam home computer was supposed to be cheap (under $600) and sophisticated enough to play games, generate tax returns, and index recipes. It was due on the shelves before Christmas 1983.

The computer was unveiled with a fanfare that surprised even Wall Street with its devotion to hyperbole. In a smoky box at the Chicago Consumer Electronics Show in June 1983, the Adam nested in its prototypical glory. The computer needed to be rolling off production lines by September to meet expected demand at Christmas—the original delivery date was August 31.

Before too much time had passed, disagreement broke out on Wall Street. The stock price started to gyrate. Rumors began to circulate that delays, production problems, and glitches in schedule were occurring. Analysts also started talking about jagged second-quarter financials: ballooning inventories from the previous year's ColecoVision videogame consoles, nonrecurring gains, odd asset classifications. The stock started slipping in earnest during the late summer.

Coleco attempted to silence detractors with daily press releases offering reassurance about production, revenues, and earnings. The stock would rally, then edge back down. The positive company press slipped in late August: Coleco made an announcement that delivery would be stalled until mid-September. Then the company flubbed a

Table 4.1 Coleco Industries, Inc., Short Interest

1983	*Number of Shares Short*	*1984*	*Number of Shares Short*
January	1,741,036	January	3,598,841
February	1,460,471	February	3,584,248
March	1,398,726	March	4,127,356
April	1,532,915	April	3,905,876
May	1,530,501	May	3,576,761
June	1,452,382	June	3,202,331
July	1,354,070	July	3,306,811
August	1,237,390	August	3,077,093
September	1,432,407	September	3,244,636
October	2,106,349	October	3,103,026
November	2,506,448	November	2,763,176
December	3,791,721	December	2,385,537

Table 4.2 Scoreboard Inc., Short-Interest

1991	*Number of Shares Short*	*1992*	*Number of Shares Short*	*1993*	*Number of Shares Short*	*1994*	*Number of Shares Short*
January	13,455	January	852,938	January	2,133,380	January	1,974,823
February	51,864	February	823,906	February	2,227,082	February	1,973,201
March	70,413	March	757,188	March	2,318,138	March	2,037,700
April	213,561	April	795,520	April	2,279,490	April	2,217,950
May	374,439	May	1,415,524	May	2,610,520	May	2,285,220
June	346,755	June	1,821,030	June	2,610,808	June	2,483,730
July	1,491,480	July	1,809,270	July	2,573,276	July	2,845,857
August	2,473,305	August	2,183,910	August	1,287,713	August	2,551,590
September	2,652,450	September	2,156,978	September	2,643,116	September	2,348,795
October	2,638,395	October	2,067,078	October	2,291,188	October	1,742,734
November	1,476,747	November	1,940,668	November	2,185,658	November	1,569,832
December	1,306,196	December	2,006,130	December	2,080,206	December	1,140,893

Source: Bloomberg Financial Markets.

demonstration on September 6. To calm the investment community, the company decided to sponsor a field trip to the factory for institutional investors and analysts. Short sellers were less than impressed with what appeared to be somewhat archaic methods of soldering circuit boards. Sure enough, computers sold on consignment were later returned for defects.

Then, the delivery date was pushed back to mid-October, and the number of units available for delivery was in question. Suppliers talked openly about canceled orders for production inputs. The September 30 10Q also showed a buildup in raw materials rather than finished goods or work in process—the production could not be spitting out Adams consistently.

But Coleco's demise did not occur in fall 1983. Although short sellers were right and momentarily jubilant, Cabbage Patch dolls—a fad from nowhere—bailed out the company and the stock price, for a while. The end was only postponed. In 1984, Coleco's management team ramped up production for their new hotter product, but the fad had passed by 1986. The company ceded to bankruptcy in 1988, with cash flow unable to support the continuous inroads of new-product optimism. Short sellers were right, but years after they made the call with assurance.

◆ *Keeping Score with Baseball*

The Scoreboard Inc. was another fad company that wrecked the nerves and the net worth of many a short seller in 1991, 1992, 1993, and 1994. BSBL was the symbol, thus its nickname Baseball. The company repackaged baseball cards and sports memorabilia and sold its wares primarily on home shopping channels.

The initial draw for analysts was the secondary stock prospectus. It was in the summer of 1991 before short sellers were beaten senseless by momentum investors, when they still thought short selling was fun and profitable. The document read like a soap—Willie Mays had "commenced an arbitration against the company out of an alleged breach of an autograph agreement . . . ,"[1] and one of the officers had a civil claim against Mays for physical assault. The head guy, Goldin, had been chairman of the board of a company that had filed for bankruptcy in March 1990 with a personal default judgment against Goldin. His son and executive vice president received a suspended sentence and three years probation for unauthorized use of credit card accounts to gain access to a computer without payment when he was a student. Thirty-three percent of revenues were booked through a company owned by a son-in-law.

The financials were slightly funny: Inventory was up by more than cost of sales; prepaids and license agreements suggested the balance sheet might have some fluff. Interesting, the short sellers thought.

Then Prudential pulled the deal—in other words, canceled the offering—and short sellers thought they had a quick one. Little did they know that baseball cards would dominate their lives for years to come.

Three months after this initial burst of short enthusiasm, the stock became a hot stock with stellar earnings growth and plenty of momentum; it quintupled and was mentioned in *Barron's* every week as someone's favorite growth idea. It traded from $7.50 to $39.00 in six months. An amusing little baseball bubble became the stock that ate your portfolio.

The 10K came out in April, and short sellers were too brutalized to look quick. When they did, they saw a classic—a theme that would be the only one that worked for the next couple of years. On the balance sheet, Accounts Receivable were up 142 percent, sales up 76 percent! Baseball was not collecting bills, for some reason. Finished goods inventory was up 82 percent, with cost of goods up 60 percent. Card sets were not selling quite as quickly as expected. Prepaids were up 144 percent—1.6 million against pretax income of $9.4 million. The only reason cash flow was positive was because of the increase in Current Liabilities. All of this belied the business plan—what should have been a cash cow business was not. Remember, they packaged cards and sold them through home shopping networks. Payments out and collections in should have matched so that the margins showed up in cash every quarter. There were two other key points in the verbiage of the 10K: 19 percent of sales were through the son-in-law to

Home Shopping, and 16 percent of sales were to QVC on consignment. In other words, 35 percent of the revenues were suspect, and, with that massive receivables growth, sales could all come back in returned merchandise.

When the first-quarter earnings were announced, they were light. Prepaids were up sequentially by almost $3 million on pretax of $2.1 million. The stock traded from $39 to $11.75 (pre-October 1993 split), and the shorts confidently added. That was the price low for years to come.

This was occurring at what was still the beginning of the conference-call phenomena. What would become an elaborate ritual with sophisticated electronic systems capable of discriminating shorts from longs was still a promotional event. At about that time, the shorts agreed not to ask questions on the Baseball call; then, in late 1993, they started raising their voices again. The denouement was August 1994 when the only voice was a lone short, probably the only live buyer left, maybe the only person on the call at all. This first call was amateur enough.

The Baseball bulls made three suggestions on the conference call: Change the symbol, get listed, and get new analysts. The company blamed the shortfall on the decline in sales of baseball cards and on low sales on Home Shopping due to a severed relationship. The second quarter would be a little tough, too, due to changed seasonality patterns, but the company expected growth in the latter half of the year with earnings of $1.75 to $1.90 for the year, sales of about $80 million. Baseball management got into the habit early on of telling investors what earnings would be. The *typical* practice is to tell the analysts who tell the Street, but, in this case, Paul Goldin did not waste time with the intermediaries.

The July quarter of 1992 was indeed lower, with down earnings and revenues, but everyone had been warned in advance, and the stock price started moving up in anticipation of the resumption of glory in the second half. By November, the stock was up to $26 (presplit), revenue growth was up 36 percent, with earnings the same. When the 10Q was finally filed and the balance sheet came out, the stock dipped down to $18 (presplit). Scoreboard came out with a real keeper of a press release: "Chairman, President, and Chief Executive Paul Goldin says the company's stock price is probably down in response to negative rumors being circulated by short sellers today. It appears the shorts are claiming that the recently filed 10Q for the third quarter ended October shows a low cash position and high inventory, Goldin notes. However, Goldin says that is 'totally untrue.'"[2] Untrue? Cash was $17,000 after Morgan Stanley had done a $7.5 million convertible private placement in August. Finished goods inventory were up huge — 127 percent with accounts receivable up 130 percent and prepaids up to $7.2 million. And this while revenues and cost of goods were down. Goldin also took the opportunity to waffle on his last earnings prediction of $1.75, saying it depended on sales on cable television in the remaining weeks of the quarter.

In early 1993, both *Forbes* and the *Wall Street Journal* announced the demise of the baseball-card collecting fad. The secondary market collapsed, with prices for cards cut in half.

When the year-end was finally announced, the stock traded down to $14 (presplit), with earnings of $1.52 and sales of $75 million. The financial statements were more of the same—cash burn, high receivables and inventories, and the intangible and other assets line growing as well. During the year, baseball had shifted the business mix away from prepackaged trading cards to more sports and entertainment memorabilia, so this growing "intangible and other assets" line was eye-catching. The 10K footnote revealed the composition of the intangible and other assets—license agreements for one thing. Inventory and intangibles were, therefore, excellent places to stash costs that management might not want to expense on the income statement to reduce earnings in current quarters. Most companies have a fair amount of leeway on how costs are attached to units—whether they expect to sell 10,000 Elvis Presley plates or 100 affects the way they expense the right or the license for those units, just like book publishing. When these balance-sheet lines jump, the concern is that the assets will never be realized, that 10,000 will not be sold. Management acknowledged on the year-end conference call that Joe Dimaggio autographed inventory was being built up prior to a television sales push.

The rest of 1993 was a nightmare for weary shorts. Baseball resumed sales on Home Shopping, expanded hours on QVC, and promised to expand margins and escalate growth. The stock was flogged by a growing number of analysts who felt this was a business, not a fad. Ray Dirks included the name in his "ShortBuster Club" stock picks. Analysts expected $95 million in revenues and $1.95 to $2.00 in earnings (presplit). Most mentioned the large short position as a bullish indicator, a drum beat that grew in the ensuing years of the bull market with any stock that had the good fortune to attract the attention of the shrinking cadre of short sellers. High short interest became reason enough to buy a stock and wait for the rush of short sellers to repent the error of their bet. Management announced a stock split for November, and the stock peaked at split price of close to $20 (see Figure 4.2), or a hair off the old high the shorts thought they had beat back in 1992.

The financial statements of Scoreboard showed good growth in revenues and earnings in fiscal 1994, with revenues higher than the previous year at $109 million and earnings slightly lower than analysts' estimates, $0.95 ($1.90 presplit). Cash flow from operations continued to be negative with debt ever rising along with receivables and prepaids.

The break came April 7, 1994, when Baseball management held a conference call and announced a restructuring, with concomitant charge of $0.33 a share, and an operating loss for the first quarter. They also addressed inventory (15 percent was old memorabilia that included

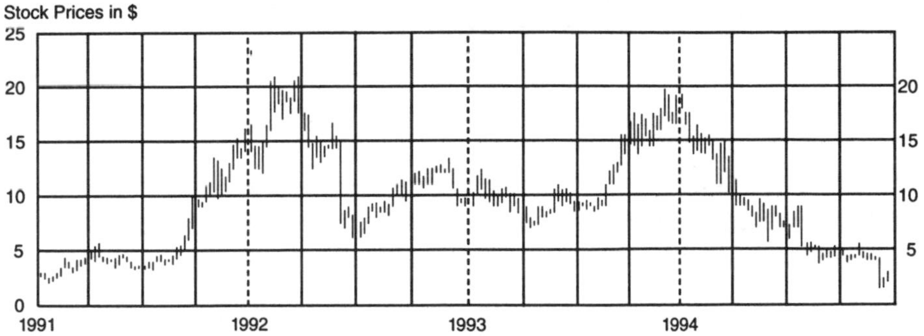

Figure 4.2 The Scoreboard, Inc., January 1, 1991–December 31, 1994. Chart from MetaStock by Equis International, Inc.

Joe DiMaggio autographed goods). Cash flow, they acknowledged, was negative but they made a commitment to achieving positive operating cash flow. When asked how they expected to do that, management had no specific plans for target inventory turnover or receivable collection—two necessary components of operating cash flow.

At the end of May, Paul Goldin died, and son Ken took over to announce the first-quarter disaster—sales $11 million versus $19 million, with finished-goods inventories up another 32 percent. It looked like Joe DiMaggio just kept signing those baseballs; in fact, the company said the largest component of inventory was Dimaggio goods, and the contract had been dropped. The balance sheet was a disaster: cash of $263,000 with short-term bank debt of $18 million; cash burn of close to $6 million in the quarter; receivables, prepaids, and intangibles high. Shorts thought years of capitalized expenses were coming home to roost. The stock traded to $6.

With bank debt and cash burn working to strangle the company, the shorts stayed with the position. On July 14, 1994, Scoreboard announced an agreement with Hallmark Cards that included Shaquille O'Neal partyware and gift wrap—surely a product designed to replace the hot fads of the past.

In September 1994, Baseball finally addressed the inventory problem with a $5.8 million write-down and another restructuring charge and notified the bank that it was in default. The conference call was the one with the eerie quiet where there was talk of a significant short squeeze. The shorts appeared to be the only ones who cared about buying and had plenty of time and supply of stock to execute the trades. By December, the stock was at $2.625, and the short sellers had made a little money.

Scoreboard was the beginning of a long series of dig-your-heels-in short positions. The momentum-growth mutual funds of the early 1990s were happy to run stocks up with high short interests; the subsequent declines had little impact on portfolio return because of the huge fund size. The short sellers, on the other hand, were slow to learn to step aside and pick their moment. Some companies, like Baseball, had no obvious indicator right before the last crash. All the analyst had to go on was the pretty-sure knowledge that the balance sheet was crammed with intangibles avoiding appropriate deduction on the income statement and that cash flow never was positive on a simple packaged product. That knowledge and the bad habit of shorting fad stocks were enough to keep the short interest at record highs through the many years of Baseball.

◆ *Marble and Brass in a Grocery Store: J. Bildner & Sons*

J. Bildner was an upscale yuppie grocery store chain that went public in the fall of 1986. It had successful stores in Boston—all brass and marble and slick displays with delivery and gourmet carryout. The initial public offering (IPO) prospectus stated that the mission was "to serve time-conscious consumers with high levels of disposable income"[3]—in other words, a big 7-Eleven with great service and home delivery for investment bankers. The stores featured imported tile, marble, European refrigerated cases, antique fixtures, and mahogany paneling and offered everything from video rentals to Brie to Pampers. It was the prospectus and its substantial information about the luxury grocery business that tipped the shorts. The Bildner escapade told shorts that anybody could get money for any business plan—for a little while. It was a simple version of the franchise mania yet to come.

The Bildner deal got off to a rocky start when the stock offering was reduced from 1,875,000 to 1,450,000 shares at the bottom limit of the price range, $13 in a $13-to-$16 proposed range.

The prospectus told readers that the company anticipated that new funds for the ambitious expansion plan would last through calendar 1987. It warned that delays in opening stores could have "material adverse effect on . . . anticipated operating results ."[4] The date was September 1986; 11 stores were running, with 24 new stores scheduled to open, according to the strategic plan, by the end of 1987. Stores cost from $350,000 to $1,800,000, with net profit margins for the industry in 1986 running 1.38 percent, according to Value Line.[5]

The prospectus also mentioned in the Risk section that "successful growth of the Company's operations will depend on continued development of management skills" and that the current team had never had responsibility for a large operation.[6] James Bildner was 32, the senior vice-president of finance was 29, and assorted other officers ranged from 32 to 42.

The first indication that the marketing plan had gone awry was observed during a visit to one of the Atlanta stores. Located in a downtown Atlanta department store, this Bildner's had a produce counter featuring iceberg lettuce near the imported cheese and wine display, and the clientele was distinctly below the yuppie standard.

A check on proposed new locations showed the Bildner strategic-marketing team to be the victim of an ebullient mall-leasing agent (although there is no evidence that the Bildner planning staff was not a willing and compliant mark). Birmingham and Atlanta, in particular, had wildly inappropriate locations. In a town where everyone has to drive, no individual chooses to drive to a mall after work, fight crowded parking lots for pricey carryout, and return home in rush-hour traffic to eat in. Walk-in traffic may work in downtown Boston, but the South is not quite ready to shift from Kentucky Fried off the main six-lane drag to shitake mushrooms through a maze of consumer traffic jams. In addition, the malls picked for locations were not necessarily in high-income locales.

A Few Small Problems

The next financial clue came with the January 25, 1987, 10K. When the document came out in late spring, the stock price was $11 to $13, after trading from $9 to $14.75 after the $13 offering (see Figure 4.3). The 10K revealed three important points:

1. The quality of earnings was poor.
2. Construction delays hurt the expansion plans.
3. Cash burn was quicker than anticipated.

The quality of earnings is a major issue with short sellers. Companies repeatedly try to include nonoperating earnings in "earnings"

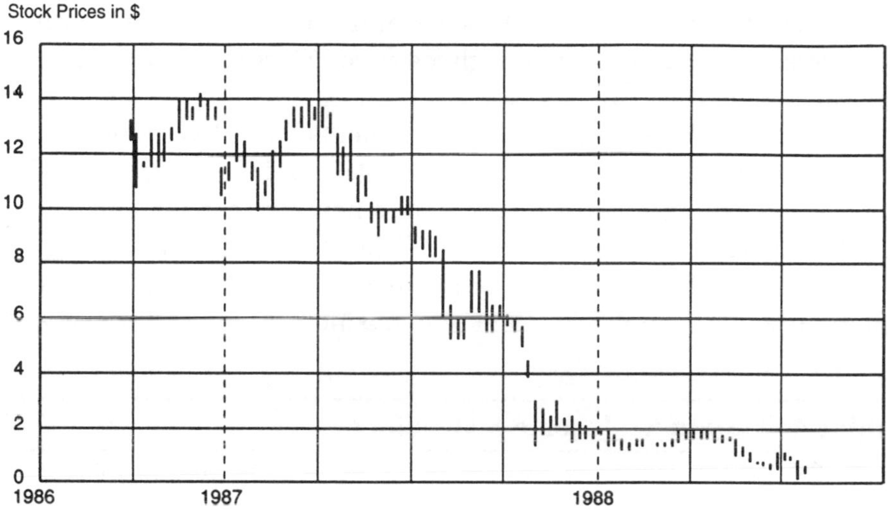

Figure 4.3 J. Bildner & Sons, Inc., July 1, 1986–September 30, 1988. Chart from MetaStock by Equis International, Inc.

to create the appearance of growth and financial well-being. This subterfuge requires the analyst to read the footnotes and the management discussion of earnings in the 10Q. Sometimes in extreme cases (Crazy Eddie in Chapter 10), the verbiage is dramatically different in the quarterly report and press releases than in the 10Q.[7]

The quality-of-earnings issue is compounded by Wall Street's electronic ritual of tape watching for earnings. Typically, most institutional players and all brokers have machines that show asterisks for news releases. Everyone is prepped in advance for the time of probable release and expected quarterly earnings per share. When the number hits the tape, the response is instantaneous. If the company is followed by a number of brokerage houses, the stock moves up if the number is above target, down if it is below. And it sometimes takes hours or days (or years in the case of Integrated Resources, Chapter 7) for brokerage analysts to get enough detail from the company to comment on the quality of earnings and the true margins. The company might be forthcoming and frank with specifics about earnings composition, but no one legally has to get a look until the 10Q or 10K is released. With the advent of fax machines, favorite analysts might get faxes way before hoi polloi. If the earnings report is a truly complex one, Street analysts might not catch the significance until the stock price alerts them to difficulties.

In Bildner's case, the Income Statement (Table 4.3) showed earnings before taxes and extraordinary credit of $681,733, versus $111,848 a year earlier—pretty good growth for a new company. A closer look at the expense lines suggested that "Other Expense, Net" was out of line: $34,781, versus $280,339 in the previous year. Note K (Table 4.4), footnote to the Income Statement, showed interest expense of $445,614,

Table 4.3 Bildner's Income Statement

	Fiscal Period Ended	
	January 25, 1987	*January 26, 1986*
Net Sales	$31,289,870	$11,353,935
Cost of Sales	16,444,774	6,263,031
Gross Profit	14,845,096	5,090,904
Store Operating Expenses	11,489,306	3,714,442
Selling, General and Administrative Expenses	2,639,276	984,275
Other Expense, Net	34,781	280,339
Earnings (Loss) before Income Taxes and Extraordinary Credit	681,733	111,848
Provision for Income Taxes	152,000	—
Earnings (Loss) before Extraordinary Credit	529,733	111,848
Extraordinary Credit—Utilization of Net Operating Loss Carryforward	87,000	—
Net Earnings (Loss)	$ 616,733	$ 111,848
Per Share Amounts:		
Earnings (Loss) before Extraordinary Credit	$ 0.11	$ 0.03
Extraordinary Credit	0.02	—
Earnings (Loss)	$ 0.13	$ 0.03
Weighted Average Number of Common and Common Equivalent Shares	4,877,057	3,310,585

Source: J. Bildner & Sons, Inc., Form 10K, 25 January 1987.

Table 4.4 J. Bildner's Disclosure of Cookie Store Gain

	Fiscal Period Ended	
	January 25, 1987	*January 26, 1986*
Interest expense	$445,614	$297,406
Interest income	(111,036)	(17,067)
Other income	(299,797)	—
	$ 34,781	$280,339

Source: J. Bildner & Sons, Inc., Form 10K, 25 January 1987.

with ($111,036) in interest income and ($299,797) in other income, for a net of the mysterious $34,781. So what is "other"?

The next step in the search for the missing "other" was the verbal explanation of earnings: "Other expenses as a percentage of sales were 0.1% in fiscal 1987, compared to 2.5% in fiscal 1986, and included a gain of $299,000 on the sale of one of the Company's cookie and ice cream stores in the fourth quarter of fiscal 1987."[8] Translated, that means the company booked a capital gain as a negative expense. With annual earnings of $529,733, quality-of-operating earnings was compromised. A more conventional and informative treatment would have been to disclose the profits from the gain as an extraordinary item, independent of operating profits. So operating earnings on sales of $31,289,870 were really $382,733, or 1.2 percent of revenues versus 2.2 percent with the gain (ignoring the tax treatment of the sale).

Next, the financials stated that the company had "experienced construction, design and licensing delays at new locations" and had deferred openings of seven stores to the next fiscal year.[9] For the first time, the company cautioned that it had made a substantial investment in New York City store locations, with no assurance of success. It also mentioned that local unions threatened problems in New York City.

New York City store checks showed one location close to both Fairway and Zabar's, two favorites of New York City shoppers for both price and quality, with a definite overlap in product. The strategic plan had failed to consider the large competitive threats across the street. The prospectus had noted that "the Company isn't aware of any competitor."[10] Most analysts on Wall Street do not do extensive site checks to determine the accuracy of execution of a company's plan. When they do, it is usually a company-sponsored trip to model locations or to a New York City location; motivated financial detectives can accumulate a bunch of relevant information easily by using their eyes. Store checks work. What you see might show variances in planned activities or weakness in strategy.

The 10K also mentioned that "the Company required more financing for expansion than originally anticipated."[11] Capital would be raised with an increased bank revolving-credit agreement and with a new offering—a convertible subordinated debenture offered for $25 million in Europe, which should surely see Bildner through January 31, 1988. In a bull market, overseas convertibles are frequently an insight into the U.S. appetite for a given security; Bildner was losing access to gold in traditional corporate finance veins. With the increased debt load, so went the margins, only in inverse direction.

Meanwhile, on the balance sheet, another red flag appeared: Prepaid expenses and other assets rose, suggesting that Bildner was not expensing items from store openings quickly. Note C (Table 4.5) to the Income Statement showed evidence of aggressive capitalization of preoperating expenses, which included such lovelies as financial planning advice. Clearly, there was a need, but the choice of consultants, if the future is an apt assessment for advice rendered, did not make it easy to expense the costs over three years. The letter from President James Bildner in the Annual Report was optimistic, assured, naive: "Over the past three years, we have successfully defined a new market—specialty food retailing—and today are on the leading edge of that niche. The coming year will be a time to build and fortify that leadership position through the innovation, energy and commitment of all of us at the company."[12]

Cockroaches: More Than One Bad Quarter

The April 1987 10Q continued the ebb. Cash was down. Prepaid expenses were up. Debt was up. Net income was only 0.3 percent of

Table 4.5 Bildner's Prepaid Expenses and Preoperating Expenses

Prepaid Expenses	*Fiscal Period Ended*	
	January 25, 1987	*January 26, 1986*
Store preopening expenses	$1,516,880	$121,533
Deferred marketing development costs	205,307	—
Packaging and supplies	417,900	66,350
Other	177,773	49,513
Prepaid expenses and other current assets	$2,317,860	$237,396

Preopening expenses relate to initial direct store operating expenses, such as rent, promotion, labor, utilities, etc., incurred by an individual store prior to opening; also included is training for employees who will be staffing new locations.

Deferred marketing development costs relate exclusively to particular future marketing campaigns, are net of amortization, and include prepaid advertising commitment fees, future promotional events, advertising time and space, and costs for marketing production for radio and television. The Company's policy is to amortize these costs over the remainder of the length of a particular marketing campaign; the balance outstanding at January 25, 1987, is expected to be fully amortized by the Company's second quarter of fiscal 1988.

Prepaid Expenses	*Fiscal Period Ended*	
	January 25, 1987	*January 26, 1986*
Preoperating expenses (included in other assets)	$1,586,583	$457,975

Preoperating expenses are those expenditures incurred by the Company in creating, developing, and negotiating leases for a new store or multiple store locations by geographic region. These costs primarily consist of legal, outside consultants (including market and location study organizations), financial planning advice, travel, regional recruitment, administrative salaries, and overhead costs related to these activities. Preoperating expenses, including those related to long-term lease agreements, are being amortized on a straight-line basis over three years. Additions and amortization for the year ended January 25, 1987, were approximately $1,485,000 and $357,000, respectively.

Source: J. Bildner & Sons, Inc., Form 10K, 25 January 1987.

revenues, even without the burden of the yet-unissued convertible interest charge. Store checks disclosed that Atlanta stores were fairly empty, and informal customer surveys indicated unhappy shoppers, even in the better locations. Meat cuts were irregular, and gourmet necessities were not always available. Clerks were not knowledgeable. The target market did not have time or interest in trying repeatedly until J. Bildner got it right.

The company responded to the cash bind and the New York City problems by slowing its expansion plans. Analysts seemed pleased: No matter if earnings growth would be slower, the change would give the company time to get back in control. The new direction "reduces the risk of a major earnings interruption as the company pursues a somewhat less rapid growth strategy," the Kidder Peabody analyst said.[13] The stock was cheap at $11, "given the company's 40% estimated 5-year normalized growth rate and prospects for earnings-per-share gains of 208% and 88%, respectively, for the next two years, we believe these shares offer considerable value for risk-oriented investors."[14] In other words, "the valuation is attractive," as the walls come down.

J. Bildner's management team made a concerted effort to pull things back together in mid-1987 when they hired a Federated executive from Atlanta-based Rich's to help run the growth. It was too late to salvage the leaky financials.

By fall, however, Bildner was admitting defeat, and expansion plans were scaled back to 23 new stores, rather than the 50 originally planned. The company had two quarters of losses and planned to close a Birmingham store and sell more assets to raise cash. The resale market for used grocery fixtures made of mahogany and brass was somewhat lower than the cost to produce them.

In December 1987, Bildner announced the closing of the New York stores. New Yorkers had never warmed to the luxurious interiors and high prices; staffing, strikes, construction delays, and location joined to deliver small sales and larger losses.

Then on July 12, 1988, Jim Bildner filed for bankruptcy under Chapter 11 with $45 million in debt and seven stores remaining.

The lessons from J. Bildner were three, all applicable to a torrid IPO market:

1. View the IPO document as a business person. Does the business make sense? Can prices be high enough to support the capital investment in glitzy store interiors? Can the necessary expansion be funded?
2. Watch for signs of potential failure, especially when the company gives you a benchmark. When the first financial clues appeared in print that J. Bildner's management was not meeting the strategic plan, the stock was still high priced—$11 to $13 per share.
3. Do not be put off by a new and unexpected cash infusion. There is usually a greater financing fool. After you think it is obvious that the business plan has failed and the appetite for cash is geometric, Wall Street will find at least one more, maybe two, fools to infuse large amounts of cash for an expected rate of return that is far below the risk they will take.

◆ *Lending to Franchisees: Jiffy Lube*

Jiffy Lube, a quick-oil-change franchise company, was a growth stock and a short sale candidate with plenty of Wall Street assistance in blowing up the balloon. It was great franchise training, with a classic set of franchise financial statements for short sellers who fought the restaurant rage in the 1990s. The story had all the drama and diversity of a multipart, made-for-TV accounting saga. Wall Street loved Jiffy Lube. The story was easy to tell, easy to sell. Americans have less time, Americans need oil changes, local full-service gas stations are disappearing: Buy Jiffy Lube; it solves a problem.

The corporate philosophy was a fine example of a poorly devised business plan: The company bet that a spectacular growth rate of franchises would swamp all competition; leave it in control of the field and, therefore, of pricing; and, in the end, offer the company a high and sustainable rate of return.

The parent company received development fees for rights to geographical areas and franchise fees for opening stores. It then sold oil and parts to the franchisees and took a percentage of revenues for the privilege of the Jiffy Lube expertise. All of this is normal franchise procedure. It is *not* normal for the parent company to assume all of the risk of many of the franchisees. Jiffy Lube took back paper (debt) for franchisee start-up expenses, and they delivered inventories of oil and parts for credit. Eventually, the balance sheet tilted over, much like a human pyramid would when one person too many is added. Getting there took several years and much agony for shorts who called the demise long before the event.

The Beginning

A *Barron's* article in December 1986 was the introduction to Jiffy Lube. The writer, Robert Barker, made some compelling points:

- "Financial strength was nothing to write home about."
- Competition was mounting.
- The stock was selling at forty times next year's earnings.
- Operating income was full of nonrecurring items.[15]

Not long after the Barker article appeared, someone wrote to *Wall Street Week* asking for a play on quick-change oil companies. The panelist answered that Jiffy Lube was one alternative. The stock price began its stellar climb, moving from $18 to $30 (presplit) over a six-week period.

The stock-buying public soon warmed to Wall Street's vision of Jiffy Lube. They could see it on the highway near their suburban homes. They could understand the concept. It reminded them of a McDonald's, and the PR was quick to capitalize on that favorite franchisor stock as a selling comparison—hamburgers, oil change—the wave of the future, convenience, speed, cookie-cutter stores.

Wall Street got behind the idea—Alex Brown, Shearson Lehman, for example. The stock went on one-decision stock lists all over town. The analysts' voices could be heard rising in harmonious support, like hounds baying at a hunt. In 1986, Alex Brown was al-

Table 4.6 Jiffy Lube International, Inc., Short Interest

1987	*Number of Shares Short*	*1988*	*Number of Shares Short*
January	48,860	January	777,588
February	76,849	February	951,005
March	200,692	March	1,564,984
April	452,327	April	1,705,528
May	422,048	May	1,756,354
June	432,853	June	2,033,572
July	628,863	July	1,956,164
August	724,550	August	2,375,752
September	717,802	September	2,557,926
October	1,066,589	October	2,604,244
November	795,101	November	2,953,684
December	751,535	December	2,737,355

ready talking about quicklubes in Britain, France, and even Japan, with earnings per share moving from $0.32 in 1986 to $1.20 in 1988.[16] Some Wall Street growth-company analysts with spreadsheet programs traditionally make earnings projections symmetrically up at an ever-increasing rate of growth.

The IPO prospectus dated July 22, 1986, foreshadowed the company's demise, as in the case of J. Bildner. Up front and out in the open under "Investment Considerations" were:

1. "Capital Adequacy. The Company requires substantial amounts of capital to provide for the acquisition and development of Centers. . . ."
2. "Sources of Income. In the past three years the Company has experienced substantial growth in income largely as a result of income from area development fees and items such as gains on the sale of real estate and Company Operated Centers. These sources, which are nonrecurring in nature and have enabled the Company to record a profit in such years, are expected to decline in magnitude. . . ."
3. "Financial and Operational Controls. Maintenance of accurate, consistent financial and operational controls over its own

operations and its network of Centers is critical to the profitable expansion. . . ."

4. "Management. Mr. Hindman has routinely facilitated the Company's funding of various projects by either loaning money directly to the Company or personally guaranteeing loans from others. . . ."

5. "Conflicts of Interest. Certain members of management are investors in area developments and franchises. The interests of such investors may conflict with the interest of the Company."[17]

You did not even have to read past page 5 to get the gist of Jiffy Lube. Like shooting fish in a barrel, the shorts said.

The Middle

In March 1987, the stock split, and aggressive buyers moved the price up its obligatory bull-market 25 percent on the announcement, to prove once again that the market really is driven by fools and euphoria. The stock peaked at $25 and change (see Figure 4.4). The first sign of real trouble came in the prospectus from the next stock deal, dated June 4, 1987, and it was a classic for a company with company officials as franchise owners. Careful readers (this time one had to read to page 34) were rewarded with a peculiarly hard-to-follow sleight of hand. James Hindman, CEO and chairman of the board of Jiffy Lube, was one of four partners in the aptly named BATH partnership, which in turn owned the franchising entity Lone Star. On March 26, 1987, before the quarter closed and the prospectus came out, Lone Star bought 24 centers and area-development rights from Jiffy Lube for $6,015,000. Lone Star paid Jiffy Lube $2,765,000 in cash, $1,625,000 in deferred-payment 10-year notes, and $1,625,000 in nonvoting stock of Lone Star. Jiffy Lube also arranged a line of credit for Lone Star and gave Lone Star reduced royalties on 13 centers initially and on all centers after year six if sales were below a certain level. What that did for Jiffy Lube was to:

- Increase revenues for the quarter by an unknown amount. Revenues for the quarter were $13,867,000, and the notes disclosed that, of the $6,015,000 Lone Star sale, the company recognized area-development fees of $935,000, franchise fees of $90,000, and a gain on sale of assets of $658,998. With income from operations for the quarter of $2,048,809, the $1,683,998 that they booked was a significant addition to earnings.

- Add $2,765,000 in cash to the prospectus balance sheet, thereby boosting cash to $2,474,018—from no cash to some cash.

The Lone Star deal was a rather productive transaction. Hindman sold 100,000 shares on the offering for $14.75 a share, or $1,475,000 total, no doubt covering any momentary outlay for his BATH. (More on BATH and Lone Star on p. 89.)

The next voice from the crowd was Ted O'glove's *Quality of Earnings* letter on July 23, 1987. O'glove noted that earnings from the 1987 fiscal year were poor quality. Nonrecurring revenues contributed

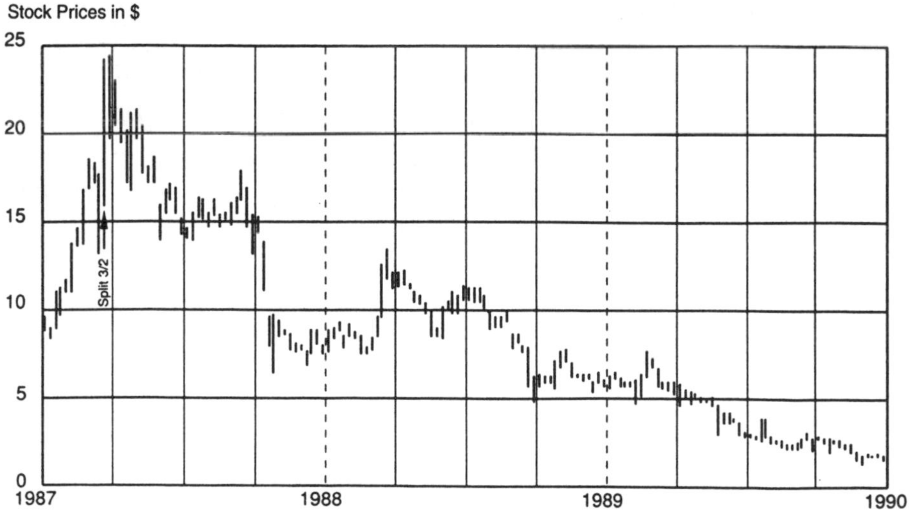

Figure 4.4 Jiffy Lube International, Inc., January 1, 1987–December 31, 1990. Chart from MetaStock by Equis International, Inc.

appreciably to earnings. His figures for after-tax, per-share contributions from nonbase business were:

- Initial franchise fees added $0.10 a share.
- Taxes and SG & A-adjusted area-development and master-license fees added $0.13.
- "Other" operating revenues added $0.03.
- Other income (interest on notes receivable and cash invested from the offering) added $0.08.
- Deferred (capitalized) expenses should have reduced earnings by $0.06.
- The Hindman transaction (Lone Star deal) mentioned earlier added $0.06.

The sum of all these nonrecurring revenues and aggressive accounting procedures was greater than the reported earnings of $0.28.[18] Even when nonrecurring earnings disappear, interest payments do not. The stock did not budge.

Then the "Heard on the Street" column in the *Wall Street Journal* pounded the stock, with short seller Jim Chanos questioning the bulls.[19] High receivables, he said; average store sales dropping, too much credit to franchisees. Hindman responded that they had to get there first and capture the market and that the store sales were not down—just more new stores in the count. Alex Brown pulled back a touch—the stock is pretty high priced, they implied, but a good grower.

The stock price dropped with the crash of October 1987 to $8, and the bears were somewhat vindicated; some covered, some waited. It looked like a broken stock.

The End, but Not the Finale

In October 1987, Jiffy Lube announced a stock buy-back of 850,000 shares—not exactly the best use of capital for a company burning cash, but a popular corporate move after the crash to calm the bloodied stockholders. Jiffy Lube, meanwhile, kept eating money and opening franchises. The December 31, 1987, 10Q showed total debt up again (this time by more than $30 million), with net income of only $0.10 a share (versus $0.09 in December 1986), down sequentially from $0.12, and margins a tad pallid.

Most analysts look at earnings and revenues versus year-ago earnings and revenues. In a rapid-growth company that adds outlets quarterly, sequential earnings can be equally interesting. Unless there is a pronounced seasonality to the product sales, revenues and net should go up each quarter.

The company also held 31 centers for resale. So the company had to sell unprofitable take-back centers as well as open new ones, doubling the burden of opening new stores. The franchise-for-sale section of a local newspaper or the *Wall Street Journal* provides the equivalent of a store check in a retail store. If franchisees are selling franchises, it means the parent has competition selling new units. If the company is advertising, the terms in the ad can be enlightening. An ad appeared in the *Wall Street Journal*, urging that "Entrepreneurs of all sizes, grab the Jiffy Lube opportunity. . . . No money down for owner/operators."[20] So the ads for centers for sale increased, offering giveaway terms.

The company made two other announcements that quarter that warmed bears' hearts: that the SEC disagreed with the recognition of area-development fees, which would require restating past earnings lower; and that the company would purchase a new headquarters for $10,500,000. Grizzled analyst wisdom says sell the stock of a company building a new headquarters that is owned, not leased: It is a top-of-the-earnings-cycle clue.

Jiffy Lube continued to run through cash at a prodigious rate. The Statement of Changes showed operating cash burn of $10.4 million for nine months, with another $17 million used for real estate—a total of $27 million—versus operating plus real estate of $11.7 million for 1986.

In February 1988, Shearson, Lehman's prospectus on a previously announced best-efforts limited partnership for the company came out:

$50 million to invest in real estate for franchisees or the company, guaranteed by Jiffy Lube. The greater fool had arrived to throw money at the company; but, unfortunately, the fools were the unwitting retail clients.

Rebirth

And then the stock price levitated again, in a palm-sweating, short-squeezing run-up in March to $13. That was a 60 percent rise. Stock was impossible to borrow. Shorts got bought in. The price ticked relentlessly up. Options traded like water. When call option volume runs up, that signals takeover rumors to observers. Some shorts recaptured lost positions with synthetic shorts: Buy a put, sell a call. The Wall Street grapevine said: Major oil company is buying JLUB for a fancy price, needs oil distribution, announced soon, probably Pennzoil. This is when one can hear the click and scratch of mechanical pencils, checking and double-checking valuations as the shorts do their version of saying the prayer beads: times revenues, times book, times earnings, times cash flow, times. . . .

And then the price settled back around $10 when the announcements failed to materialize. The June 30, 1988, 10Q was reassuring to shorts. Centers for resale were up to an astounding 70. Dogs that were returned to the parent because they were not profitable were draining cash as the parent tried to turn them around and find a buyer. Total debt was up again, by $25 million, with an operating loss on the income statement for the first time.

Even more amazing was the nature of the new, soon-to-be-long-term debt. Jiffy Lube or their investment bankers had found insurance companies willing to buy a private placement of $58 million at reasonable rates: 10.97 percent on the 10-year bond. Shorts called to find out buyers' names so they could short insurance companies willing to take on so much risk for so little return.

Jiffy Lube's stock price steadily declined after the operating loss, with occasional price flurries when takeover rumors surfaced. Shearson pulled their rating on the stock, reducing it to a sell—only 10 days after an investment pool of Shearson executives filed to sell 100,000 shares.[21]

The September quarter continued the decline with one new twist: more debt, more centers for resale (up to 81) requiring new advertising to attract franchisees. For the first time, the ugly specter of write-offs was raised: The company increased the credit-loss provision because of "significant increases in the outstanding balances of accounts and notes receivable and to provide for possible losses on receivables with franchisees who are experiencing financial difficulties."[22] Because a large proportion of assets on the balance sheet were franchisee-backed, significant franchisee defaults could collapse the balance sheet, destroy the book value, and throw the company into default of debt covenants.

And Default, Finally

And that's exactly what the company announced on February 9, 1989: a write-off (or special charge, as executives called it) of $39.2 million that threw Jiffy Lube into default of debt covenants. Of the write-off, $10.6 million was a charge for "resizing" Chairman Hindman's partnership (24 percent Hindman-owned), presumably the Lone Star/BATH arrangement that had created cash and earnings for the 1987 stock offering. A television station in Philadelphia added to the bad news when it aired a show on bad customer service at a local Jiffy Lube, dropping car counts in that market by 70 percent.

A comparative look at the Jiffy Lube balance sheets for year-end 1986 and 1988 tells the story of the company's demise. Franchisee-backed assets escalated from approximately 45 percent to 79 percent of total assets, while debt as a percentage of total capital declined slightly but nonetheless remained too high relative to dubious and illiquid assets. The company had no cushion to withstand the shock of weak sales or weak franchisee financial condition. The balance sheet, when analyzed with a healthy measure of skepticism, showed that assets might not be real and liquid.

The critical variable in franchise growth stories is obviously growth. If a company quits adding new franchisees, earnings and revenue growth halt. In a business like oil changes, cost of entry is not very high, so competition is fierce. A 10-percent price cut during a price war can decimate store margins. If the stores lose profitability, franchise growth slows, and franchisees slow payments to the parent (for the franchisor equivalent of a run on the bank—money out, none in). If the parent subsidizes all the growth of new stores, slow payments can kill already tenuous cash flow. And after cash burn escalates, the debt burden climbs and finally the asset side deteriorates as franchisees lose their ability to pay. The parent cannot bail fast enough.

In retrospect, the bankers said the problem with Jiffy Lube was easy money. Given plenty of financing by banks, Wall Street, and insurance companies, the urge to spend was too compelling. In an effort to throw the growing cache of funds out the door, Jiffy Lube lost control, lent to increasingly weaker franchisees in bad locations, and also tried to expand more and more quickly. An austere money environment certainly begets more conservative business practices for the likes of Jiffy Lube.

Jiffy Lube continued its rush to restructure and return to profitability. Real estate went on the block. The new headquarters was slated for a sale/leaseback. Unprofitable stores were relentlessly slashed. The stock price settled around $2.50. Pennzoil infused cash for 80 percent of the stock, thereby diluting existing shareholders (and edifying short sellers who managed to stay short), and paid off Hindman handsomely for not working.

Jiffy Lube taught one bull-market lesson soon to be repeated in the 1990s: In the long run, it is the equity and the junk-bond holders who take the torpedo hit for poorly conceived business plans, not the insiders or the investment bankers.

Scoreboard, J. Bildner's, and Jiffy Lube showed the student of IPOs how to evaluate a business plan, watch for execution, then dissect the financials for signs that the plan's failure had not been reflected in the income statement. The patience required to track the trail of failure is a critical skill for short sellers avoiding the wrong stock or the wrong time in a growth company's price trajectory.

◆ *Notes*

1. The Scoreboard Inc., Prospectus, 21 May, 1991, 22.
2. Dow Jones PIR, Scoreboard, 21 December 1992, 1.
3. J. Bildner & Sons, Inc., Prospectus, 22 September 1986, 3.
4. Ibid., 17.
5. *The Value Line Investment Survey*, 45, p. 3, no. 23, 10th ed., 23 February 1990, 1498.
6. Bildner, Prospectus, 5.
7. The best books on detecting accounting gimmickry and quality-of-earnings problems are Bernstein's *Financial Statement Analysis* (Homewood, IL: Richard Irwin, Inc., 1983), Thornton O'glove's *Quality of Earnings* (New York: The Free Press, 1987), and any book or article by Abraham Briloff. There are also several monthly services that detail ongoing problems.
8. J. Bildner & Sons, Inc., Form 10K, 25 January 1987, 18.
9. Ibid., 13.
10. J. Bildner & Sons, Inc., Prospectus, 22 September 1986, 19.
11. J. Bildner & Sons, Inc., Form 10K, 25 January 1987, 19.
12. J. Bildner & Sons, Inc., Annual Report, 15 May 1987, 8.
13. Barbara L. Kahn, "J. Bildner & Sons," Kidder, Peabody & Co., Incorporated Research, 12 May 1987, 1.
14. Ibid., 3.
15. Robert Barker, "Greaselock?," *Barron's*, 22 December 1986, 16.
16. Charles Glovsky, "Jiffy Lube International, Inc.," Alex Brown & Sons, Incorporated Research, 29 October 1986, 1.
17. Jiffy Lube International, Inc., Prospectus, 22 July 1986, 4–5.
18. Thornton O'glove, *Quality of Earnings Report*, 23 July 1987, 66–67.

19. Randall Smith, "Heard on the Street," *Wall Street Journal*, 1 October 1987, 71.
20. *Wall Street Journal*, 6 October 1988, B10.
21. Stephen Taub, "Shearson's Nifty Lube Job," *Financial World*, 15 November 1988, 8.
22. Jiffy Lube International, Inc., Form 10Q, 30 September 1988, 16.

5

High-Multiple Growth Stocks, Part 2: High Returns, Faltering Growth

The very backbone of a bull market is growth—new products, new presentation, new technology—spectacular growth opportunities that offer an investor the portfolio appreciation of the next Xerox. Short sellers itch to short these stocks. More savvy investors know how to own them, then sell them twice. There is almost always a bell ringing on the growth stocks that have one product. Shorts get killed trusting their intuition and common sense; longs get killed with their belief that the company can always expand to one more market. Chapter 4 dealt with fads that looked like new businesses. Chapter 5 is simply new products and how the growth cycle gives you clues at inflection points. The two relevant concepts that define the analytical task are pipeline fill and sustainable growth rate: *Pipeline fill* gives the revenue curve its shape; *sustainable growth rate* sets the financing needs for that curve.

Beverages

The year of the brave new beverage on Wall Street was 1993. The big guys, Pepsi and Coca-Cola, were thought to be slackers in understanding the taste preference of the new-age consumer. Water was chic: Clearly Canadian blossomed early on as a stock-market phenomenon and almost as quickly faded. Both the growth-stock guys and the short sellers got their appetites whetted with a whole new sector.

The three most tradable entrees were Cott Corporation, the Canadian generic cola company; Snapple for flavored ice teas; and Starbucks for coffee and coffee houses. Wall Street analysts could taste them, see them on the shelves at neighborhood delis, and argue the merits of a whole new taste experience that could expand to the world as soon as Manhattan was drowning in the new-age drinks. By the end of 1993, Cott traded at 69 times the last 12 months earnings, Snapple at 61 times, and Starbucks at 75 times.

◆ *Cott Corporation*

Cott Corporation did an equity deal in February of 1993, and that was probably the first time short sellers looked at the company. This was the period when business magazines were heralding the advent of the smart consumer who bought generic products and shunned the magic and higher prices of brand names. Cott produced a generic cola that taste tests said tasted better than Coke and Pepsi, or so the company reported. Why not?

The stock traded at around $28 in U.S. dollars, up from $9 a year before, and the prospectus had a couple of points of note. For those veterans of the Baseball wars (Chapter 4), the points were interesting but not actionable—most short sellers stayed away and watched, or they shorted, got burned, and quickly covered. First, the stock was pricey at 80 times fiscal (January) 1993 earnings, but that was not unusual in early 1993. Second, the prospectus mentioned lower margins and lower selling prices, and that was odd on a hot new product. Third, the "other asset" category on the balance sheet was large relative to pretax earnings. The footnotes told you that the company amortized deferred development costs, including new packaging costs, over three years—aggressive because it overstates current earnings and costs that should be expensed are not. Fourth, the director and officer list violated the more-than-two-with-the-same-last-name rule: There were three Pencers on the roster, including an insurance broker and what looked to be a Wharton M.B.A. dropout. Insiders had sold around a million shares since October 1991.

A little digging suggested Gerald Pencer's business background was the kind of record that short sellers love. His previous publicly traded company Financial Trustco Capital had wrecked with subsequent accusations of overstated assets and income. The stock had dropped to $2 from $19. Consistency in management style is one attribute that cheers short sellers. Most corporate managers reproduce the errors of the past with remarkably regular frequency and inspire their corporate culture with the same consistency of mismanagement.

The Oppenheimer analyst David Goldman was the first in the United States on the Cott bandwagon (not a surprise because Oppenheimer was the banker on the equity deal)—earnings of $0.95 in fiscal year 1994 were expected to be up from $0.35 the previous year. With the price at $34, Goldman suggested investors wait for a better buying opportunity. By April, with the fourth-quarter results out and the stock at $36, he got more aggressive: "The Cott story seems more compelling today (with the stock at $36) than it did a year ago (when the stock was at only $9) . . . our estimates could have a significant upward bias."[1] He went on to mention that the bottom line had been helped by a lower than expected tax rate and fewer shares outstanding to offset the effect of lower margins.

At the end of April, the stock was rocked from its $38 high down to $28 (see Figure 5.1) on news that Coca-Cola was ready to take the gloves off and lower prices to regain share. The shorts lamented their lack of involvement and their timorousness in such perilous times, and then the stock took off again. Morgan Stanley issued a new purchase recommendation, effusive in its praise of the new private-label business.

Analyst Howard Penney mentioned Cott's dependence on Wal-Mart in his report—34.3 percent of sales in fiscal 1993—as a negative, and the shorts had been mindful of the fact since the first. Longtime short wisdom (if there was such a thing in 1993, after the trying years that went before) says to short a stock when the Wal-Mart pipeline is

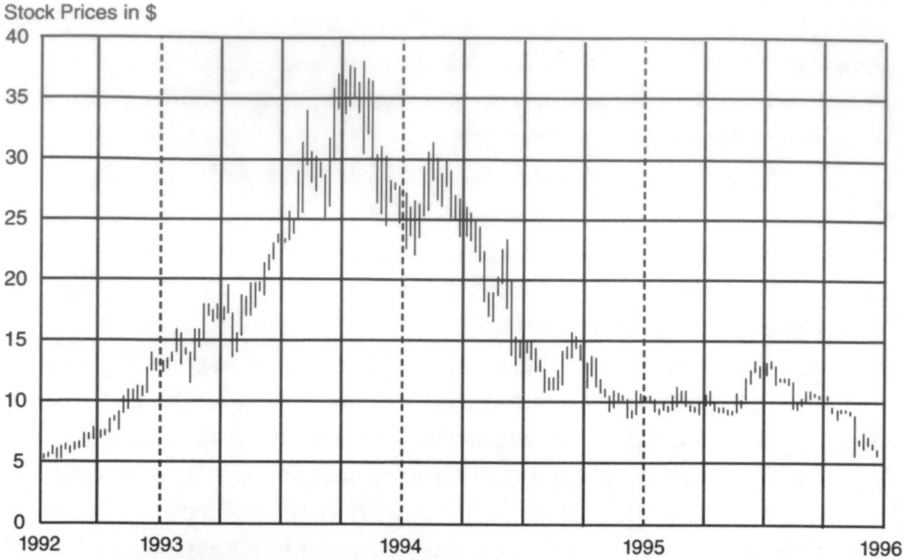

Figure 5.1 Cott Corporation, June 1992–December 1996. Chart from MetaStock by Equis International, Inc.

full. *Pipeline fill* refers to the process of filling the distribution channels' inventories: If the product is sold to the consumer from stores, the manufacturer must produce and deliver the product to every available store outlet. Pipeline fill on a new product rollout gathers momentum as more and more "doors" are opened; sales momentum crescendos as bigger and bigger accounts are added. At some point, the pipeline is full—every store has a shelf of product, and the growth rate is purely what the consumer consumes. So the revenue or top-line growth rate drops from huge to high teens or, even worse, single digits. That is the death of a growth stock. Thus, when Wal-Mart is full, the product is pretty much at the top of the growth curve. That is usually when a company starts talking international expansion, right before the end when they almost always enthuse on prospective sales in Russia and China. Further, Wal-Mart is known to be a tough bargainer, not always pleased to give the supplier extraordinary profits, so profit margins might drop. Some shorts were foolish enough to let all this hubbub go to their heads, and they shorted and watched the stock double.

Second quarter 1993 results were fine, and the stock split two for one and traded to $38 (postsplit) on November 1, right before the third-quarter earnings announcement.

During that time of jubilance for the growth-stock junkies, a couple of things happened. The proxy came out, for one. Nobody reads proxies (more on that in Chapter 13) except for those vicious rumor mongers, the short sellers. The proxy showed that the Pencers were getting a pretty good deal: The five executive officers made $2.635 million Canadian in fiscal year ended January 30, 1993 (including $1.4 in a profit plan), plus personal benefits of $117,000, plus aggregate net value of options exercised of $5.645 million. That is with company earnings from operations at $22.5 million for the year, net earnings of $12.8 million. In addition, there were certain odd transactions in the past in which officers and directors seemed to benefit extraordinarily from company purchases of minority interests in Cott Beverages USA and Retail Brands Inc. Four employees of the company and a consultant had received over $13 million in stock in exchange for their minority interest in Cott Beverages USA (an interest that chief operating officer Fraser Latta had gotten as part of his employment agreement), a practice that serves to keep the expense of salaries off the income statement and capitalize it as goodwill on the balance sheet. In addition, it appeared that a substantial chunk of insider stock had been sold in the previous 10 months, no doubt to pay for the option exercise.

Shortly after the proxy came out, a report "not for reproduction" circulated that rehashed the accounting practices, the insider take, and the competitive environment. It got folks riled again.

Finally—and all this before the third-quarter-earnings release—the bell rang. Oppenheimer analyst David Goldman let his enthusiasm get the better of him—he quit his cushy analyst job in October and went to work for Cott as the investor relations officer. That was within weeks of the top tick on the stock price. The only other time in memory that short sellers have gotten such a toothsome signal was when home-infusion company T2 Medical included a picture of its favorite analyst in its annual report, the most accurate timing clue that beleaguered short sellers got on what had been a horror of a short.

Before the earnings were announced, Pepsi Canada talked price cutting, and Cott stock felt the hot breath of competitive pricing from a giant. On December 9, 1993, the third quarter came out right on the estimate, with gross margins much improved, 17.7 percent up from 15 percent. The kicker was the balance sheet. Inventories were up 137 percent year over year, with cost of goods up 110 percent and that from a company where inventories had grown slower than cost of goods (see Table 5.1). Other assets were up sequentially by close to 5 million, almost one-third of earnings from operations of $16.5 million. Short sellers that had stayed away started trying to borrow the stock to sell it.

In March, *The Financial Post* noted a Cott director stock sale of $2.3 million Canadian. Insider sales were hard to follow on this one because Canadian reporting practices were different from the usual procedures. What seemed clear, however, was that insiders sold frequently and got stock options to replace some of what they sold.

The fourth quarter was finally released on April 7, and the inventory numbers were up again, 85 percent year over year, with cost of goods up 44 percent. Other assets were up by more than 8 million as well. One excuse the company offered for the high inventory level was the use of more returnable bottles, but the magnitude of the increase made that a ridiculous explanation. The stock price started down in earnest from the mid 20s where it had settled since November.

In May, Cott directed analysts to slightly lower estimates because of higher SG and A (sales, general and administrative expense) spending for the European ramp-up. Oppenheimer continued to be an aggressive buyer, stating that the problem was that investors had been spoiled by triple-digit growth.

The press piled on with Gretchen Morgenson's article in the June 1994 *Worth* magazine. The article delineated Pencer's past, the insider sales, and the spurious accounting practices, complete with an analysis by an independent authority who stated that cash was a problem. Cott responded with a one-of-a-kind document from their own accounting authority, one Dr. Roman Weil at the University of Chicago, who stated that Cott's accounting policies complied with generally accepted accounting principles (GAAP), were appropriate with the company's

Table 5.1 Cott Corporation Inventory Analysis

	FY93				*FY94*			
	Apr	*Jul*	*Oct*	*Jan*	*Apr*	*Jul*	*Oct*	*Jan*
Cost of goods sold*	$41,370	$74,078	$68,339	$93,329	$105,251	$163,983	$143,583	$134,452
Annual change	—	—	—	—	151%	121%	110%	44%
Inventory*	$30,374	$37,849	$35,226	$44,910	$53,776	$66,433	$83,503	$83,137
Annual change	—	—	—	—	77%	76%	137%	85%
Days inventory				44	47	37	53	55

*Numbers are hundred thousands.

Table 5.2 Cott Corporation, Short Interest

1993	Number of Shares Short	1994	Number of Shares Short
January	408,200	January	5,413,243
February	575,104	February	6,362,223
March	1,134,840	March	5,833,379
April	1,110,402	April	6,730,932
May	1,737,014	May	7,276,405
June	2,465,744	June	8,125,240
July	2,763,290		
August	2,874,639		
September	1,961,206		
October	1,895,872		
November	2,237,799		
December	3,671,321		

Source: Bloomberg Financial Markets.

business, and did not mask a pending cash crisis. The point (more in Chapter 6) for short sellers was not whether the accounting was legal, but whether aggressive accounting practices masked the true earnings and assets of the company. So the much documented debate was amusing but had little to do with what the stock price would do. The Oppenheimer analyst dismissed it all as "rumors and sloppy journalism."[1]

By early June, it was over. Cott released its first-quarter report with weaker than expected profit margins and a week later, took analyst's estimates down again. The stock slipped 36 percent in a week to $14.50 U.S.,"setting the table for strong long-term growth," Oppenheimer said.[2] Oppenheimer finally downgraded Cott to a market performer in October, with the price at $12 and yet another analyst covering the stock.

◆ *Snapple Beverage Corporation*

Snapple showed up earlier in the short screen than its beverage buddy Cott with the October 1992 initial public offering (IPO) memorandum. The stock was priced at $20, and it was hot from the outset, opening at $31. Its growth story really caught fire in the spring of 1993 when Wall Street noticed that every wife, child, and construction worker in their local deli drank Snapple's flavored ice teas. Short sellers thought it was silly—water and a tea bag at premium beer prices, with Coke and Pepsi competing for the beverage pie. At 64 times 1992 earnings and 31 times 1993 estimates in March, the shorts felt pretty confident—one of many ill-timed, blood-curdling valuation bets in the 1990s.

Earnings and revenue showed spectacular growth: The company declared a 100 percent stock dividend for June 1993, and the stock responded with a parabolic climb to $30 postsplit by September.

All year, the press had been riding the new-age beverage company about competition. *Forbes* and *USA Today* (via Dan Dorfman's column) nattered on about Coke and Pepsi and Nestea and price-to-earnings multiples of 156 times 1992, 55 times 1993. But the truth was that revenues were up over 100 percent in the first half of 1993, with a triple in earnings per share, stellar cash flow, and a clean balance sheet.

The shorts were embarrassed and talked about short squeezes.

Snapple announced an offering in September of 8 million shares of insider stock, which took director and officer ownership from 38.7 percent before the IPO to 30.2 percent after the secondary—not horrifying for a holder but enough to cure a short squeeze if that had been a factor in the ascent.

The stock broke back to $20 in the fall and winter—the price appeared to be seasonal as well as the product—then rallied to a new high of $32 by February 1993.

For those who were watching, the first fundamental sign of problems appeared in the third-quarter announcement made in November 1993. Cash flow from operations was less than $1 million in the quarter (it had been almost $4 million at the same time the previous year), and the culprit was receivables—up 198 percent, with sales up 133 percent. Slow-pay summer customers, perhaps. The number told investors to pay attention but maybe not short. Despite the high return on equity—over 40 percent in 1993—the growth rate was higher, so cash flow mattered.

The March-earnings announcement of the 1993 year-end was the perfect short-sale signal, but one could wait for the June quarter's undeniable confirmation and still make good money. Inventories were up by 153 percent with cost of goods up 106 percent in the fourth quarter and days of inventory up to 50 from the previous year's 45 (see Table 5.3). The company explained the increase as seasonal buildup before a gangbuster summer. December cash flow was fine because the wayward receivables had been collected. The stock price was still around $24 and would trade above $28 in the coming months.

When the March quarter was announced, inventories were up again, 180 percent, and cost-of-goods growth was 98 percent—still growing for summer tea sprees at 89 days, versus 64 a year ago. Something had changed at Snapple about inventory management.

The Morgan Stanley analyst reduced his rating in July purely on price—24 times 1994 estimates seemed pricey now. Meanwhile, the bulls talked about vending machines and the boost that would give sales momentum.

The stock air-pocketed to $14 in August with the earnings announcement (see Figure 5.2). Earnings per share were light—analysts expected $0.21, not the $0.19 Snapple delivered. Operating margins fell. But the kicker was the inventories, a confessed problem now, up again and not seasonal buildup any longer. Executives told analysts that a buildup of 4 million to 5 million cases would depress the next quarter's sales. Apparently, the pipeline was full, wholesalers were overstocked, and there was nowhere to go with the excess tea. Quaker Oats finally took it over for $14 a share after months of grousing by shorts and longs alike. It proved a difficult drain on Quaker profitability in the years that followed, with seeming perpetual inventory problems once the tea-drinking public was steeped.

The Snapple story was a great lesson for growth-stock players and short sellers alike: Store checks and valuation be damned, inventories are key in a one-product company rolling out in a new-era industry. If they build up, it is almost always because the product is not selling as planned.

Table 5.3 Snapple Inventory and Accounts Receivable Analysis

	1992			*1993*				*1994*	
	June	*Sep*	*Dec*	*March*	*June*	*Sep*	*Dec*	*March*	*June*
Sales revenue*	$64,054	$86,905	$54,507	$65,417	$129,955	$202,911	$117,722	$134,015	$243,019
Annual change	—	—	—	—	103%	133%	116%	105%	87%
Accounts receivable*	$28,480	$27,868	$17,428	$28,948	$59,124	$83,111	$53,010	$71,283	$124,356
Annual change	—	—	—	—	108%	198%	204%	146%	110%
Days receivable				39	64	67	37	45	65
Cost of goods sold*	$41,063	$53,203	$32,833	$38,326	$75,585	$117,338	$67,476	$76,030	$142,077
Annual change	—	—	—	—	84%	121%	106%	98%	88%
Inventory*	$18,147	$20,462	$16,166	$29,163	$34,641	$44,086	$40,924	$81,721	$102,182
Annual change	—	—	—	—	91%	115%	153%	180%	195%
Days inventory				64	63	61	50	89	93

*Numbers are hundred thousands.

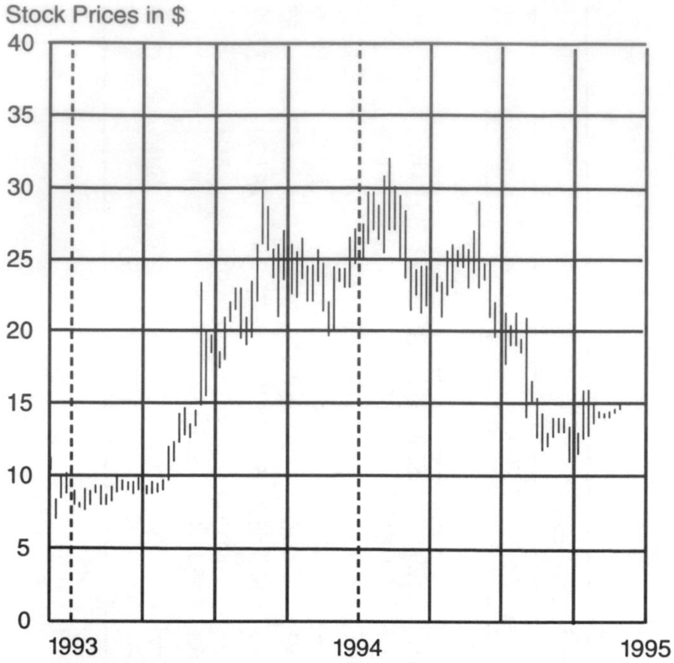

Figure 5.2 Snapple, December 1, 1992–December 31, 1994. Chart from MetaStock by Equis International, Inc.

Table 5.4 Snapple Beverage Corporation, Short Interest

1993	*Number of Shares Short*	*1994*	*Number of Shares Short*
January	2,202,724	January	9,522,428
February	5,265,524	February	9,319,433
March	5,844,024	March	9,591,123
April	6,562,368	April	9,297,894
May	11,135,608	May	9,873,187
June	12,392,320	June	9,559,030
July	7,761,766	July	9,299,559
August	9,220,958	August	6,077,833
September	10,649,442		
October	10,137,888		
November	10,247,541		
December	9,840,694		

Source: Bloomberg Financial Markets.

◆ High Tech: Media Vision

Media Vision Technology, Inc., was another hair-raising growth story of the 1992 IPO class, with definite similarities to Coleco and Miniscribe (phantom inventories) for short sellers who still had memories. There was no way to play this one rationally, no way in retrospect to avoid the pain or to time it right. Snapple and Cott, for all the agony, had a reasonable progression of financial clues if the short seller stayed objective. Not Media Vision.

Somewhere in the summer of 1992, a prospectus on Creative Technology Ltd. (CREAF) was published. The stock was priced at $12 and the business duly noted by avid prospectus readers. Then in November, a competitor, Media Vision, filed a deal and priced the stock at $15. By the first quarter of 1993, both stocks traded at $33. Media Vision followed the first offering with a 2-million-share secondary with 1 million shares of insider stock while the stock was in the $20s in April.

What these companies did was make sound and video products for personal computers, add-on boards that allowed personal computer (PC) users to play video games on their computers. This was after Nintendo and Sega had seduced a large percentage of the under-35 male population into compulsive game playing, so the market for additional game platforms was greedy and growing.

In the spring of 1993, Jeff Perry at Kynikos Associates came out with a research piece called "Unsound Boards" that said that the prospective profits over years for these products were substantially less than the market caps of the companies; in other words, a discounted-cash-flow analysis made the prices look silly. Valuation had gotten a touch hysterical. Perry projected a worldwide PC base of 65 million units for households and 150 million for business (high numbers, he said), with sound cards in roughly one-third of the households and one-quarter of the businesses, minus the number of cards already installed—19 million households and 34 million business units for the possible end market over time. The current average unit selling price was $150 to $160, and both Media Vision and Creative Technology expected that lower-priced chips would replace the current kit by 1994 and sell for around $15 to $25. So Perry used a price of $80 for the household model and $25 for the business model to get a total size of market of $2.37 billion. Because the two companies already had competitors, he gave them 50 to 60 percent of the market at current company margins, for total prospective profits for Media Vision of $37 million and Creative of $180 million, versus market capitalizations (equity times number of shares plus debt minus cash on the balance sheets) of $380 million for Media Vision and $1.25 billion for Creative. This, Perry pointed out, was for companies that spent collectively $10 million on research through 1992 in a market that already had over 45 sound boards and multimedia upgrade kits in the stores in an industry that was characterized by short product life cycles and rapid change. The product was clearly a commodity product with margins soon to collapse.

The shorts told growth stock players to worry if the product life cycle was shorter than the days of inventory on the balance sheet, which brings me to the next point: The financials were never pretty for Media Vision. By March, anyone would have shorted the stock, even a reformed short seller bent on steering clear of dumb valuation plays. Media Vision in March was insider selling, high receivables, single-digit return on equity, a nutsy valuation, a fad product—a layup—until it climbed and climbed and made everyone feel like it had to be a new industry standard with great products to follow. Short sellers felt that they must have missed something (much like they would feel in 1996 with Iomega).

To back up a bit, Montgomery Securities was the most outspoken proponent of a soundboard in every house. They were the lead manager in the Media Vision IPO offering in November and followed up after the allotted quiet period with a rousing recommendation the end of December when the stock price was at $21. Montgomery was a force to be reckoned with in the 1990s growth stock business—they got wide sponsorship for their crop of seedlings. "Multimedia, a New Era in personal computing," said Montgomery analyst Paul Fox. Triple-digit top-line growth, he projected, with earnings of $0.88 in 1993.[4] He was right on the first count.

Fox went on to talk about liquidity and cash flow. Because the

Table 5.5 Media Vision Technology, Inc., Short Interest

1992	*Number of Shares Short*	*1993*	*Number of Shares Short*	*1994*	*Number of Shares Short*
December	4,049	January	67,837	January	2,615,926
		February	318,921	February	2,740,459
		March	624,499	March	2,340,868
		April	680,256	April	1,920,705
		May	919,105	May	2,973,722
		June	937,905	June	3,291,691
		July	1,183,573		
		August	1,384,937		
		September	1,656,308		
		October	2,026,765		
		November	2,470,010		
		December	2,428,556		

Source: Bloomberg Financial Markets.

company outsourced manufacturing and did very little research, the primary cash drain was the growth in inventory and receivables needed to support burgeoning sales. Payables (via vendors) are expected to finance inventories to some extent, so Fox thought Media Vision would be only slightly cash-flow negative in 1993. He was brave enough to give inventory and receivables estimates for the year end 1992 and 1993. Baseball in its first drop had taught short sellers that when cash flow logically should be neutral and is massively negative, something stinks. The Montgomery analyst, therefore, set the stage for expectations, presumedly after a chat with management to guide his assumptions.

The bigger point on cash appetite in a growth company is a concept called *sustainable growth rate*. It is an easy thing to remember and a killer ratio to track. Sustainable growth rate says that a company can grow at the rate of return on equity times the retention rate without going to the capital markets. The return on equity (ROE) is pure and simple: net income divided by equity on the balance sheet. In this case, 1992 net income was $3.2 million, equity was $56.4 million. The *retention rate* is the percentage of net income that the company does not pay out in a dividend. Media Vision and most growth companies pay no dividend, so the retention rate is 100 percent. Thus, Media Vision's sustainable growth rate in 1992 was 5.7 percent, far below the growth plans and prospects of the company. What all that means is that growth companies with low ROE have to go to market early and often and, if the prospects for eager buyers decline due to market conditions or failing financials, they have big trouble. That is also why a really high ROE makes for a lousy short sale—the company can finance its growth without caring a fig what the Wall Street pubahs think about the business plan.

So that was how the stage was set for the year to come with Media Vision and its magnificent multimedia machine. By the time the March quarter was announced in April, several other analysts had recommended the stock, and the estimates for 1993 were up to $1.23. The Cowen analyst was predicting three years of triple-digit growth. The shorts were encouraged because receivables were up huge again; management said 80 percent were booked late in the quarter. The other current asset line on the balance sheet was up $1 million with operating income of $5 million. Inventories, management said, were mostly raw materials, only about 5 percent in finished goods. That was the first of many misleading statements—when the 10Q came out, finished goods were 20 percent of total inventories, a point of note in a hot product where demand supposedly exceeds supply. In addition, management was now talking about a new multimedia publishing division that would produce CD-Rom titles for the Christmas season. When a company switches or expands its business line into something completely different, it generally means management fears that growth will slow in the main line. When they expand into a highly competitive business that costs money for product development (like software game titles) when the base business eats money as well, you sit back and watch with relish for the train wreck to happen sooner. The problem was that the stock price did not allow too much complacency and joy in the short camp.

When the second quarter was announced, the shorts had another nasty triple-digit revenue quarter, but inventories doubled relative to cost of goods and finished goods tripled sequentially, up to almost $16 million. The reported earnings of $0.24 included some oddities: a one-time gain ($0.02), lower-than-expected tax rate ($0.01), lower number of shares ($0.01), but still higher by $0.03 than analysts' target number. Inventories, management said, were growing in response to a very fine second half. Estimates went up for the year to $1.30.

Somewhere over the next couple of months, the dialogue between CEO Paul Jain and the short sellers heated up. Short sales were up to 9 percent of the shares outstanding, and Jain started talking about disappointing them. Herb Greenberg of the *San Francisco Chronicle* wrote his first column on Media Vision, mentioned the perilous receivables and inventory levels, and quoted Jain as saying that both would be fixed soon, that sales would shortly be spectacular. Meanwhile, the price of the kits in stores was coming down, and original equipment manufacturers' (OEM) sales were in the offing; both meant lower margins, if higher volume.

Jain sold stock, and the price chopped from $20 to $28 all summer, giving short sellers a necessary respite and a little hope. Remember, Snapple and Cott also were causing trouble that summer.

When Media Vision announced a convertible deal in October with Montgomery as lead banker, nobody was surprised. The company needed money to support the growth drain. Insider ownership had dropped to 18.6 percent from 39.3 percent after the first stock offering. The other announcement in the prospectus was a probable range for the third-quarter earnings and revenue, as well as assurance that inventory turns would improve and receivable days drop. When the quarter was announced, all those good things came to pass, and Jain was properly jubilant at besting the shorts. The stock started higher. Jain exercised options and sold stock at $33.

Short sellers remember the tail end of 1993 as the "Critical Path" nightmare. Institutional investors, whether short or long, go to conferences at which companies give presentations and answer questions. Shorts, in particular, go to repeated presentations to see if anything changes. For example, when Picturetel stopped talking about blockbuster technology and started talking about synergistic corporate solutions back in the early days of picture phones, the shorts figured that competition was gaining momentum and it was time to pile on. So with a pesky position like Media Vision, short sellers went to every growth conference and convertible road show to check out Paul Jain and the sound-card story. What they saw was the "Critical Path" video over and over and over. "Critical Path" was the highly touted first CD-Rom game of Media Vision's purported unending product flow of hot software—10 game titles out for Christmas—that was going to sell like crazy. Jain said that 100,000, maybe 200,000, of "Critical Path" would sell within three months. It was a lousy sexist video segment that annoyed already annoyed short sellers no end: a superwoman on a conveyor belt with a villain, if memory serves. At one of these many meetings, Jain showed a slide with Dell mentioned as an OEM. When questioned, he responded that the sound card was simply included in the Dell mail order catalogue like any other product.

Herb Greenberg commented again in the *Chronicle* about the improbable chance of sales hitting 100,000 for "Critical Path," with the top title in the industry at 150,000 after nine months. He also noted that Media Vision was capitalizing software costs, not expensing them.

The shorts figured out somewhere in December they had better call the big software retail chains and ask after the fate of "Critical Path." One chain in particular noted that they did not have it, had not been called by a salesperson on it, and, therefore, could not sell it over Christmas. That was news. But it did not make the spike to $46.50 from Christmas euphoria in January any more fun.

On February 17, 1994, shorts sellers were dreary about earnings prospects—after all, nobody ever stiffs an investment banker the quarter after a deal. So short sellers were glued to their speaker phones and their scrolling news after the market close for the year-end conference call. By now, estimates were up to $1.40.

What happened was $1.40—no upside surprise. What happened was inventories and receivables were back up again after the first-quarter clean-up. Other current assets and other assets almost doubled sequentially—increases so big they almost ate operating earnings. Payday, it looked like to weary soundboard shorts.

Indeed, the stock started dropping the next day but stabilized in the $20s. It took Jain's March disclosures to crater Media Vision to $11 (see Figure 5.3). On March 24, after a cheerful Wall Street meeting a week earlier, Jain announced a first-quarter loss due to price cuts and

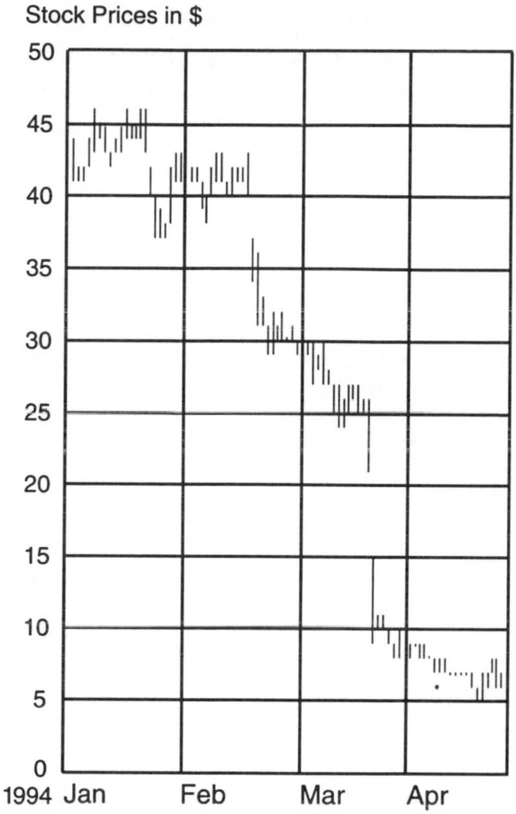

Figure 5.3 Media Vision Technology, Inc., January 1994–June 1994

shipment delays. By May, Jain was restating the last quarter of 1993 to an undisclosed loss, and the stock was at $5.

Herb Greenberg continued to dig away for the *Chronicle*. What had happened at Media Vision was beyond anything the short sellers could have surmised. Insiders, he said in his May 9, 1994, article, said the company engaged in "channel stuffing," discounting at the end of the quarter to boost sales. They also shipped millions of dollars of upgrade kits that documents show could not have been assembled yet, as well as defective units. They shipped units, booked revenues, then took them back the next quarter. Jain, it turned out, had engaged in similar practices at a previous company. The company facilities manager received bills for warehouses she did not recognize and assumed returned inventory was dumped there.[5] Greenberg wrote as recently as April 1996 that the company had actually capitalized its 1993 Christmas party—a new high in creative accounting. Jain, as yet, has not filed a formal response to charges.

Media Vision was a hot-growth, new technology company that nearly scared shorts into prolonged inactivity. But the frauds spoil shorts, the lack of substantive clues giving us false courage to short stock with triple-digit top-line growth. Growth is a good stock to own and a great stock to short if you can time both sides of the pyramid.

◆ *Notes*

1. David A. Goldman, "Cott Corp.," Oppenheimer and Co., Inc., research, 16 April 1993, 2.
2. Gabriel D. Lowy, "Cott Corp.," Oppenheimer and Co., Inc., research, 12 May 1994, 1.
3. Gabriel D. Lowy,"Cott Corp.," Oppenheimer and Co., Inc., research, 10 June 1994, 1.
4. Paul G. Fox, "Media Vision Technology, Inc.," Montgomery Securities Research, 31 December 1992, 2.
5. Herb Greenberg and David Dietz, "Spectacular Rise and Fall of Bay Area High Tech Giant," *San Francisco Chronicle*, 9 May 1994, A6.

6

If You Can't Read It, Short It

Public financial statements are disclosures of the financial underpinnings of publicly traded companies. The intent of the 10K is to explain the business of the company and to give audited financial data supporting that business. Theoretically, shareholders should be able to understand what underlies their equity in assets and liabilities, what earnings power drives the company, and whether the company can support that business with operating, financing, and investing cash flows. Footnotes to the financial statements should explain, expand on, and disclose additional information to the public.

Most companies write reports that are comprehensible to a person with a fair knowledge of accounting terminology. Some companies write reports that are impossible to follow, even for accounting experts. Experience suggests that if you cannot understand a report, officers are hiding something worse than you expect. It is almost an iceberg phenomenona: If you find five or six serious questions in financial statements, you can be sure that there are many more that you cannot see. If a call to the company for explanation receives a garbled response that sounds suspiciously like the company official is speaking in tongues, you have got a live one.

The corollary to the disclosure dilemna is that most analysts are afraid to admit that they do not understand accounting or accounting terminology. So the cycle is self-perpetuating: Chief financial officers do not explain; analysts do not ask.

The simplest form of financial obfuscation is detected by tracking the growth in receivables versus the growth in sales. Outsized growth leads the analyst to search out policies on booking revenues and collecting cash. National Education did a fine job of confusing the best students of footnotes with their multiple recognition policies.

The next level of complexity combines costs and revenues—the company manages earnings by delaying expenses and accelerating revenues. The asset side of the balance sheet rises as prepaid expenses build, and net income stays consistent, always upward by a comfortable growth rate. Companies that have perfect growth rates should always be carefully studied for gimmickry on the balance sheet—in particular, burgeoning prepaid expenses and deferred costs. Autotote had aspects of their financial statements that were intriguing to wrestle with, in particular incomprehensible assets and disappearing depreciation.

Financial institutions are the most challenging of all the industry statements. Valuing assets and ascertaining recurring earnings in banks and insurance companies is an exercise fraught with peril. A passing knowledge of which rock to turn over can save an investor from the problem of crumbling footings on a highly leveraged institution.

◆ *National Education*

National Education was a Wall Street darling in the late 1980s, a comfortable concept stock with notable personage Barry Goldwater on the board. Unfortunately, the company's accounting stance did not mimic Goldwater's conservative political philosophy.

The company sold two types of education: re-education, or training for corporate and government employees (for example, a program to introduce a new computer system or product); and technical-vocational training. Popular wisdom said the stock was recession resistant because more people would need to be retrained in a downturn. Demographics also favored the concept: A smaller labor pool meant that corporations would have to reeducate, reuse, and retrain existing employees. The eyecatcher, again, was the financial statements.

What Receivables?

The first clue was that accounts receivables were up significantly year over year: 90 percent year over year, with sales up only 15 percent. Allowance for doubtful accounts, meanwhile, rose only 12 percent. Long-term receivables, or contracts receivable, were also up 100 percent. Receivables can be up by more than sales for several reasons:

1. The company acquired a company, and the acquisition is not yet under control—collections do not have the same billing cycle or terms for sales, for example. If the acquisition was a large one relative to sales, the relationship of year versus year in receivables is not comparable.
2. The company is booking revenues too aggressively—for example, a three-year contract recognized at the front end, so that receivables stay high because the rate of payment is slow.
3. The company changed its credit policy to easier terms or is giving incentives for sales, thereby jeopardizing future sales.
4. The company is having trouble collecting from customers.

Building accounts receivables is a cost to the company because investing in business already booked hurts cash flow. Timely collections are sensible in a growing business because growth eats money by definition.

The first step in analyzing National Education's receivables was to check to see if any major acquisitions had skewed the receivables comparison. Note 2 (Business Combinations) said that National Education acquired Spectrum on December 19, 1988, which was accounted for as a pooling-of-interest. Spectrum had provided $24 million of the $457 million of revenues for the combined companies—certainly not enough to increase receivables by $75 million.

The next step was to flip through the verbiage in the financial statements for disclosure, comment, observation—anything helpful to explain a large change. But they revealed nothing. National Education apparently did not feel that a $75-million increase merited a mention.

Note 1 (Summary of Significant Accounting Policies) was the next stop to see what accounting principles apply to the company's statements. Under Revenues and Costs, more confusion: National Education had a lot of different contracts, all booked with different assumptions. There were three major types of training contracts:

1. "Rental contracts revenues under ad hoc month-to-month arrangements are recognized when usage occurs," but "under resident library arrangements, customers agree to use training courses for a period of time, and revenue is recognized for the contracted course usage." So when do they book it—up front or throughout the contract?
2. "Custom contract revenues under time and materials contracts are recognized as costs are incurred, and revenues from fixed price contracts are recognized using the percentage-of-completion method." Not as cash is received.
3. "Industrial contract revenues are recognized when cash is received with appropriate recognition of estimated expenses relative to servicing such contracts."[1]

The note tells the interested reader that National Education books revenue at different times under different assumptions, suggests that the company has some leeway in the time to recognize revenues, and implies that the accounting methodology does not always match cash payment. How companies book revenues is a particularly quarrelsome issue for analysts: There are many ways to fool around, and technology and training companies are two categories of regular abusers. Revenues booked should have a consistent relationship with collection—if a company ships now and collects in 60 days, the accounts receivable schedule should consistently mirror that policy. So rising receivables versus sales or a lengthening number of days in receivables should always trigger a question: Something has changed, it says. In National Education's case, the resident library verbiage was especially troubling: How do they track use, and do they book two or three years at the outset of the contract?

The 1988 Annual Report also showed that an unusual charge in 1987 made the 1988-to-1987 comparison in earnings per share look good—$1.57 versus $0.03. Furthermore, the large acquisition of Advanced Systems in late 1987 with subsequent cost cutting on overhead from economies of scale gave the expense side a kick lower that probably would not be duplicated in later years.

Acquired intangible assets (from the acquisitions) was a sizable balance-sheet line of well over $89 million, with total assets of $422 million and stockholders' equity of $185 million. The notes said that the assets consisted of rental contracts, product and text materials, course development costs, and copyrights. These assets are being amortized over a period "not to exceed 40 years." Educational manuals? Over a long period? How long? Not longer than 40 years. Seems pretty aggressive with the massive amount of change in technology and software, some of the areas of National Education's expertise. Management has discretion on booking intangibles, creating a productive source of earnings management.

Management Changes Its Mind

The real signal on National Education occurred when Jerome W. Cwiertnia, president, quit on March 16, 1989. He chose the conclusion of his presentation at the Shearson Selected Growth Conference to make this announcement. Cwiertnia had an advantageous employment contract: He got annual compensation of $695,251, including a special bonus applied to a tax loan—his aggregate loan was $176,734. He also received 150 percent of his salary times the number of years worked, or $1.38 million, if he was terminated. All of this was small relative to David Bright, the chairman of the board and CEO (his termination pay was $7.373 million, a later bone of contention). But this corporate largesse came to Cwiertnia in every instance *except for voluntary resignation under certain circumstances*. He resigned voluntarily. He potentially gave up millions and walked—unless, of course, the resignation was friendly and the terms of his contract included this particular circumstance. The stock dropped five points in 20 minutes and then rallied to $21 to 22 in the months following (see Figure 6.1). Analysts appeared unconcerned about Cwiertnia's contract or the affability of his departure.

The confusing financials with mounting receivables and the resignation of a key person were enough evidence to short the stock. The vocational-training business has come under repeated fire for spurious accounting practices, low collection rates, and bogus students—*Barron's* had an article titled "Schools for Scandal" on January 2, 1989. The smoke should have suggested that a casual analyst could not expect to decipher reality from financial statements in this particular industry sector.

Analysts on the Street, however, were reassured and comfortable. As a group they "bah-humbugged" the accounting issue, rationalized Cwiertnia's resignation (change of life, wanted his own company), and dismissed growing receivables (new billing system). Merrill Lynch analyst Arthur Rade commented on April 17, 1989, that he expected

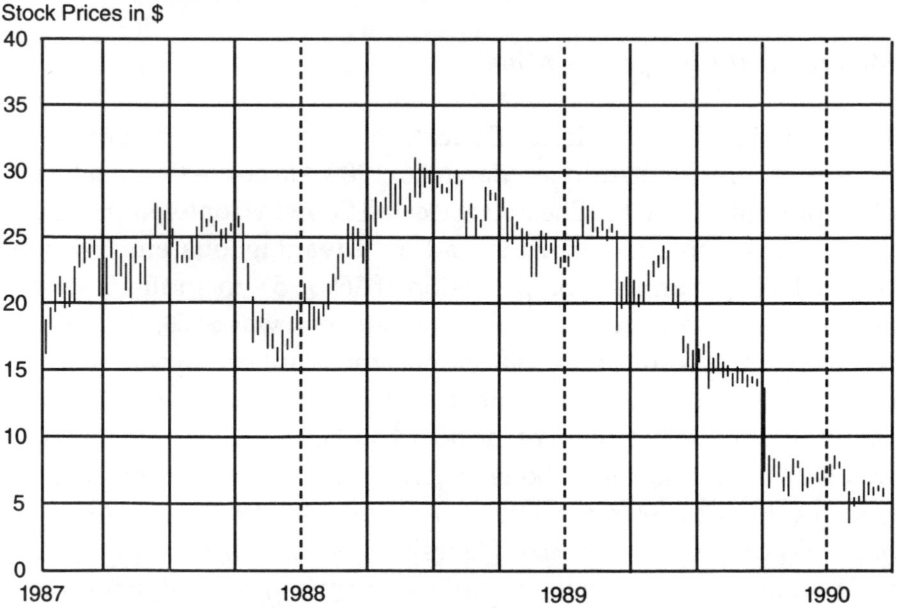

Figure 6.1 National Education Corp., January 1, 1987–March 31, 1990. Chart from MetaStock by Equis International, Inc.

$1.90 for 1989: "Quite attractive," he said, "growth averaging about 18%."[2] Morgan Stanley's Ram Capoor also liked the stock, stating that the change "reinforces our recommendation . . ."[3]

Management met with analysts at the end of May and suggested that revenues and earnings might be a little light for the quarter. Everyone simultaneously dropped year estimates a nickel or a dime. The Shearson analyst appeared to be nervous about cash flow and accounting and kept the rating at 3-1 (Hold short term, buy long term).

Troubled waters did not clear quite as quickly as the Street had hoped. *Barron's* ran an article in the June 5 issue that talked about student default rates at vocational schools. National Education had five schools listed with defaults over 40 percent. The stock hiccuped, the company reassured the Street that the numbers were old, and analysts rustled nervously like sheep in a pen.

But that was not all. As they said on the Street, another shoe dropped (this sucker was a centipede) when the company announced on June 12 that the quarter would be below last year because of "account reassignments and lengthened sales cycle."[4] The stock traded to $16. Analysts affably lowered their year estimates to $1.50 and some went to "hold" on the stock, a trifle late for investors. Dean Witter's Fred Anschel refused to follow the herd, however: "Buy," he said. "Target $24 to $27."[5]

The stock dropped from $16 to $13 when the company announced a second-quarter loss on July 19, 1989. It was much bigger than expected, even after the company's June meeting. Some analysts went to a "sell." Merrill's Rade said, "Adolescent crisis, rather than terminal illness," but clearly a loss of confidence had occurred.[6]

Cwiertnia Comes Back

Analysts again rallied around the company when David Bright quit (presumably because of the doglike earnings), and Cwiertnia was reinstated. The honeymoon was short-lived, despite company reassurances that "the other shoe wouldn't drop."[7]

When the 10Q came out, it showed prepaid marketing expenses up to $42 million, with accounts receivable down a little and operating cash burn of $21 million, versus $11 million from the previous year. National Education also charged off $4 million. The verbiage explained that "the second quarter results include an unusual charge of $4 million resulting from all issued and estimated future customer credits arising from the reconciliation of customer accounts following the conversion to a new management information system at Applied Learning."[8] The company topped previous obfuscatory verbiage with this explanation. What did they mean? Perhaps the receivables were bad because the computer system did not track usage correctly? Eventually, the company admitted to receivables problems from booking 60 percent of revenues on the signing of a three-year contract in the Applied Learning division, resident library section. Tighter revenue-recognition policies were instituted.

Throughout the National Education saga, analysts seemed content to listen to management explanations and direction without asking tough questions. As a group, they lowered estimates and ratings at the prodding of company officials. They appeared to be unconcerned about employment contracts and the ensuing lawsuit by the deposed David Bright over payment of his contract. They failed to understand that the accounting issues masked important negative developments, whatever they were.

On February 1, 1990, the stock was at $4. Most Wall Street analysts no longer cover the stock; it went off the recommended list of major firms, with eight analysts sending the stock to Siberia. Nobody remembered to change estimates or to comment. National Education quietly slipped off lists without announcement. The disappearing-analysts phenomenon, however, should not be considered a sell-short signal: When Wall Street analysts forget they have a stock under coverage, worry if you are long, but it is probably too late to short.

◆ *Autotote*

Autotote Corporation (TOTE) in 1993 took accounting mumbo jumbo to new heights. Not only could casual readers not understand the financials, but first they had to find the unfiled statements and then translate the insider sales from doubletalk trades. It made National Education look like a walk in the park.

It was probably the spectacular price move that attracted attention to Autotote—from $7 to $50—before it split two for one. The company made sports-wagering and racetrack-betting terminals—designed, operated, manufactured, and serviced computerized wagering systems. A quick look at the July 31, 1993, 10Q—the most recent piece of financial evidence—made an analyst scramble for the more elaborate disclosure of the 1992 10K. The July 10Q had $2 million in cash; extraordinary growth in receivables, inventories, prepaids, and other assets; and cash burn from operations of $26 million in the nine months. The stock was also trading at twice the forward-earnings multiple of competitor GTech and four times Video Lottery.

The 1992 10K showed that nobody had a prayer of figuring out whether this stock made money or not. First, TOTE used percentage of completion on revenues from major contracts for the sale of totalisator systems based on delivery and acceptance of product. Second, service contract costs were amortized over the life of the contract, "including expected renewals, which is 15 years or the actual life of the contract if not renewed."[9] Including expected renewals? Pretty outrageous, short

Table 6.1 Autotote, Short Interest

1993	*Number of Shares Short*	*1994*	*Number of Shares Short*	*1995*	*Number of Shares Short*
February	40,335	January	1,760,110	January	3,153,951
March	120,066	February	1,898,331		
April	125,661	March	2,094,934		
May	184,098	April	3,485,674		
June	233,878	May'	5,510,533		
July	202,168	June	6,028,037		
August	382,394	July	6,270,459		
September	317,162	August	5,857,018		
October	383,112	September	6,088,289		
November	603,269	October	5,750,311		
December	1,551,332	November	5,561,995		
		December	3,453,115		

Source: Bloomberg Financial Markets.

sellers thought. Software was capitalized. Product development was capitalized. Patents, trademarks, marketing rights, and employment agreements were capitalized. Deferred installation costs were included in property and equipment and amortized. Inventory included equipment held for firm wagering service contracts that would later be transferred to property and equipment—that did not make much sense because inventory was bigger than backlog. In other words, management had complete discretion on when to expense costs and book revenues. The negative cash flow suggested TOTE was not making a dime. So the stock was shorted and watched.

TOTE was keen on announcements. The ticker was hot with acquisitions, new proposals, partial contracts, sales, and, of course, investment banker Oppenheimer's resounding buy articulations. Earnings were supposed to be $0.35 for the October 31, 1993, fiscal year and $0.70 for 1994.

By the end of January, the stock price was around $25, postsplit (see Figure 6.2).

Companies have 90 days to file 10Ks with the Securities and

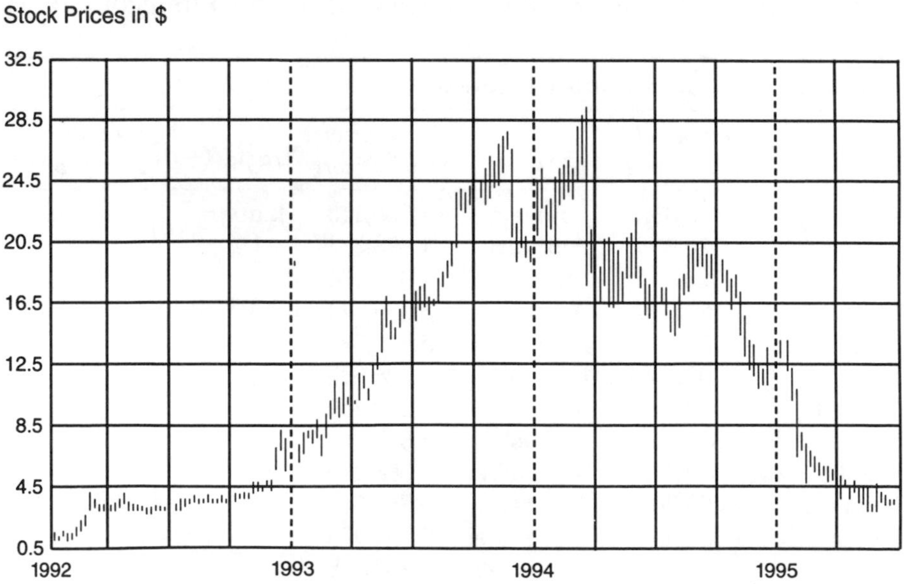

Figure 6.2 Autotote, January 1, 1992–June 30, 1995

Exchange Commission (SEC). That meant TOTE had to announce year-end earnings and file financials before February. It hardly ever happens that a company is late filing. After all, big accounting firms audit the statements—they know the rules, and chief financial officers (CFOs) know the rules. So when TOTE failed to file, shorts added to positions and waited for the Form 12b-25 (Notification of Late Filing) that appeared on February 1 at the SEC. TOTE explained that complicated foreign acquisitions made them late—but they released earnings anyway, $0.33 for the year. How, said the shorts, can you figure earnings without a balance sheet?

The stock spiked to $29 while shorts waited for the erstwhile 10K. Oppenheimer reiterated their buy. Montgomery initiated coverage with a buy and even forecast a balance sheet—more than the company would do.

TOTE released first-quarter earnings on March 21, 1994. Montgomery was at $0.06, Oppenheimer was more optimistic at $0.09. TOTE reported $0.06, with higher costs and a lower tax rate. Chairman and CEO A. Lorne Weil said the company was pleased at success despite bad weather and earthquakes in two major markets.

There was still no 10K, no balance sheet from October.

The next lightning bolt for short sellers occurred March 24, 1994, just days after earnings were released. It was small print. A fed filing for TOTE came across the tape, an amended 13D update that said Weil had entered into a five-year swap of 500,000 shares of stock with Bankers Trust and agreed to pay any appreciation above $26.7769 per share in exchange for interest and depreciation. That, said short sellers, is a sale.

Floyd Norris at the *New York Times* was quick to catch the insider trade as well. The deal had been struck March 18, before the earnings release, before the 10K was finally filed on March 23. Bankers Trust was thought to hedge the transaction with a short sale, therefore driving down the price and up the short interest. There was some question as to whether the trade needed to be disclosed because the executive still had the stock and the voting rights. The SEC finally ruled in September 1994 that the use of an equity swap constituted a sale.

Lorne Weil responded to questions about his innovative transaction after the stock dropped 10 percent. He said the bank would pay him a return according to a complex formula and implied it was purely an income stream.

The January 31, 1994, 10Q came out amid the murmur of activity. The two documents, 10Q and 10K, had a few points worth waiting for. TOTE had hired a new CFO in February, maybe for faster financials. The company had made acquisitions, so the numbers were not comparable. A new convertible debenture provided cash of $40 million, but cash was already down to $10.5 million by October 31 and $7.6 million by January 31. The 10Q mentioned liquidity needs, possible equity offering, or bank borrowings to finance growth. Cash flow from operations was mysteriously positive at year-end with a new investing line in the cash-flow statement called "Expenditures for equipment under wagering systems contracts." That line together with the increase in other assets and "payment for operating rights" wiped out the piddling virtue of $13 million in operating cash flow with a $72 million hit. There was more of the same in the first quarter. It looked like their easy accounting system for expensing costs was inflating the balance sheet with all manner of capitalized costs. The stock price dropped with the controversy but stabilized in the $16 to $20 range through October.

The middle of April, TOTE announced a $100 million contract with Caliente Group for a video gaming, race-and-sports network throughout Mexico. The shorts got a letter from a Mexican attorney that said that Mexican federal law prohibited gambling but allowed some sports betting (horse racing) under limited circumstances. There was much talk of whether the contract was of substance. Analysts duly raised estimates for 1995 to $1.10.

In May, the *San Diego Business Journal* ran an article on Caliente Group. An official was quoted when queried about the TOTE order as saying, "There is no commitment for so large an order. We have only a handful of machines."[10] It mentioned the possible regulatory restrictions as well.

Earnings for the second quarter were announced in the middle of May with the April 30, 1994, 10Q filed June 14. The balance sheet had a real keeper of a line on it—accumulated depreciation dropped by

$10 million sequentially, with property and equipment up by $1 million. There was no explanation in the verbiage. Accumulated depreciation can drop for several reasons: (1) the company sells something or otherwise unloads property that is depreciated; (2) the company changes the life of the asset; (3) the company changes the salvage value. None of this information has to be disclosed, but it usually is. If the company unloads an asset, it generally shows up in the cash-flow-for-investment section; or, maybe, the gross property and equipment line might drop by a similar amount. When asked, company officials declined to comment. If TOTE, in fact, changed their depreciation schedule, earnings could have been massively inflated in the quarter. On the other hand, there could have been an easy explanation related to a purchase by a client of a wagering system previously used under a service contract. But the magnitude was enormous relative to the operating income of less than $7 million in the quarter. So it raised enough of a question to convince growth players to sell the stock if they still owned it and if they happened to watch disappearing depreciation.

By early 1995, the stock was under $5 when the company announced for the second time in two years that financial filing would be delayed. The auditors apparently had questions about the amortization of assets and the timing of revenues that were as yet unresolved. Weil explained the price drop as an industry phenomenon. Gambling was out of favor. Maybe, he said, some of it was due to disappointing earnings for the fiscal year—a loss, after all was said and done, from one-time charges.

The accounting mumbo jumbo stocks should lead a stockholder to conclude: If you own it and cannot understand it, sell it. If you do not own it and cannot understand it, consider selling it short if you think the obscurity is just the tip of the iceberg.

◆ *The Weasel: Western Savings and Loan*

The problem for an analyst is how to detect, by reading their public histories, which companies are built on worthless and illiquid assets before the market realizes the disparity. Particularly in the financial sector, company portfolios are akin to blind pools. For example, it is difficult to ascertain the quality of loans in a bank portfolio.

Western Savings and Loan Association, or "the Weasel" as it was dubbed by short sellers, was an Arizona savings and loan (S&L) that the market priced above any rational valuation. In 1986, the stock traded above $20, despite book value of $6 and a Standard & Poor's write-up that alluded to the inflated balance sheet.

The questions about the Weasel's market valuation rested on two concerns:

1. What was the equity after adjustment for odd, unpriceable assets: securities, loans, and real estate?
2. What were recurring earnings, if any?

It took a couple of years for the market to resolve those issues to satisfaction.

Background

Western had a colorful history. The Driggs family had run the S&L for three generations, and son Gary Driggs, who had control in the 1980s, was the architect of the assets. After a downturn in the early 1980s when significant losses threatened to sink the 20-percent family-owned company, Gary Driggs pulled Western out of a death spiral with an infusion of approved capital in the guise of Western preferred stock (considered capital by regulators), which he swapped for land.[11] In 1983, he helped another S&L improve its capital base when he booked a gain on real estate that Western sold to Broadview Savings and Loan for preferred stock, a note, and cash. The preferred stock quit paying interest quickly—in 1984—but it stayed on in the financials at the original swap price. The Broadview Savings stock became a cornerstone for shorts' asset evaluation.

Gary was famous in Phoenix for his economics sound-and-light shows. He would pack the Arizona Biltmore with business people and

Table 6.2 Western Savings and Loan Association, Short Interest

1986	*Number of Shares Short*	*1987*	*Number of Shares Short*	*1988*	*Number of Shares Short*
January	151,800	January	360,600	January	240,580
February	135,900	February	360,600	February	243,990
March	79,800	March	293,700	March	361,140
April	72,100	April	287,045	April	459,212
May	53,400	May	319,000	May	743,575
June	65,800	June	339,010	June	576,643
July	277,200	July	351,506	July	616,442
August	263,200	August	371,545	August	612,282
September	267,500	September	411,446	September	583,061
October	268,200	October	413,216	October	649,641
November	255,700	November	291,803	November	666,476
December	289,100	December	269,994	December	814,051

use multiple projectors and pulsating-jazz soundtracks to communicate his ever-bullish view on the economy of Arizona. He put his shareholders' money where his mouth was.

By 1986, Gary Driggs had shifted the mission of the S&L in an effort to hedge the vagaries of interest-rate swings. He had been strung out in the early 1980s on a huge interest-rate bet with the S&L portfolio. The December 31, 1986, 10K chats about his new strategy:

> Western Savings availed itself of these new investment opportunities by aggressively diversifying its operations with investments in real estate and in the securities of other companies in an effort to produce non-interest income. Western Savings believes that the problems experienced by the industry over the last few years as a result of volatile interest rates demonstrate that a strategy of diversification is important for future growth and stability.[12]

Detecting Asset Values: Hide and Go Seek

In practice, this strategy meant that the balance sheet changed (see Table 6.3). On the asset side, direct investments steadily grew to 16.5

Table 6.3 Western's Balance Sheet (dollars in thousands)

	1986	*1985*
Assets		
Cash	$ 92,461	$ 54,788
Federal funds sold—at cost, which approximates market	85,000	—
U.S. government securities—at amortized cost (market value of $698,940 and $466,277, respectively)	707,334	475,304
Mortgage-backed securities (market value of $380,504 and $483,421, respectively)	372,594	484,930
Loans receivable, net	2,995,312	2,686,857
Accrued interest receivable	47,495	44,785
Real estate		
Loans with additional interest provisions, accounted for as joint ventures, net	197,665	186,111
Acquired for development or investment, net	571,601	493,104
Acquired in settlement of loans, net	30,885	23,368
Capital stock of the Federal Home Loan Bank—at cost	26,213	22,500
Investments in affiliates	66,920	51,662
Other investments—at cost	88,786	94,378
Office properties and equipment—at costs, less accumulated depreciation and amortization	173,843	76,873
Goodwill and other intangible—at cost, less accumulated amortization	32,271	33,650
Other assets and deferred charges	58,725	56,287
Total Assets	$5,547,105	$4,784,597
Liabilities and Stockholders' Equity		
Deposits	$3,813,475	$3,279,691
Advances from Federal Home Loan Bank	450,000	450,000
Securities sold under agreements to repurchase	836,292	694,518
Notes payable	91,654	39,332
Advances from borrowers for taxes and insurance	10,219	10,910
Accounts payable and accrued expenses	52,621	46,284
Income tax liabilities	43,730	28,883
Subordinated capital notes	121,130	121,904
Total Liabilities	$5,419,121	$4,671,522

percent of assets, or $915 million of $5.5 billion. It got attention, from a quality-of-assets perspective. The Federal Home Loan Bank Board (FHLBB) had exhibited interest in the "direct investment" category as a percentage of regulatory net worth when it issued its first regulation on the subject in 1985. Western had stockholders' equity of $128 million on December 31, 1986, including preferred stock with liquidation value of $55.2 million and common equity, then, of $72.7 million.

What were these assets? First, Western had $571.6 million in real estate development projects in six states. The bank also stated that it "expected to expend up to $975 million toward the development of such projects, excluding capitalized interest, over a period of 10 to 20 years."[13] So that is okay—real estate always goes up, thoughtful investors must have said.

Investment securities were the next category. According to information right out of the December 31, 1986, 10K (see Table 6.4), Western had invested $155.7 million carrying value of assets in a grab bag of companies. How much were they worth? The Weasel's "estimated market value" column (Column 4) is mostly footnotes. Footnote 5c of the Consolidated Financial Statement said, "Many of the investments held by the Association are not publicly traded; accordingly, market value is not readily determinable. In the opinion of management, the estimated aggregate market value of the above investments approximated cost at December 31, 1986 and 1985."[14] Of these investments, John Driggs was a director of America West Airlines, Inc., and Gary Driggs was a director of Newell Co. and Thousand Trails.

Can a reasonable market value be calculated? Start at the top of the investment security list with Thousand Trails. Trails was a notorious campground with memberships that sometimes forgot to pay after the initial sign-up fee. Negative cash flow had pushed the common stock price from the $20s to $2.9375 by December 31, 1986. After earning $1.8 million in 1985, Thousand Trails lost $50.4 million in 1986 and was in talks with lenders to restructure debt. Western's exposure to Trails was $22 million in common stock and $30.1 million face value in subordinated debt, with a carrying cost of $15 million.

Table 6.4 Western's Odd Assets (dollars in thousands)

	December 31, 1985		December 31, 1986	
	Carrying Value	*Estimated Market Value*[1]	*Carrying Value*	*Estimated Market Value*[1]
Common Stock				
Thousand Trails, Inc.[2]	$24,438	$19,861	$22,000	[6]
Newell Co.[2]	27,224	38,276	29,876	$46,710
Broadview Financial Corporation[3]	1,030	404	1,030	350
Charter Federal Savings and Loan Association	696	1,087	0	—
Other	4,243	4,397	5,347	5,332
Total	$57,631	$64,025	$58,253	
Cumulative Preferred Stock				
Del E. Webb Corporation	$11,465	[4]	$11,465	[4]
Broadview Savings and Loan Company (with warrants)[5]	35,000	[4]	35,000	[4]
Convertible Preferred Stock				
America West Airlines, Inc. 9.75% convertible[7]	6,000	[4]	0	—
America West Airlines, Inc. 10.5% convertible	14,820	[4]	14,820	[4]
Subordinated Debt				
Del E. Webb Corporation, variable rate	2,866	[4]	2,866	[4]
Finalco, Inc., variable rate	10,413	[4]	10,413	[4]
Thousand Trails, Inc., 14 5/8%	0	—	15,044	[6]
Public Utility Bonds	7,845	6,723	7,845	7,344
Total	$88,409		$97,453	

[1]Market values reflect the last reported sales price of the security on the date set forth and may not be indicative of the current market value of these investments.

[2]At December 31, 1986, these investments are being held for sale; however, there are certain restrictions which must be met in order to transfer ownership. See Note 5 of the Consolidated Financial Statements, at Item 8.

[3]The Association is holding these shares for investment.

[4]No active public trading market exists for these securities.

[5]Broadview Savings has declared but has not paid six semi-annual dividends aggregating $12.6 million as of December 31, 1986. Western Savings believes that it is unlikely that Broadview Savings and Loan Company will pay dividends of $2.1 million due June 30, 1987, and December 31, 1987, and is unable to predict whether Broadview Savings and Loan Company will pay dividends thereafter. See Note 5b of the Consolidated Financial Statements at Item 8.

[6]In the opinion of management, the combined value of Thousand Trails, Inc., common stock and subordinated debentures approximated $37,044,000 at December 31, 1986. Management relied upon the advice of an investment banker and market quotations in determining such value, which is substantially higher than the quoted market value.

[7]In April 1986, America West, Inc., redeemed all of the shares of the 9.75% convertible preferred stock held by the Association at a premium of $468,000.

The value of the Association's investments in other companies will fluctuate as a result of changes in the economy in general, the stock market, and the business of the companies in which the investments are made and as a result of other factors outside the control of Western Savings. In addition, securities for which there is no active trading market or the transferability of which is otherwise restricted by contractual provisions or applicable securities laws are not liquid investments and thus Western Savings may not be able to dispose of them at the most opportune time to minimize losses or maximize gains.

Source: Western Savings and Loan Association Form 10K, 31 December 1986.

Footnote 6 of Table 6.4 said that the values of the securities are "substantially higher than the quoted market value."[15] The number of common shares owned was 2.4 million, or less than $7.2 million at current market, certainly "substantially" less than the $22 million carrying value. Notes to the financials also mentioned that Western had committed up to $50 million on two credit lines to Thousand Trails, $48.4 million outstanding at year-end, collateralized by real estate operating properties and receivables—no doubt the famous uncollectible ones. The total hook on Weasel's books was $85.4 million for the Trails investment.

Newell Co., in contrast, was a home run for Western, having almost doubled from the original cost of $29.9 million. Western owned 1.73 million shares worth $27 each on December 31, 1986, or close to $46.7 million, for a profit of $16.8 million. The securities were held for sale as soon as the details of transfer could be worked out.

Broadview Financial Corporation, however, was in arrears by $12.6 million on the preferred dividend and below capital requirements, with asset writedowns from construction lending mounting. Broadview common stock traded in November 1986 around $2 a share. Clearly, Broadview stock was worth something less than the $1 million for the common stock and $35 million on the cumulative preferred carrying value.

Del E. Webb, American Air West, and Finalco were all in business and the securities were unpriceable.

The wary analyst who tried to calculate a value for the Western portfolio might adjust for Trails, Broadview, and Newell and give the other securities the benefit of management's valuation skills. Adjusted values would be:

- $7.2 million for Trails common.
- $45 million for Newell.
- $0 for Broadview common and preferred.
- $7 million for the Trails bond.
- $52.8 for other securities.

The total of priceable securities equals $112 million, for a loss of $43.7 million on the portfolio—and that is without considering the Trails receivables.

In addition to high direct-real-estate exposure and the investments in unpriceable securities, Western also had, of course, large exposure to real estate and construction loans ($347 million) and mobile home and property improvement loans ($801 million). Equity was $128 million, net worth $248.3, with regulators requiring a minimum net worth of $154.1 million. Western was close to jeopardy on required levels of capital, if the portfolio was carried at more realistic values.

Income Statement and Insiders

What about earnings? No doubt, all those real estate and securities profits resulted in regular increases; the added risk of the portfolio must have yielded abnormally high returns. But that was not the case: Earnings per share were $1.80 for 1986, versus $2.32 in 1985, with net income of $30 million, versus $36 million in 1985. "Other income," including gain on sale of loans and investments and income from real estate, was $127 million in 1986, versus $109 million in 1985. Western also capitalized large amounts of interest—$35 million in 1986, $29 million in 1985.

Meanwhile, the Driggs family was not doing too badly with the company. John (chairman of the board) and Gary (president and chief executive officer) made $414,016 each in 1986. Net realized value of stock options was $366,393 for John and $1,574,100 for Gary. Mortgage loans from Western to John totaled $500,000 at 9.5 percent and to Gary, $602,119 at rates from 6 to 11.75 percent. Their sister, Lois Cannon, had a PR job in Laguna Beach with the company's West Coast arm.

To summarize, the 1986 10K showed an interested investor that stated book value was probably too high and earnings were not necessarily recurring. With a price-to-book ratio of over three times and price-to-tangible-book of six times, Western Savings was trading on hope for earnings growth, real estate appreciation, or, perhaps, a takeover (unlikely, according to family comments).

Why Write It Down?

Western Savings had a better year in 1987. It included a very peculiar financial transaction—an asset swap that was impossible for an outsider to value. Western took a loss of only $1.3 million on the whole Thousand Trails package of assets—the $50 million receivable loan plus the securities. Western traded it to Southmark for a package of securities that included: a $35.5 million Southmark subordinated convertible debenture, $10.9 million in preferred Southmark stock, $23.2 million in Visa participation rights, a $21.5 million participation in two collateralized real estate loans, and $9.5 million of Thousand Trails' campground memberships. Whew! What could they do with the campground memberships? Recreational vehicle (RV) hookups were no trouble at all when a major capital-eroding loss disappeared into the air.

A check of the 1987 financial footnotes showed that Broadview preferred was still carried at cost, with no writedown in sight. Newell Co. had been sold for a gain.

Net income was up nicely, $33 million versus $30 million in 1986, with $161 million contributed from other income—$78.9 million from real estate. But stockholders' equity declined from $128 million to $116 million. Western had bought in common stock—1.8 million shares that cost close to $30 million.

The asset shuffle continued in 1988 when Gary announced with the second-quarter earnings a prospective sale of branches for a $26 million gain and continued sale of real estate, loans, and investments for profits. For the quarter, earnings were down versus the previous year, and, more telling, real estate acquired in settlement of loans had more than doubled to $219 million. The real estate environment in Arizona was adding to the pressure on Gary's asset strategy. Earnings appeared to be hard to come by, even with swaps and sales.

Management declared a dividend, then reneged, and offered stock in its place.

In May 1988, *Forbes* noticed the disparity between stock price and asset value in a lovely article by Allan Sloan. He elucidated the shuffles and swaps and alluded to capital in "increasingly short supply."[16]

Western Savings and Loan Association is no more, taken over by regulators, finally, and the auditors' hands were slapped for their whimsical accounting treatment. Gary and family resigned in December 1988, with the stock selling at around $3 per share (see Figure 6.3). The $6.2 billion thrift is reported to be the probable third largest thrift bailout, with a taxpayer price tag of $1.7 billion and repossessed real estate of $637 million, with an additional $295 million in speculative loans and $46 million in junk bonds. The Broadview Savings preferred might be written down by now and the economic sound-and-light show quiet this year at the Biltmore.

The Western exercise should teach a prospective buyer or seller to read the footnotes and try to price the securities and assets on the balance sheet—or, at least, to read an S&P sheet on a company that

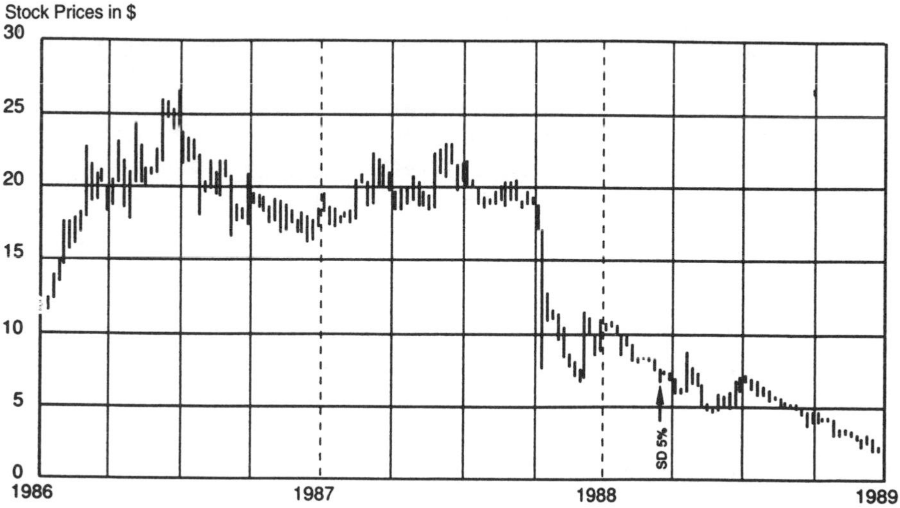

Figure 6.3 Western Savings and Loan, January 1, 1986–December 31, 1989

issues a lot of probably convertible, preferred, privately issued, no-market securities that sit on the balance sheet like a hippo thinly disguised as a race horse.

◆ *Insurance Companies: Who's on First?*

Any asset that does not have a ready market is fair game for asset shuffling. Junk bonds, real estate, mortgage pools, funny preferred stocks, convertibles, and notes all work just fine when a company is bent on optimistic valuations. Insurance companies, like banks and thrifts, are grounded on portfolios. All business, especially in life insurance companies, is irreparably linked to the underlying assets: Payment of benefits, ability to write new business, and solvency are all functions of the stocks and bonds held by the company.

"Insurance Company Insolvencies," a February 1990 report by the Subcommittee on Oversight and Investigations of the U.S. House of Representatives, comes down hard on the insurance industry for this asset-shuffling skill. One of the main weaknesses that the committee noted was unreliable information:

> Much of the information used to measure solvency by state regulators, industry participants, and ratings services is simply unreliable as a basis for accurately determining an insurance company's financial condition. Most such information is provided by insurance companies themselves, with no verification by regulators, independent auditors, or qualified actuaries. Information may also be outdated and based on "guesstimates," omissions, creative accounting, and even bold-faced lies.[17]

Insurance companies are a great place to hone financial statement detecting skills.

How to Glue Your Attention to Tiny Print

The most important point about insurance companies is that everybody but Joseph Belth (a one-person vigilante on abusive-insurance company practices) hates to read insurance companies' financials.[18] Rumor has it that some investment bankers working on acquisitions of insurance companies do not even look at the Schedule D of potential targets. And that leads to point number two: The few people who do understand insurance companies speak in unknown tongues (like saying "Schedule D," when they really mean "the portfolio") so nobody else can understand. It creates a massive market inefficiency.

Insurance companies are regulated almost exclusively by individual states. The state insurance commissioners have responsibility for overseeing the financial stability of the companies licensed to do business in their state. A voluntary association, the National Association of Insurance Commissioners (NAIC), creates uniform standards for examination and is the acknowledged authority on financial standards. It is the most important source for valuation of securities and other assets and is a quasi-legal body because of its widespread acceptance by state authorities.

The following are the most important points about insurance company financial statements (skip this section if you bore easily).

1. All insurance companies are required to file annual financial statements, which are available for public inspection with the state insurance department. Called "annual statements"—blue books for life companies, yellow for property and casualty—the financials are on standard forms dubbed "blanks." Copies of the statements can be obtained at the insurance department in a state's capital if the insurance company of choice will not send them. They are filed in March.

2. These statements require different accounting practices (called "statutory accounting"), so they will not match generally-accepted-accounting-principles (GAAP) accounting used with 10Ks and 10Qs and annuals. The driving force of statutory accounting is liquidity; for example, acquisition costs are expensed immediately, not over several years. The spirit of the rule is the determination of solvency or of claims-paying ability—which makes it easier for a financial detective to

analyze. Statutory accounting is quasi-cash accounting, close to tax accounting. Here is a quick road map to life companies (remember that the forms, page numbers, and line numbers are standard):

- Page 2 tells you the assets: bonds, stocks, real estate, and policy loans.
- Page 3 tells you the liabilities and surplus: the interest maintenance reserve on line 11.4 , the asset valuation reserve on line 24.1 (more later), and the surplus on line 37.
- Page 4 is the income statement with net income (line 33), realized capital gains and losses (line 32), and unrealized capital gains and losses (line 36).
- Page 5 is cash flow.
- Page 10 is the detail of income and gains and losses by type of security.
- Notes to Financial Statements tell all the dirt: who owns the company, what dividends were paid to the owner, prohibitions on dividends paid, and information about transactions between parent and subs.
- Schedule A is real estate: Part 1 owned, Part 2 sold.
- Schedule B is mortgages, Part 1 owned, lines 13 and 14 foreclosed and transferred to real estate, and acquired by deed in lieu of foreclosure. Schedule B, Part 2, Section 3, is mortgages in process of foreclosure.
- Schedule BA, Part 1, shows other long-term investments, such as real estate joint ventures and partnerships.
- Form for Calculating the Interest Maintenance Reserve and the Asset Valuation Reserve gives the breakdown of the reserve component.
- Schedule D tells the details of the investment portfolio. Schedule D, Part 1, lists the bonds held, with the book value, cost, market, interest collected, and NAIC designation as of December 31.
- Schedule D, Part 2, Section 1, lists the preferred stocks, and Schedule D, Part 2, Section 2, gives the common stocks. Schedule D, Part 3, shows all the stocks and bonds acquired for the year and from whom. Schedule D, Part 4, lists stocks and bonds sold or redeemed with gain or loss. Schedule

D, Part 5, gives those stocks and bonds acquired and disposed of in the same year.

3. All of this fits together in one number called surplus.

   Surplus = Assets – (Liabilities + Capital).

   In other words, surplus equals retained earnings. In the words of the Life Management Institute accounting textbook by Paul Zucconi, "The proper valuation of assets and liabilities is most important to the accuracy of the surplus total."[19] Surplus provides the cushion for surprises and it provides funds for expansion. It is the heart of the company. It also determines how much the owner can take out and whether the regulators take over.

As you can see, the insurance commission makes the companies publish everything an analyst needs to know. But it requires patience to read all those tiny numbers and try to track reality.

An analyst wants to know the possibility that problems in the portfolio will eat through surplus (that is like eating through the net worth). Clair and Joseph Galloway, in their blockbuster insurance accounting textbook *Handbook of Accounting for Insurance Companies*, said that policyholders' surplus is not meant to imply value of the company, but is "intended to measure the strength of the company for regulatory purposes. . . . Because of conservative statutory accounting practices, including the exclusion of nonadmitted assets, the policyholders' surplus does provide an estimate of minimum financial strength of the company available for policyholders."[20]

The NAIC suggests that life companies reserve for possible problems in the investment portfolio by establishing a reserve account that reduces surplus, much like banks must have reserves for loan losses. In the early 1990s the NAIC divided the old reserve (the mandatory securities valuation reserve—MSRV) into two pieces: the asset valuation reserve (AVR) and the interest maintenance valuation reserve (IMR). Also like banks, life companies have a direct relationship between problem assets and reserves. The NAIC does this with the AVR, which is a liability of the company—an increase in AVR causes a decrease in surplus. AVR is made up of two components: a default component for credit-related losses on bonds, preferred stocks, and mortgages and an equity component for all types of equity.

The IMR is intended to capture realized gains and losses unrelated to credit quality changes. This reserve amortizes gains or losses into income over the life of the investment and is a policyholder liability, not a valuation reserve. The AVR requirements concerning portfolio reserves follow. Publicly traded stocks are automatic 20-percent reserves times a weighted average portfolio beta factor; preferreds are from 3 to 22 percent.

In 1990, the NAIC instituted new categories for bonds that rely more heavily on rating services than the previous categories did.

The categories are:

NAIC Designation	Rating Agency	Maximum Accumulation
1	AAA/Aaa, AA/AA, A/A	1%
2	BBB/Baa	2%
3	BB/BA	5%
4	B/B	10%
5	CCC/Caa and lower	20%
6	In or near default	20%

Insurance companies do not have to write down defaulted bonds by more than 20 percent until bankruptcy is declared unless the investment officer is of a conservative bent. So the burden of reality for risky assets rests on either the regulating arm or conservative management, whichever comes first.

Capitol Life: An Integrated-Resources Hazardous-Waste Holding Tank

The point of the analysis is to determine from the financials the likelihood that problem assets can eat up surplus. A simplistic, but useful, approach is to add up illiquid, risky assets to get a problem-asset total.

Then add back accumulated MSVR (as it was called in 1988) to surplus for the assets you have spotted. Finally, divide the adjusted surplus by the perceived problem-asset number to see what the coverage is before the regulators' hornet's nest is stirred or a capital infusion is necessary.

Capitol Life's capital structure as of December 31, 1988, was:

Assets	$1,900,327,685
Liabilities	$1,834,267,556
including MSVR of	$ 46,447,775
Surplus	$ 61,560,309

So the surplus is the cushion.

The next step is to go over Schedules A through D and make subjective decisions about which assets are potential problems—in other words, to critique the NAIC's valuations.

- Schedule A shows $8.5 million in real estate, of which $3.9 million represents mortgages foreclosed on from Schedule B.
- Schedule BA has $30 million in real estate partnerships.
- Schedule D has $249 million in 20-percent reserve CCC or in default bonds, so add back $49.8 million to surplus.
- Schedule D also has $43.5 million in notes and bonds of subsidiaries and parents, including a $38-million note from its parent, Integrated, designated 2 percent. The 20 percent NAIC designation is on only $1.5 million of the total, so add back $1.14 million to surplus.
- Common stock shows $137.2 million in stock of affiliates, including $123.2 million in Realty Investors. Add back $27.4 to surplus for the necessary 20-percent MSVR for common stocks.

This list sums it up:

Problem Asset		MSVR Addback
Real estate	$ 8.5 million	—
Venture capital	30 million	—
Bonds, rated CCC or in default	249 million	$ 49.8 million
Subsidiary notes/bonds	43.5 million	1.14 million
Stock in affiliates	137.2 million	27.4 million
Total	$468.20 million	$78.34 million

The total is $468.20 million for potential-problem illiquid assets. Add back the accumulated MSVR of $46.5 million because the full $78.34 million has not yet reduced surplus to avoid double deducting. Adjusted surplus is $108 million, so coverage is one-fourth; that is, if one-fourth of the problems materialize, Capitol Life is in trouble. MSVR is $46.5 million, or one-tenth, and therefore provides some small protection.

This exercise reveals to an analyst the pulse of the company. If Integrated and Realty Investors gets in trouble (see Chapter 7), there is no room in surplus and certainly little already anticipated in MSVR. The bugbear is clearly the securities of parent and affiliates, so a pessimist needs to watch Integrated and Realty, not just the insurance company. The NAIC, meanwhile, thought Integrated Resources looked good enough to require only a 2-percent reserve, and that says loud and clear, DO YOUR OWN WORK.

Insurance companies have a lot of leeway on the carrying value of securities, particularly when the stocks or bonds do not have a public market value. As a critical bystander, all you have to do is cast doubt on the quality of some of those assets to avoid owning the parent stock. If you question a significant number of assets relative to surplus, short the parent.

More Rules of the Insurance Game

According to GAAP rules, no gain or loss is realized when controlling or controlled entities swap securities. The security must be sold to a third party in order to take realized gains. Statutory reporting (the conservative, cash-based accounting that figures surplus) is more lenient in this regard: The transferring company can recognize a gain or loss, which will affect the surplus of the company selling the security, which in turn affects how much cash money the parent can take home.

Most states also have limitations about how much money can be pulled out of a company by the parent. A typical restriction reads that all of the net income (sometimes, operating profits) or 10 percent of surplus may be paid out to the parent. This limitation is always spelled out in the Convention Statement in "Notes to Financial Statements." Companies can, however, pay out interest to the parent on surplus debentures (a capital infusion that is neither cat nor dog, debt nor equity) as long as adequate surplus exists and the state regulators are happy.

All that means is that it is harder to repatriate money to the parent than it seems and it is also harder to generate accounting gains by swapping securities between subsidiaries.

Unrelated companies can certainly help out in tough times by owning each other's securities. And, in the event of problems with the issuer, they can also neglect to write down those securities—as in the case of First Executive with its holdings in terminal companies, Integrated Resources and Southmark.

New games appear in the insurance industry as fast as analysts learn to track the old ones. Reading Convention Statements, however, significantly lowers the chance of being broadsided by fast-swapping mavens.

The conclusion from studying insurance companies, as it is for all the accounting mumbo jumbo stocks, is that the tough stocks to analyze are usually the most lucrative because they are generally the most overvalued (or undervalued, but definitely mispriced).

◆ *Notes*

1. National Education Corporation, Annual Report, 31 December 1988, 28.

2. Arthur Rade, Merrill Lynch Research Report, 17 April 1989, from National Education Corporation Excerpts, 1 August 1989.
3. Ram Capoor, Morgan Stanley Research Report, 24 May 1989, from National Education Corporation Excerpts, 1 August 1989.
4. Arthur Rade, Merrill Lynch Research Report, 12 June 1989, from National Education Corporation Excerpts, 1 August 1989.
5. Fred Anschel, Dean Witter Reynolds Research Report, 13 June 1989, from National Education Corporation Excerpts, 1 August 1989.
6. Arthur Rade, Merrill Lynch Research Report, 19 July 1989, from National Education Corporation Excerpts, 1 August 1989.
7. Ram Capoor, Morgan Stanley Research Report, 21 July 1989, from National Education Corporation Excerpts, 1 August 1989.
8. National Education Corporation, Form 10Q, 30 June 1989, 7.
9. Autotote Corporation, Form 10K, 31 October 1992, 35.
10. Penn Crabtree,"Caliente pulls the plug on video gaming machines," *San Diego Business Journal*, 23 May 1994, 3.
11. Allan Sloan, "Phoenix's Wild West Show," *Forbes*, 30 May 1988, 38.
12. Western Savings and Loan Association, Form 10K, 31 December 1986, 39.
13. Ibid., 15.
14. Ibid., 59.
15. Ibid., 16.
16. Sloan, "Phoenix's Wild West Show," 38.
17. U.S. House of Representatives, Committee on Energy and Commerce, Subcommittee on Oversight and Investigations, *Failed Promises: Insurance Company Insolvencies* (Washington, DC: Government Printing Office, 1990), 4.

18. Joseph Belth writes a wonderful newsletter for insurance company nuts called *The Insurance Forum*, P.O. Box 245, Ellettsville, IN, 47429.

19. Paul J. Zucconi, *Accounting in Life and Health Insurance Companies* (Atlanta: LOMA, 1987), 210.

20. Clair J. and Joseph M. Galloway, *Handbook of Accounting for Insurance Companies* (New York: McGraw Hill, 1986), 255.

21. Joseph M. Belth, *The Insurance Forum*, 17: 4, 102.

7

Money Suckers: Coining Money to Live

Some companies require great gulps of capital to stay alive, even during periods of economic expansion. When operations fail to prime the pump of free cash flow, financial markets irrigate the basic business. To fund a company that goes to the markets routinely, the debt or equity buyer must assume one of two things: that the company either will eventually earn enough money to pay back the obligation or will make a reasonable return on equity or that the assets on the balance sheet will appreciate enough so that a sale will cover the outstanding obligations. Like carnival barkers, these companies promise that the view from front row center will someday be worth the admission price.

In order to fund the future, money must be obtained continually. Debt, equity, partnerships, private placements—all the financial instruments—are used. Integrated Resources is the best example of a capital guzzler in recent years. Medical start-up companies are another. In the 1980s, money was easy to get; companies prospered without earnings and without free cash flow. As the banker said about Jiffy Lube, easy money was the problem. When the market appetite for new debt and equity disappeared, so did the companies.

The Nine Lives of Integrated Resources, Inc.

Integrated Resources takes honors as one of the longest term short positions (except perhaps CopyTele). It seemed like a layup in 1986, but it took until June 1989 to default on the layers of debt. At least once or twice a year, short sellers would yell, "Timber, there she goes," but the stock would defy gravity and bounce back. Its demise marked the beginning of the junk-bond debacle, and its financial history covers lessons on cash-flow analysis, insurance-company leverage, real estate shenanigans, and insider transactions.

New Tax Law Death Blow to Shelter Companies

When the Tax Reform Act of 1986 was passed, business looked hard for the companies that made money selling tax shelters. When a fundamental change occurs in the business environment, there are two strategies to follow for the short seller: short the marginal company or short the institutional favorite. Both strategies have proponents. The institutional favorite is the quality company with good growth, pretty financials, and a large number of institutional stockholders. Institutional favorites crash more quickly than marginal companies because large numbers of portfolio managers rush to dump the stock of the favorites when the analysts are finally convinced that the industry has been dealt an irreparable blow. If the company management is astute, they might dig their way out of the cave-in before the institutions exit. The marginal company, on the other hand, has shaky financials, bad management, and a history of aggressive but often poorly executed business strategies. Problems develop more rapidly when no support exists, either financial or managerial. The stockholder base is less sophisticated: They are slower to sell, they pay less attention, or, even worse, they are composed entirely of friends of the company. The price takes forever to reflect the reality of the company condition.

Integrated Resources was a marginal company. Revenues came from three areas: life insurance companies, direct-participation investment programs, and money management. Privately offered investment programs (tax shelters) provided the bulk of the revenue and net income—more than 69 percent of investment-program revenue in 1982 to 1984, which in turn was 77 percent of pretax income. A change in

Table 7.1 Integrated Resources, Inc., Short Interest

1987	*Number of Short Shares*	*1988*	*Number of Short Shares*	*1989*	*Number of Short Shares*
January	584,305	January	325,028	January	615,760
February	718,614	February	347,728	February	757,701
March	626,119	March	408,113	March	1,057,170
April	591,986	April	441,395	April	1,010,221
May	563,048	May	447,095	May	1,038,495
June	543,170	June	482,120	June	1,365,330
July	524,856	July	497,320	July	2,632,226
August	586,570	August	504,220	August	2,208,990
September	572,969	September	490,320	September	1,925,123
October	575,257	October	453,020	October	1,564,903
November	539,103	November	455,070	November	1,234,121
December	440,518	December	489,878	December	997,833

the tax law should certainly affect Integrated's net income, unless the company could reposition itself rapidly.

Why was Integrated a marginal company? The 1986 10K and proxy held the clues.

Greedy Management or Valuable Leaders?

First, the Zises brothers—Selig and Jay—and Arthur Goldberg, were the executives of Integrated. You could hardly go wrong with the brothers and company. The granddaddies of creative compensation planning, the Zises, got paid for just about everything that happened at Integrated: You expected to see a percentage of the pencil purchase order go to the Zises. A few highlights from the proxy are:

- Selig owned 6 percent, Jay 5.4 percent, of the common; "other family members" owned 3.5 percent, Goldberg 2.3 percent.
- Total salary + bonus + compensation for the five top officers was $5,855,920. The top 21 executives as a group earned over $15 million. The company earned $49,812,000.

- The bonus package included a minimum of 5.5 percent of pretax profits and a guideline of 10 percent of pretax profits before unusual charges and credits. An additional 5.7 percent went to other executive officers.

In 1985, the company even paid medical costs not covered by insurance policies for the Zises's father and brother, $22,342 and $16,018, respectively. Corporate headquarters was a daily family reunion: Everybody got paid, and everybody had a job. Father Bernard got $125,000 in consulting fees, $27,500 in bonuses, and $417,000 in allocated partnership losses. Brother Seymour was an insurance agent and registered representative and got a hefty cut. Jay's wife made a paltry $100,000. In 1985, Integrated gave the printing company of the Zises's brother-in-law $922,115 in printing business.

Integrated also had a creative stock-bonus incentive plan: When grantors exercised the stock option, they paid 5 percent in cash and the balance in installments over the vesting period. But each grantor was also entitled to a bonus equal to the installment payment when it was due. The executives, therefore, paid just 5 percent cash money for their stock.

Selig also bought a condominium in Manhattan from the company. Integrated bought it for $1.4 million in 1982 and added $170,000 in improvements. Selig improved it another $275,000. The appraisal in 1986 was $1.825 million, or a little less than the purchase price plus improvements; so Selig bought it for $1.55 million. Manhattan real estate was apparently flat for four years in the mid-1980s.

Chief executives paid no money management fees to the company's subsidiary money manager, although they had funds under management—waived fees were $49,208 each a year. They had, of course, disability, life insurance, and "additional personal benefits." Officers also purchased interest in limited partnerships, and the company granted bonuses in the amount of the capital contribution. Officers were also allocated $18.2 million in losses from the partnerships before the limited partners were admitted, presumably to shelter their salary/bonus packages.

For the 1981-to-1985 period, Integrated paid officers and directors approximately $50 million under compensation, bonus incentive, reimbursement for partnership investments, life insurance, and medical reimbursements. In 1986, a stockholder sued, claiming excessive compensation was paid to executives.

Challenging Financial Statements

The financial statements of the company were as edifying as the executives' perks. The December 31, 1986, 10K was a long and enlightening document. First, on the balance sheet (see Table 7.2), equity as a percentage of assets had dropped from over 20 percent to under 10 percent in a year—not a lot of cushion for bad times.

Next, the assets looked a little funny: What was real and bankable? Notes and receivables were 22 percent of assets. Were those due from investors in old partnerships that were no longer attractive? Were they from partnerships with negative cash flow? Were they collectable?

Notes to the financials explained a little. Of the $692,010,000 due from investment programs, $231,409,000 was due from limited partnerships and $131,227,000 from investors in partnerships, and $299,395,000 represented deferred fees and contract rights. Deferred fees? Yes, Integrated booked revenues from future rental proceeds and proceeds realized on sale of property up front when it closed the partnership. If the deals turned sour, not only were receivables and assets inflated, but the company also would have to reverse revenues previously realized.

Keep in mind that shareholders' equity was only $505,711,000—10 percent of assets. Common stockholders' equity (less preferred stock) was $145 million—2.8 percent of assets. With that as a base, $299 million of the assets was aggressively booked revenues based on future events. Common equity has an impact on how much money can be raised in hard times—eroding equity capital affects bargaining and credit standing in the markets. The composition of capital was an important trail sign to track Integrated's demise.

Prepaid acquisition costs were $445 million, up from $203 mil-

Table 7.2 Integrated Resources Balance Sheet (dollars in thousands)

	December 31, 1986	December 31, 1985
Assets		
Cash	$ 69,473	$ 41,536
Investments:		
Held by life insurance subsidiaries	2,178,550	388,992
Short-term investments, at cost (approximates market)	34,230	25,205
Equity securities, at lower of cost or market (1986—cost $28,740, 1985—market $44,256)	26,039	43,830
Other	85,723	67,677
	$2,324,542	$ 525,704
Notes and Receivables	1,149,808	935,993
Property, Equipment and Improvements, at cost, net of accumulated depreciation and amortization of $24,773 and $16,029	52,066	40,904
Prepaid Acquisition Costs of life insurance, investment programs and value of acquired insurance in force	445,392	203,068
Assets of Separate Accounts	948,469	275,395
Other Assets	62,301	49,775
Intangible Assets, net of accumulated amortization of $5,494 and $4,449	84,617	38,193
Total Assets	$5,136,668	$2,110,568
Liabilities and Shareholders' Equity		
Future Policy Benefits and Claim Reserves	$2,541,423	$ 362,227
Short-Term Loans	200,960	281,585
Accounts Payable and Other Liabilities (Note F)	248,428	207,740
Deferred Income Taxes	101,873	109,905
Liabilities of Separate Accounts	948,469	275,395
Senior Indebtedness	111,411	134,743
Subordinated Indebtedness	478,393	276,607
Commitments and Contingencies		
Redeemable Preferred Stock	—	13,088
Shareholders' Equity	505,711	449,278
Total Liabilities and Shareholders' Equity	$5,136,668	$2,110,568

Source: Integrated Resources, Inc., Form 10K, 31 December 1986.

lion, a big jump. Notes, again, explained a little. Prepaid acquisition costs on investment programs had gone from $89 million to $193 million. Prepaid acquisition costs, remember, are costs that the company decided to defer expensing until later. They can be commissions paid to salespeople, costs of acquiring the business from another company, or costs of putting a partnership together. Integrated looked like it was attempting to manage earnings by deferring expenses. Not only does that not match cash flow (you pay now, collect later), but it puts future earnings in jeopardy. If revenues should slow (say, because the tax law changed), the company still has expenses to deduct every quarter, even without revenue—an interesting balance-sheet structure for a company in flux.

Second, from the income statement, an optimistic Wall Streeter would infer that maybe Integrated has already straightened out the basic business questions and the resulting cash flow will strengthen the balance sheet. Pretax operating income was $39 million, down from $56 million, and $23 million of that (you have to check the notes for this number—see Table 7.3) came from realized gains in the life insurance portfolios. It is hard to get cash money out of a life insurance sub: It might look pretty on consolidated income statements, but there are some restrictions on its use and repatriation back to the parent (Chapter 6).

Table 7.3 Gains in the Insurance Subsidiaries (dollars in thousands)

	1986	*1985*	*1984*
Fixed maturities	$ 82,244	$29,759	$17,436
Equity securities	1,384	1,296	424
Mortgage loans on real estate	21,052	1,474	—
Policy loans	7,207	3,577	1,998
Short-term and other investments	12,354	1,998	2,155
	124,241	38,104	22,013
Realized gains	23,169	5,478	1,841
	147,410	43,582	23,854
Investment expenses	1,474	326	280
	$145,936	$43,256	$23,574

Source: Integrated Resources, Inc., Form 10K, 31 December 1986.

Net income of $18 million (before preferred dividend) looks a little pallid, next to the Zises brothers' income, but it is tough to run a company.

Shifting Focus: 1987

Integrated decided to change the product emphasis to income-producing partnerships, variable annuities, and money management. The company, as it diversified, continued to assure the public that the basic business was intact: The Japanese purchase of Integrated's property, 666 Fifth Avenue in New York City, by Sumitomo was widely publicized as a coup for the company, although it was not booked as a gain until a subsequent quarter. What followed in 1987 was a year of inventive earnings management.

The first quarter of 1987 was a victory for Integrated as far as the company was concerned, with "advances in revenues and income per share from continuing operations," despite conservative accounting.[1] Well, not exactly. Income from operations was $11.7 million, down from $12.5 million, and cash flow continued to deteriorate.

A short lecture on cash flow is in order: *Cash flow* is defined as "net income plus depreciation, amortization, and deferred taxes." Cash flow from operations generally takes into account working capital as well. An analyst wants to know how much cash is available to the company for expansion, dividends, stock purchase, or retirement of debt—in other words, what is the financial flexibility of the company? That means making subjective decisions about the business of the company and what cash flows relate directly to that business. Some examples are: (1) a furniture-rental company must continually refurbish rental furniture or revenues slow; so the analyst tempers the depreciation add-back number to take this into account because depreciation is a direct cost of doing business; (2) when analyzing retailers, adjustments must be made for inventory and receivables because they have to have inventory to sell;

(3) when analyzing a cable production company, produced programming is surely a cost of staying in business. End of lecture.

Integrated was in the business of buying property, then repackaging the property into partnerships, selling the partnerships, managing the partnership property, and then selling it. So cash flow should be reduced by purchases of property and increased by collections—that is not investing, it is the basic business. The March 31, 1987, 10Q cash flow defined in those terms was an outflow of $24 million, compared to an inflow of $31 million in March 1986 (operating cash flow from the Statement of Changes minus the purchase of property and investments plus collections—see Table 7.4). And that is without deducting for preferred dividends, which are not a necessity of doing business, although they are a factor in financing.

In the second quarter of 1987, management thought the company had turned the corner. Sharply higher results heralded the transition. Integrated had discovered the roll-up. Income from operations of $23 million, versus $13.3 million in 1986, was backed with solid declines in cash flow. Six-month cash burn was ($190.9 million) versus ($54 million) in 1986. Management mentioned in the notes to the 10Q that part of the increases in net income (no disclosure yet on how much) had come from "restructuring public net lease real estate limited partnerships."[2] Integrated folded 13 limited partnerships into New York Stock Exchange depository units and collected a fee one more time on partnerships they had previously packaged, sold, and booked as revenue.

The stock price returned to health with a move off September 1986 lows of $16.25 to $30 by July 8, 1987. Everybody was happy, especially the Zises (Selig sold a little stock—41,000 shares—in the early fall). *Value Line* commented that Integrated's business was booming; they predicted an earnings growth rate of 30 percent in 1988, after more than tripling in 1987, and rated the stock "2" for timeliness.[3] "A Resourceful Turnaround," *Fortune* announced after panning the stock in June 1986.[4]

The stock price peaked at $32.875 in the fall.

Table 7.4 Integrated Resources Statement of Changes (Unaudited) (dollars in thousands)

	Three Months Ended March 31,	
	1987	*1986*
Operating Activities:		
Net cash (used in) continuing operating activities	$ (5,406)	$ (5,920)
Investing Activities:		
Net cash (used in) discontinued operations	—	(2,924)
Purchases of property, equipment, and improvements, net of sales	(1,740)	(5,779)
Purchases of investments, net of sales	(47,482)	(317)
Net collections on notes and receivables	30,611	43,038
Net (increase) in other assets	(4,500)	(6,973)
Net cash (used in) provided from investing activities	(23,111)	27,045
Financing Activities:		
Shareholders' equity:		
Issuance of capital stock	—	70,998
Redemption of preferred stock	—	(13,088)
Preferred dividends	(7,325)	(9,187)
Debt:		
Increase (decrease) in short-term loans	46,620	(237,001)
Issuance of subordinated indebtedness	—	287,207
Early extinguishment of subordinated indebtedness	—	(118,050)
Payments of indebtedness	(11,618)	(4,268)
Net cash provided from (used in) financing activities	27,677	(23,389)
Net (Decrease) in Cash	$ (840)	$ (2,264)

Source: Integrated Resources, Inc., Form 10Q, 31 March 1987.

The Drop

The third quarter of 1987 was another good one, not up sequentially but still $22.5 million in operating earnings, versus $4.5 million in 1986. Cash flow was ($244 million) versus $8.2 million for nine months. The cash burn was ameliorated by new long-term and short-term debt. Shareholders' equity as a percent of assets was now 8.6 percent. Income for the quarter included the gain on the sale of 666 Fifth Avenue.

Wall Street never warmed to Integrated. Drexel, Burnham, the investment banker, was really the only advocate of the stock. Maybe that was because there were too few shares outstanding or because the company did not tempt the Street with fees on new-issue stock deals. Most firms on the Street sold Integrated's private partnerships in the early 1980s, so this lack of interest was odd. It helped the shorts. The stock escaped the notice of the investment community, so a short squeeze never developed, even toward the end when it was a lay-up.

But the stock was something of an institutional favorite. The 1987 10K noted that Templeton Funds owned 15.8 percent of the company and Equitable had another 14.4 percent. *Value Line* periodically liked the stock. And, of course, the Drexel daisy chain owned paper and bonds and a little stock. First Executive had 6.9 percent of the common, $27 million in bonds (the 10.75 percent of 1996 bonds), together with $39 million book value of preferred stock.

The stock chopped along in late 1987 and early 1988—$16 to $24 was the range (see Figure 7.1). When the 10K came out around the end of March, equity per share was listed in the 10K as $21.97, and income was $2.98, up from $1.06.

The 10K had a particularly interesting footnote: A change in amortization of prepaid acquisition costs in the fourth quarter added $0.97 to earnings. Net for the quarter was $0.97 from continuing operations. The change was not booked as an extraordinary item.

To recap the earnings for the year: The second-quarter growth was from fees for the roll-up; third-quarter growth was the sale of a building; fourth-quarter growth was an accounting change. Throw in a gain from termination of a pension plan and fees from previously

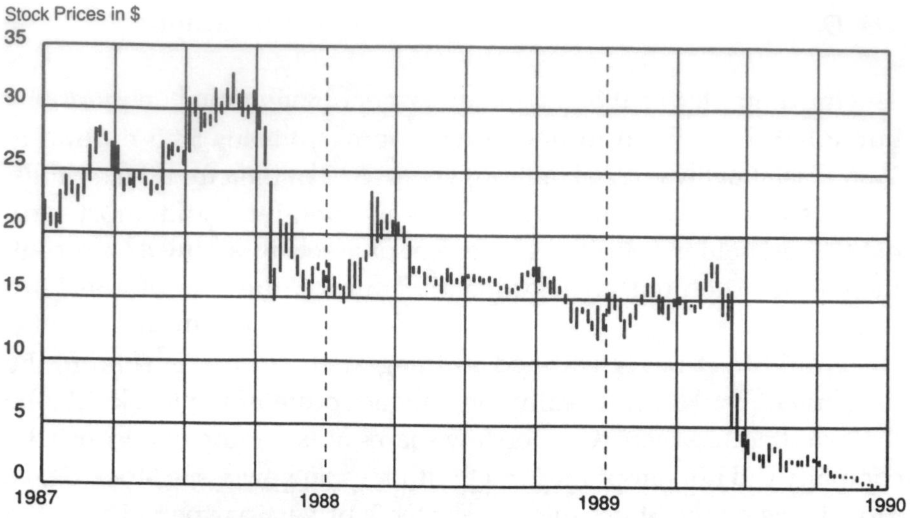

Figure 7.1 Integrated Resources, January 1, 1987–December 31, 1989

syndicated programs. Integrated was having a tough time generating recurring operating earnings, even as debt climbed.

Pretax income was down in the first quarter of 1988. The new amortization schedule helped the comparison by $0.20, but interest expense was up. The 10Q again stated that the company "will continue to require additional funds from sources other than operations."[5] And accounts payable was up from $270 million to $426 million in just three months. Integrated needed financing. Who would lend to a company with disastrous operating cash flow and deteriorating ratios, down to less than 8 percent equity to assets, in a dismal business climate for new real estate partnerships?

Who, indeed? Drexel announced a senior subordinated-note deal in the summer of 1988, just $100 million. Who bought? Insurance companies, primarily, and S&Ls.

Integrated itself owned two insurance companies—Integrated Resources Life and Capitol Life. The insurance subs, in turn, owned a fair amount of Integrated and Integrated affiliate paperstocks, bonds, and notes. The insurance company portfolios turned out to be a problem (Chapter 6).

Integrated Resources Life's 1988 Convention Statements showed

$41 million in Integrated and other subsidiary debt, acquired in 1988, and $3.5 million in common stock (including Integrated's American Insured Mortgage Investors Series), plus $6.2 million in book value of Diasonics stock, a company that Integrated senior was trying to acquire. And that is in a life company with total assets of $3.086 billion and a surplus of only $77.3 million (up from $51.1 million after Integrated contributed a note to a surplus of $15 million). Integrated Life also owned $17.8 million in real estate. Of the bond portfolio, 24 percent was classified in the 20-percent-reserve category (meaning high-yield junk bonds).

Capitol Life looked worse. It owned $38 million in a promissory note of the parent acquired in 1986 and $2 million in demand notes of Integrated Life. But the real clunker in Capitol was $187.56 million invested in the stock of subsidiaries, mostly Realty Investors, a real estate holding company. Twenty percent of the bond portfolio—$249 million—was in the maximum reserve category, and the company owned an additional $8.5 million in real estate, with a current value of $5.6 million. Capitol had assets of $1.9 billion and a surplus of $61 million after paying the parent an $8 million dividend in 1988, according to the 1988 Convention Statement.

The insurance companies were clearly unhealthy. They were perilously close to running through surplus if the parent floundered. So the entire Integrated empire, not only the parent, looked shaky.

The quarter ending June 30, 1988, was uneventful, and the stock continued to wallow from $15.50 to $20.75. Operating income was down, $17.2 million versus $23 million, despite revenues of $414.5 million versus $289 million. The comparison of net income was not as bad as that of operating income because of tax-rate decreases.

The bond deal went off without a hitch in August, and the proceeds were used to pay down short-term debt.

The September 1988 earnings announcement showed that the struggle for earnings was losing ground. Pretax was $9.5 million versus $22.5 million. The earnings gains of the previous year were tough to match. Equity as a percentage of assets was down to 7.1 percent. Cash resources were disappearing, and only $7 million was available for dividends from the life companies.

Insiders Stampede to Exit

On December 21, 1988, Integrated was trading around $14 a share. The Zises brothers sold 900,000 shares to ICH Corp., an insurance company, for $21 a share! ICH announced that it would buy another 7.5 million to-be-issued shares to gain control of the company.

Short sellers went wild in greedy anticipation of the certain crash. The big trigger, the clue that the game was up, had been announced by the company. But, one more time, the stock did not drop to single digits. It was a gift—the fat lady sang loud and clear and wore a "the end is here" sign. Takeover greed appeared to be supporting the price: *Value Line* said avoid, despite potential for near-term price rises if the company fetches another buy-out proposal. The shorts used the disparity to short more.

A little history here: ICH owned 20 percent of First Executive. The company had been involved in several other mergers or buy-outs with Drexel clients that had fallen through. ICH did not have much credibility as anything but a Zises bailout vehicle.

The market mulled the proposal and the stock price dipped to $12. One or more of the convertible preferred holders sold 562,000 shares at a low. Rumors continued off and on of a new suitor—maybe JMB, the real estate company. Lawsuits proliferated against the brothers. It looked like the end.

But nothing ever happens fast on Wall Street. The stock stabilized, ran up to $16 and change, backed off a little, and stalled. On March 22, 1989, Integrated announced earnings for the year and stockholders might have been reassured. After-tax income from operations was up dramatically from the paltry September quarter—$20 million versus $15.3 million in the previous year. Earnings per share for the year was $2.42. Former president and new chief executive officer Goldberg made comforting noises about limited partnership sales, the executive equivalent of toasting marshmallows on the embers of Carthage.

Then on May 16, 1989, Integrated announced that first-quarter results would be late and that there would be a net loss after preferred dividends. (Companies have 45 days to file 10Qs with the SEC after the end of the quarter, and 90 after the end of the fiscal year.)

The stock spiked again, up over $17. Buyers said there would be a takeover for sure at higher prices. Look at book on the stock anyway, the bulls continued; all that real estate was not even valued at market. And the great retail sales network was peerless, according to advocates—a sure thing. Some financial services company would jump at the value.

Shorts felt a little like this particular dead dog would not ever keel over. It had been years—and six months since the death blow. But it felt like more than a lifetime. Who says short sellers are short-term market players? They already had their list of bondholders and stockholders and all the concentric circles of other companies that would be affected when the various Integrated securities dropped in price after the blasted stock finally bit the dust.

Around June 14, 1989, the company admitted cash was a problem. The stock obligingly dropped to $12, down 3.375. But bulls thought bankers and investment bankers would help out, swap money for collateral on new loans, or that the company could sell some assets. Then Drexel balked, and it was all over. The stock traded to $5—finally.

And everyone said, "Oh my, it was so sudden, just out of the blue." *Value Line* owned Integrated commercial paper in the money market fund, the fall had been so quick. And the company was so healthy just yesterday, said Wall Street—except the short sellers, who sadly punched into their HP-12C calculators the present value/future value/years to figure the annualized returns from being short this dog for years.

The most important lesson from Integrated, one that should have been obvious (but perhaps not in the 1980s), was that banks and other short-term lenders (Drexel, in this case) control the destiny of a company that has negative cash flow. The lenders decided to foreclose. Nothing had changed with Integrated; the spigot was just shut off. Assets might be undervalued on the balance sheet, but if a company's particular asset (be it a buggy whip or real estate) is illiquid when it needs funds, the asset does not count for much except as collateral for bonds or bank loans. Leopold Bernstein can lecture in his *Financial Statement Analysis* that financial structure and working capital affect the essential flexibility of management to react to varying economic environments, but, until you see a big one topple, you really do not believe how important capital structure can be. Companies do not cause bankruptcies, banks do. But the companies build the gory mare's nests of financial statements.

After playing footsy with debt holders for six months, Integrated filed for bankruptcy in early 1990.

◆ *Summit Technology, Inc.*

In the early 1990s, biotech companies got growth buyers and short sellers charged up. The companies could not be figured with certitude either way. What short sellers knew was that the companies ate money; what investors did not know was whether earnings per share would ever darken the income statement. Money was made and lost on either side.

When Summit Technology, Inc., was first noticed, it looked easier than the pie-in-the-sky stocks for the analysts who had troubled their pro formas with biotechs. Summit was the child of David Muller, "a college dropout and former carpenter and sewer installer."[6] Summit went public in 1987, raising $6 million after an initial private placement in 1985 of $3.5 million. What Summit made was the promise of unassisted vision for nearsighted folks. Stock symbol BEAM, Summit manufactured and marketed an excimer laser system that corrected vision by carving a slice off the cornea. The machines were sold in Europe and Canada from 1988 on.

The earliest voice of the bears was Mark Roberts at Off Wall Street Consulting Group, Inc. He produced an early research piece called "Blinded by the Light" in September 1990. He stated that BEAM would not get FDA marketing approval for U.S. sales until 1995, suggested that BEAM had a weak patent position versus competitor VISX, and insisted that market-size projections were ludicrous. He was right on all three counts. Unfortunately, he also recommended sale of the stock; that was with the stock price around $11 (split adjusted). It dipped to $7 in the ensuing months and never looked back on its run to $39 that lasted until early 1996, as long as Integrated Resources.

BEAM was like the biotechs and the internet stocks in that, to own it, a person had to believe the company would make a whole lot of money—some day. At its peak, the market capitalization of BEAM was three-quarters of a billion. The argument centered on the same point as the Media Vision argument—the market size and the eventual profit potential. Unlike Media Vision, the company had negligible sales and no profits for years and years. BEAM was a stellar example of Wall Street's patience and forbearance in the business of hope. What the bears forgot was the short maxim to wait to short until reality can be proved—in other words, wait until the machine is approved in the U.S. market and the earnings or lack thereof are apparent to all.

Back in 1990, with the market cap at $160 million, Mark Roberts opined that earnings were years off and speculated on the market size. Irving Arons of Arthur D. Little's Product Technology Section (a consultant also used by BEAM) was quoted as having reduced his estimates from 4 to 5 million procedures performed annually within five years of approval to 2 million a year. That meant about 1,000 machines in operation, or 400 machines a year at $300,000 per machine—for a total U.S. market of $120 million, with strong competitor VISX sure to gain a healthy market share. BEAM's machine, unlike VISX's, could not correct astigmatic myopes—one-half of the market.

Bulls noted the 12,000 U.S. ophthalmologist population and the 100 million people with corrected vision, 60 million of those with nearsightedness, 30 million visually impaired with contact lenses. All these statistics suggested a market really too big to predict.

In late 1991, VISX went public, too, creating twice the documents and a two-horse race.

BEAM's profitability strategy by 1991 was based on a razor/razor blade. The company had an erodible mask in development that allowed the doctor to treat astigmatisms and that improved success or ease of use in vision correction—the point being that the machine sales were secondary to the erodible-mask sales for future profitability. VISX understood the market dynamics, too; a per procedure fee (due to its patent position) was the key to VISX earnings. So, early on, it looked like both companies knew that machine sales at $500,000 a pop to docs would not get them out of red ink.

In February 1992, BEAM announced year-end 1991 earnings of $0.04 from operations on revenues of $22 million. A year earlier, bulls had expected $0.20 on revenues of $22 million. Remember, BEAM had been selling machines in international markets for several years.

BEAM stock price hit a high in March 1992 (see Figure 7.2) when the FDA accepted the company's PMA filing for a more limited use of the laser (PTK or PhotoTherapuetic Keratectomy not the broader business opportunity of PRK, PhotoRefractive Keratectomy). That high was hardly to be broken until late 1995. The three-year hiatus in jolts to short sellers portfolio profitability encouraged the bears and made the wait for approval and earnings seem whimsical. Meanwhile, the bulls started talking eventual takeover—always a good sign for bears—by Iolab, a subsidiary of Johnson & Johnson or Bausch & Lomb. Both VISX and BEAM were evaluating a per procedure fee in the U.S. market.

The year 1992 was nondescript for BEAM bulls and bears, except for a couple of changes. *Barron's* pounded on BEAM a bit, and the Piper Jaffray analyst came to the company's defense: "proper valuation is much like certain other words such as truth or beauty, i.e., very debatable and much in the eye of beholder. Furthermore, should Summit succeed in creating a major new medical market for refractive correction, it could, and we are inclined to believe it will, prove justified. . . . our recommendation to buy the stock is conditioned more by the fear of being left out than by fear of overpaying."[7] The big change was Pillar Point Partners, a partnership between BEAM and VISX to hold the patents and licenses and to collect royalties; the split was advantageous to VISX. BEAM's balance sheet, meanwhile, deteriorated, with receivables and inventories mounting. The company burned $6.5 million from operations and $1.8 on additions to property in 1992 but still had cash of almost $9 million.

In 1993 the debate about safety and efficacy continued: What was the incidence of glare disability or necessity for further vision correction after the procedure? Various panels and conferences would argue the questions for several years.

BEAM moved ahead in England in a joint venture with an optical chain, a predecessor to the centers it would open in the United States in 1996, in an attempt to capture more than the machine sales and to

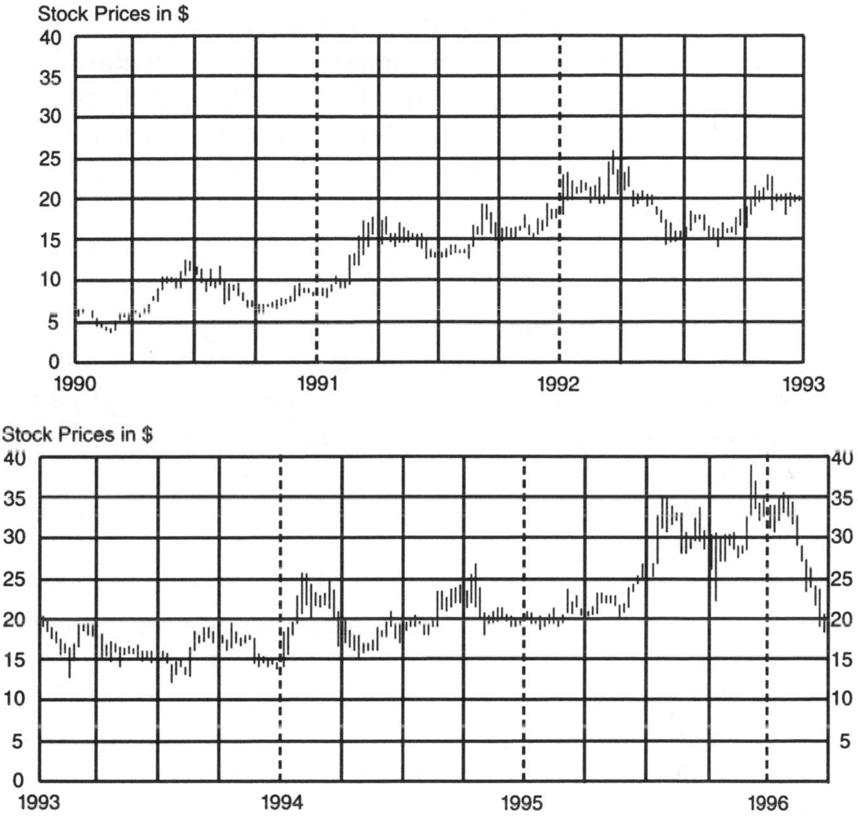

Figure 7.2 Summit Technology, January 1990–April 1996. Chart from MetaStock by Equis International, Inc.

score ephemeral earnings. In July 1993, BEAM offered 1 million shares in a secondary to shore up the balance sheet. When the third-quarter report came out, it was clear the company would have been out of cash without the deal. Sales were down sequentially and year over year with slower European sales. The 10Q also raised the question that Pillar Point Partners might be challenged under the antitrust laws.

When year-end 1993 was announced, sales were down, uncollectible receivables had been written down by $2.4 million, the loss per share was up ($0.59), and cash flow from operations was a burn of $7.65 million, with addition to property and patents of another

$8.5 million. No closer to profits than back in 1990 the shorts said as they waited for the next round of company announcements.

In the first quarter of 1994, BEAM laid off 32 production employees and had down revenues again. The second quarter was equally sad, with six months revenues at $9.5 million, versus $14.9 for the previous year's first half. The stock price's new high belied the financial condition as news circulated that BEAM's FDA application would be considered in October. Mark Roberts predicted a Fall 1995 approval and hoped for sooner, to put the speculation about profitability finally to rest. He delineated the Justice Department's possible interest in Pillar Point and suggested that the two companies were not exactly happy bedfellows. The $250 proposed per procedure fee, on top of the hefty machine price tag and high machine-maintenance costs, was not popular with the ophthalmologists' community. In Canada, docs paid $15 to 20 per procedure.

After the pre-FDA flurry of activity, BEAM stock price dropped again when the FDA requested more information to prove safety and efficacy—more time, more money.

The 1994 year-end was less revenues and greater loss per share ($0.94)—anaylsts had been at $0.37 earlier in the year—but the year showed slower cash burn, due to lower inventories and receivables, probably because of lower sales. BEAM by this time had an accumulated deficit of $30 million, with proceeds from stock offerings in the past four years of $47 million. Whoever owned this sucker was waiting on some kind of a payoff.

The year to sell the stock finally was 1995. It took off in earnest before the expected autumn approval date, ran to $35 in late summer and to $39 before the year-end in anticipation of a profitable first quarter with, no doubt, many, many machines shipped. BEAM, in fact, received approval in October, and VISX was expected to get it within months; so bulls and bears alike could finally see how many contact lens wearers flocked to their eye doctors to get vision corrected with lasers.

The stock was $18 by April. Analysts high-flying finally-it's-time-to-bank-it estimates for 1996 were already ebbing lower—Smith Barney had moved from $0.85 in January to $0.56 by February. When BEAM announced the first quarter, it was a surprise—loss of $0.11 per share, with declining revenues and a loss from vision correction centers. Insiders were selling, and the FDA announced an inquiry about an information leak of competitor VISX's filing information. Morgan, Stanley reduced the rating from a *strong buy* to a *hold*. BEAM announced an acquisition, a contact-lens mail-order company, one more attempt to create a vehicle that made money out of a company that appeared to some to be in the business of stock offerings. By summer, the stock price was single digits, with the losses mounting higher than even the shorts had dared suggest.

It remains to be seen whether the BEAM procedure for vision correction becomes the standard—until the next technology advance makes it obsolete. What is pretty clear is that, so far, the appetite for cash has not been matched by the payback to stockholders, unless they were smart enough (unlike short sellers) to sell on the FDA approval when hope becomes sales, or lack thereof.

The vision wars of the 1990s point firmly to the most prevalent mistake of short sellers: They are often shortsighted about the duration of hope for a new industry and for concomitant stock-price decreases. Stock-price parabolas can sometimes appear to bend back on themselves, but the rate of return on the short position might look like net income on a vision company in the interim.

During a bull market, equity offerings, with an occasional convertible debenture, are the financing instrument of choice for the companies with no earnings that require great gulps of cash to shore up the day-to-day business of trying to make money some day.

◆ *Notes*

1. Selig A. Zises, Arthur H. Goldberg, and Jay H. Zises, Integrated Resources, Inc., First Quarter Report, 31 March 1987, 2.

2. Integrated Resources, Inc., Form 10Q, 31 March 1987, 10.

3. *Value Line*, 18 September 1987, 2066.

4. "Follow-up," *Fortune*, 28 September 1987, 15.

5. Integrated Resources, Inc., Form 10Q, 31 March 1988, 14.
6. Susan Caminiti, *Fortune*, 20 February 1995, 31.
7. Edward Mutsch, "BEAM," Piper Jaffray Inc. Research, 2 June 1992, 3.

8

If You Can't Fix It, Sell It

During a period of recurring buy-outs and mergers, any company can see an immediate rise in share price by announcing that the company seeks to sell part or all of its assets. During a time of prosperity and economic expansion, the companies that cannot earn a respectable living are left no recourse but to sell out or restructure if the level of the stock price aggravates shareholders or if a raider notes the underlying assets. Three categories of opportunity appear in a bull market: (1) the restructured and heavily indebted company close to a stumble, (2) the "for sale" but not sold company, and (3) the company with deteriorating earnings that attempts to create the appearance of health with sale of assets.

In the first category, the restructured companies, or stub stocks, were easy shorts: Harcourt Brace Jovanovich is a prime example. Close attention to the quarterly financial statements told the story over time. Texas Air, by virtue of its leverage, was a stub of sorts with perennial assets for sale.

In the second category, the short sellers, as sharp-eyed asset evaluators, were among the first on Wall Street to question the subsequent stock-price surge and to benefit from "for sale" signs. Corporate finance departments in search of fees continue to break trails for shorts looking for absurd prices. Assets, however, are hard to value in a greater fool environment—before a stock is shorted, the maximum buy-out value must be lower than the stock price. In the 1980s, leveraged buy-out (LBO) artists were always around to state publicly that they could pay a zillion times cash flow for any pig's ear. Cooper Companies, Agency Rent-a-Car, and Kay Jewelers were examples of companies for sale. In the 1990s, this was a tougher trade for the shorts because companies were sold for high multiple stock and became accretive.

In the third category, management sold assets to support the illusion of earnings. Morrison Knudsen Corporation failed to fix the decline in basic business profitability, padded the income statement with tag-sale profits, and ended up with a shell.

◆ *Harcourt Brace Jovanovich Escapes Maxwell's Money*

Harcourt Brace Jovanovich, Inc., went through a number of changes in financial structure from 1987 to 1989. With each twist in the tale, short sellers were confident that the disparity between the capital structure and the earnings power of the business would drive the price of the recapitalized stub stock lower.

In 1987, Harcourt Brace Jovanovich (HBJ) recapitalized in a massive effort to escape the clutches of lusting acquirer Robert Maxwell. The cash-flow requirements of the new debt were ponderous, and short sellers decided after copious pro formas that the company could not support the new structure even after slashes to expenses. Jim Grant commented in the October 5, 1987, *Grant's Interest Rate Observer* that the new HBJ seemed sensitive to interest rates and to small economic slowdowns—in fact, to any adverse breeze that created revenue dips. He used HBJ as a paradigm for the highly leveraged corporate phenomenon, the antithesis of Graham and Dodd's safety and value.[1]

In November 1988, HBJ again modified its capital structure under yet another refinancing that included extending debt maturities, loosening restrictive covenants, and issuing 10.5 million new shares of common stock. The stock deal was ragged, but First Boston moved the product at $9.50.

Although the new interest burden seemed heavy, HBJ and Wall Street appeared to be cheerful about prospects for the three divisions. "Will not sell assets," management announced unconditionally, despite

Table 8.1 Harcourt Brace Jovanovich, Short Interest

1988	*Number of Shares Short*	*1989*	*Number of Shares Short*
January	688,933	January	1,011,275
February	650,842	February	833,838
March	1,066,889	March	867,495
April	1,378,761	April	1,250,723
May	1,329,648	May	1,191,152
June	338,490	June	1,105,775
July	668,316	July	2,084,067
August	691,875	August	2,553,254
September	720,553	September	2,715,713
October	843,996	October	3,145,210
November	885,535	November	3,044,787
December	970,507	December	4,005,125

previous rumors to the contrary.[2] Common wisdom was that the theme parks group would supply the growth, publishing would coin money, and the insurance company would provide a safety if the company needed to sell something.

In September 1988, Oppenheimer analyst Joseph C. Frazzano projected cash flow of $550 million in 1989, with asset value of $28 to $32 per share. After the deal, he adjusted his cash flow down to $510 million for 1989. Asset value was projected confidently at $26 to $28 per share. The stock price was around $9. "Very attractive," he said, and pointed to the operating efficiencies of 1988.[3] That was at the end of 1988.

Short sellers disagreed. They calculated cash flow for each division, gave it a multiple, and came up with a negative value for the company after debt and preferred stock were subtracted. The parks group, they felt, was a problem, eating money even after substantial capital improvements in recent years. Attendance was rumored to be dropping, ticket prices were escalating, and cost reductions might hurt comparisons with competition if acreage started looking seedy. Publishing, with the textbook division, might see the same level of shrinkage that the school-age population saw—gross national product at best

(GNP) level growth, with not much more room for margin improvement after the initial round of cost cutting.

It was a stalemate. Wall Street pounded the table, particularly Gabelli & Company, Inc.'s, Elizabeth Bramwell and Oppenheimer's Frazzano. The shorts snarled and pointed to the debt.

Then first-quarter 1989 earnings came out. HBJ had elected to take a hit in the publishing division. Sampling and marketing costs for new editions were high, and college returns of unsold textbooks were a month early—affecting earnings in the first quarter, not the second. Publishing revenues in elementary and secondary declined as well. No problem. Sea World had higher attendance and higher per capita spending. Bulls gulped and regrouped; shorts said, "I told you so, and the book margins are shot, too." And things went along again.

One point that made HBJ different in short-sale annals was that the big float (72-plus million shares outstanding), the institutional following, and the Wall Street participation all combined to make it an easy stock on which to have an opinion. So the shorts were outspoken, playful, and haranguing, and the longs were assured and hyperbolic. HBJ, all in all, was pretty good fun in a boring market.

HBJ Sells Shamu

The real drama came when HBJ announced in June 1989 that, after all, the company would sell their parks, including Sea World and Shamu. Shorts shrieked with glee that HBJ had come to this—and so quickly. The only source of growth was going on the block. To the shorts' collective amazement and disbelief, the longs ballyhooed, too. Billions, they said. Many, many billions. Huh?

So the two camps settled down to name calling, spitting, and cursing. The argument revolved around what multiple of cash flow parks would sell for and what that would subsequently do for the balance sheet and cash-flow statement of the parent. The admirable disclosure of HBJ made the numbers easy to come by. Depreciation and amortization for parks was $37 million in 1988, and net income was $62 million from continuing operations, for a total of $99 million in cash flow. Shorts said, recent sales of parks suggested that 12 to 13 was a realistic, possibly optimistic, multiple for cash flow, so call it $1.3 billion for the sticker price. Longs said, you're outta your mind—$1.75 billion. Then the bulls figured out that was not quite enough and raised the number once, then twice, until some optimistic soul actually mentioned $3 billion, 30 times cash flow. Only if they sell Shamu for sushi, said the shorts. Disney will buy, said one analyst with assurance. The Japanese, definitely, said another. A bunch of old fish, countered shorts.

Both camps then retreated behind closed doors to pro forma cash flow on their computers. The crux, of course, was what the sale would do for the company's post-sale cash flow and, thus, for HBJ's ability to pay PIKs (payment-in-kind securities—which converted to cash interest in the early 1990s).

If HBJ sold parks for $1.3 billion and paid taxes on the gain (the assets were on the books at around $470 million), it could pay down 12 percent bank debt of $900 million (not the high-coupon, noncallable-until-1990 debt), thereby reducing interest payments by $110 million. If free cash flow from parks was supposed to be $120 million the following year, the transaction was a push. It meant that the company was desperate. If, on the other hand, parks sold for $3 billion, reducing debt by $2 billion and interest by $240 million, with only $100 million in projected cash flow, the sale was a win. The assumptions made all the difference.

Somewhere in the middle of all this, earnings for the second quarter were announced. Publishing did not look any better (increases were due to sales shifting from third quarter to second), and parks was down in revenues—lower attendance due to competition—but margins improved because of more cost cutting. Disney does not have to cut costs, shorts taunted.

With every round of rumors, the stock lurched higher, accompanied by the stomachs of tapped-out shorts. Maybe there was someone dumb enough to pay 30 times cash flow; stranger things had happened in recent years. Texas Air, another big-cap short favorite, was also running to new highs, with stories about many planes sold for very high prices, indeed. So the shorts were morose. They lost their taunt and settled down to a bunker mentality; or more appropriately, they emulated American Brigadier General Anthony C. McAuliffe's attitude in Bastogne when surrounded by Germans requesting an unconditional surrender: "Nuts," he is reputed to have said and hunkered down to wait for George Patton.

On August 14, 1989, *New York Times* reporter Thomas Hayes announced that "people close to the company" said an agreement would be signed soon: "Disney, MCA, and Anheuser-Busch each have the financial muscle to pay $1.5 billion or more."[4] Short shock treatment, it seemed at the time. With every announcement, the stock lurched higher.

And then the announcement came in September: $1.1 billion to Anheuser-Busch. Cash interest would be reduced by $115 million. The stock dropped $4.125 within 24 hours to $12.125. The shorts cheered and hung on for more. The stock settled around $9 and change (see Figure 8.1).

The next salvo came in October when the company hinted that cash-flow estimates were still a little high on the Street. Company officials were said to have guided Frazzano to a lower number. Ana-

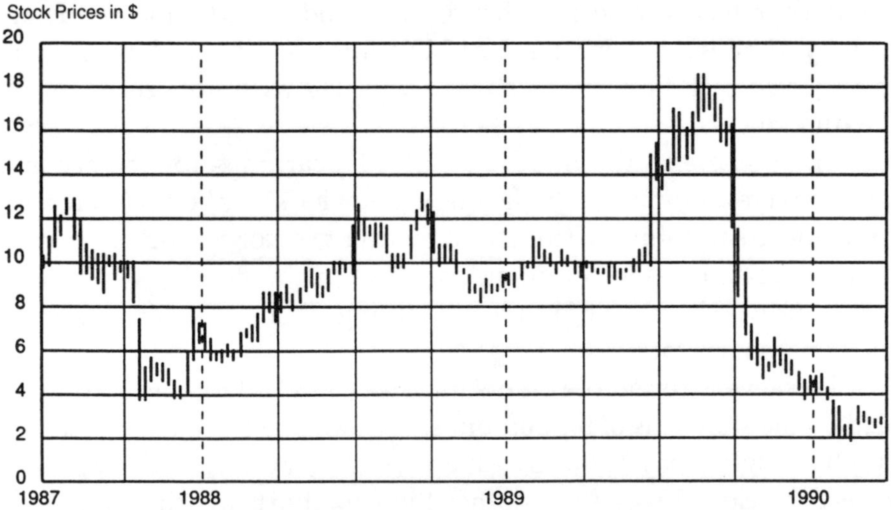

Figure 8.1 Harcourt Brace Jovanovich, July 1, 1987–March 31, 1990. Chart from MetaStock by Equis International, Inc.

lysts backpedaled, sweated, and made furious phone calls. Everyone speculated on soon-to-be-announced earnings. The company was unavailable for comment. Shorts shorted more, gleefully. The stock kept going down.

Frazzano started to get worried with the stock at $5 plus. His October 26, 1989, report mentioned that the stock might take three to six months to recover. His 1989 cash-flow number was then around $260 million (down from $510 million), with 1990 at $300 million. Asset value was $22 per share, with the target price of the stock $15 to $16. "Considerably undervalued," he still said.

Third-quarter earnings came out. Publishing was pallid. Margins had continued to decrease. Sales were a mite disappointing. Operating income from publishing, even without write-offs, was $50 million less than the previous year.

And the shorts smiled and stayed short. There was never anything there, they said; where do those guys get those silly numbers, anyway?

HBJ flurried around its $3 base for a while. One rumor had Canadians buying part of the publishing division for a whole lot of money; then talks were terminated. Short interest doubled again. The debt stayed too high for remaining income. HBJ ran out of assets to sell and declared bankruptcy.

◆ *Texas Air: Flying with Frank*

One cannot very well talk about HBJ without mentioning Texas Air Corporation because that was the other stock that made shorts bone weary in the summer of 1989. Texas Air never went up for sale, but Wall Street decided it had takeover sizzle.

Texas Air, like HBJ, was a stock that was worth more as parts than as an operating company. In other words, analysts added up all the prices of bits and pieces, subtracted the elephant-sized debt, and got numbers far in excess of the stock price. Texas Air was worth $26 plus, they said. The stock initially traded around $9 and shot up to the $20s about the same time that HBJ was at $18.

Table 8.2 Texas Air Corporation, Short Interest

1988	*Number of Shares Short*	*1989*	*Number of Shares Short*
January	627,645	January	1,088,449
February	695,973	February	1,570,924
March	612,330	March	2,726,953
April	572,436	April	4,069,267
May	527,873	May	3,535,667
June	627,086	June	3,459,665
July	792,736	July	3,679,215
August	695,136	August	3,673,092
September	978,091	September	3,363,949
October	1,024,032	October	3,820,634
November	997,267	November	6,229,967
December	1,177,390	December	6,872,002

The bull side rested on several points: Airlines were hot (all the airline takeovers were flying); slots and planes were worth a lot; and, as soon as Frank Lorenzo could get rid of that nasty union or sell Eastern, operating profits would look a whole lot better. The bull side was espoused by Ken Heebner of Loomis and Sayles, Michael Steinhardt, Drexel Burnham, and many brokerage houses on the Street.

The bear case was spearheaded by Jim Chanos. First, shorts felt that you could not go wrong with a record like Frank Lorenzo's: several bankruptcies and a personality that unions appeared to dislike. Second, shorts believed that the liquidation value was lower than bulls anticipated and that the cash burn in a shaky airline could be mammoth. By the end of 1988, Texas Air's consolidated balance sheet had negative equity and loss per share of $18.88 in 1988 and $12.58 in 1987, with positive cash flow dependent on new debt and property sales.

Long before the battle of summer 1989 raged, bulls on the stock had calculated the net asset value (NAV) of Eastern and the subsequent stock price of Texas Air, should they manage to remove the troublesome child. Michael Derchin of Drexel Burnham added up the assets of Eastern (planes, shuttle, South American routes, the Caribbean routes, Atlanta and Miami hubs, and so on), subtracted the debt, assumed that net operating losses (NOLs) and investment tax credits (ITCs) would shelter the gain and Texas Air would net from $16 to $38 per share plus Continental and System One, of course.[5] So Texas Air, indeed, looked cheap to the bulls with the stock trading around $12.

Events moved along through the end of 1988—never a dull moment with Frank Lorenzo. Scandinavian Airline System (SAS) announced an alliance with Texas Air in October, leading the bulls to speculate that SAS might combine with the union to buy out Eastern. Donald Trump offered $365 million for the shuttle, but the purchase was held up in court. Texas Air quit paying dividends on four preferreds, but not because of a cash bind, said analysts—just a small problem with debt covenants, negative net worth, and all that.

The new year came. SAS announced that it owned 6.3 percent of Texas, and union negotiations with the machinists were expected to be a mite testy. Derchin lowered his Eastern NAV to $16 to $24 but thought that discounted normal earnings for Continental/System One (minus that nasty Eastern) were $5 to $7 per share.[6] The stock price was $15 at the end of January 1989 (see Figure 8.2).

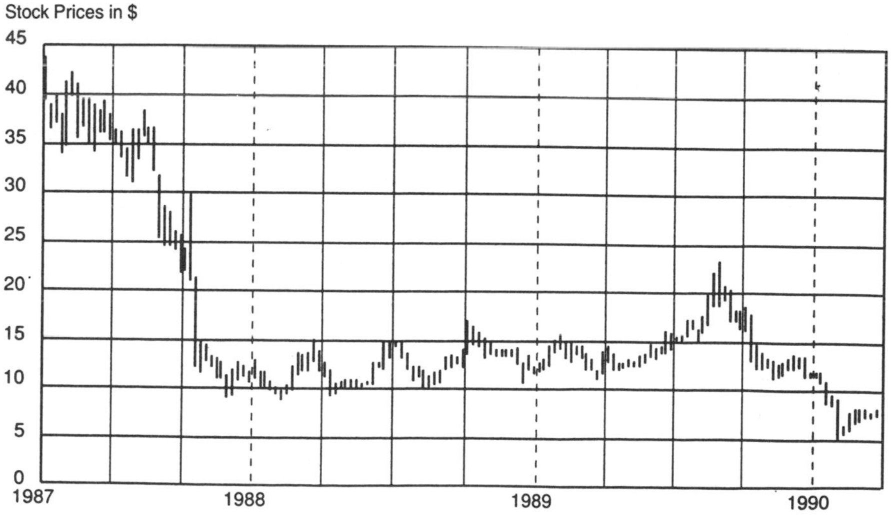

Figure 8.2 Texas Air Corp., April 1, 1987–March 31, 1990

Easy Money Isn't

The short sellers were short Texas Air before the Eastern strike, and, when the machinists went out in March 1989, shorts were pleased but not surprised. When the pilots and the flight attendants joined in sympathy, the shorts sat back to wait for a quick conclusion. The stock, however, baffled them—it did not drop.

Floyd Norris's *New York Times* column on March 9, 1989, recapped the struggle. Michael Steinhardt said that Texas Air was "worth more dead than alive." Norris quoted one bull estimate of the Eastern sale at $1 billion (equivalent to $27 per share), but Jim Chanos disagreed. He pointed out that only two years were left on the lease of the Miami repair facility, and he noted that Eastern's planes were old.

Lorenzo responded with the confidence of practice; he declared bankruptcy for Eastern on March 9, 1989, but the move did not work quite as well as it had with Continental. Times had changed. But the investing public was not yet aware, and the stock moved up.

Things deteriorated for the shorts; they would not have another confident high like the strike for months. First Peter Ueberroth decided to buy Eastern, then reneged after hostile encounters with creditors and disagreements about interim control. Analysts were highly confident that Lorenzo could sell off the odd pieces and rebuild the core. The Trump shuttle sale was completed. South American routes were sold and then not sold.

The noteworthy part of the Texas Air episode was the speed, or momentum, of the ascent as more and more buyers jumped on the bandwagon. There was nothing rational about it: It was a greed frenzy. The psychology of the summer of 1989 was that many managers felt left out by the takeover rage. They wanted badly to believe. Analysts like Drexel's Derchin came out with nice rows of numbers that added up to a lot. So the institutions bought, and then bought more. The valuation numbers went higher as the stock price went up, just like earnings estimates on a rising growth stock.

The shorts were flabbergasted, but unwavering. As Kynikos Associates analyst Scott Bessent said, "What made Texas Air a wonderful short was that, even if you believed some of the absurd valuations, our model showed that the company was going to lose $18 to $20 per share before the end of the year. So even if the bulls were right in August, the stock would be at least 50 percent lower by December."[7]

Part of the final price frenzy and unrelenting volume surge in a stock like Texas Air is that, toward the end of the parabolic price run, weak shorts get scared and cover and strong shorts run out of shorting room. The positions dwarf the usually well-diversified short portfolios, and managers short in smaller size, if at all. So there is unabated buying, with none of the balance or hesitation of the first part of the advance: white knuckle stuff. The shorts' conclusion was that Parkinson's Law of Short Selling should be: "The stock price expands to fill the available short capacity and last iota of patience, particularly when it's a no-brainer."

After the demise of the United Air Lines deal in October 1989, airline assets were not quite as valuable to stock buyers. So in the fall, Texas Air declined from its summer hysteria and floundered as Eastern beat its planned numbers for planes and revenues, then did not. Robert McAdoo of Oppenheimer castigated sellers in his October 16, 1989, report: "The doubters continue to promote the idea that Texas Air is a great short-sale idea . . .. Our target for Texas Air is still $25 to $30 per share by the spring of 1990, based on the realization in the market that Texas Air will have succeeded in fixing its problems by that time."[8] He reported what Texas Air would earn if they made one-third, one-half, and 100 percent of American Airlines' margins—as if Frank could turn Texas Air into American Airlines by spring.

In January 1990, Ken Heebner of Loomis unloaded his 5 million-share position and clipped the stock back to $6. Astronomical losses continued to mount. McAdoo missed his price target in the spring of 1990. Lorenzo finally got ousted from Eastern in April 1990, and the shorts made a little money for a whole lot of pain.

◆ *Kay Jewelers Sells Out (or Tries to) at the Annual Sale*

Kay Jewelers was a growth retailer with well-known problems. In the *Wall Street Journal* "Heard on the Street" column on January 4, 1990,

Table 8.3 Kay Jewelers, Inc., Short Interest

1989	*Number of Shares Short*	*1990*	*Number of Shares Short*
October	42,244	January	1,340,903
November	228,943	February	2,013,435
December	366,868	March	1,856,247
		April	1,908,418
		May	1,894,047
		June	1,852,564

Roger Lowenstein pointed out that same-store sales were down, inventories were up, and receivables were deteriorating. Apparently, Kay had offered credit too leniently in order to promote sales. While receivables were factored (sold for ready cash) to NCNB, they were recourse back to Kay for defaults, so that Kay carried the liability for problems. A problem with receivables meant losses, but, more important, it also meant a subsequent tighter credit policy and lower revenues.

Meanwhile, consumers had been on a spree for years, and fad jewelry had held a spot in the purchasing pocket of middle-mall America. Kay already had locations in malls, but that position could deteriorate, particularly with mall anchors dropping like flies with department store bankruptcies.

The shorts were interested in Kay and aware that a buy-out was a possibility, as Lowenstein had mentioned. A sell-out by the company was sensible, except for one problem: debt. Kay was already leveraged. It had also been the recipient of acquisition rumors before—in July 1989—and the stock had moved up to $23 from $16 (see Figure 8.3). That was after a $6 million write-off in the spring of 1989 for bad debts and an optimistic assessment by company officials for a strong Christmas bailout. Some short sellers sold stock in January 1990.

Then on February 1, 1990, Kay suspended the dividend and announced a weak quarter. Toward the end of the month, Kay announced that it had hired First Boston to shop the company. The stock spiked with eager buy-out groupies running the price to $17. The shorts acted

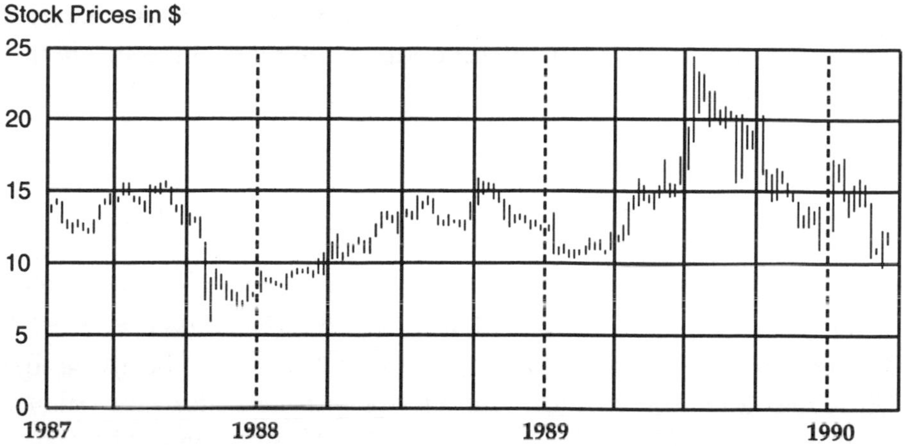

Figure 8.3 Kay Jewelers, Inc., April 1, 1987–March 31, 1990. Chart from MetaStock by Equis International, Inc.

so fast that all available stock to borrow for shorting was gone in a heartbeat, so the options took the brunt of short interest with puts immediately overvalued. The Swiss shareholders were said to be particularly interested in doing something, buying or selling, but a denouement of some sort was desired.

The shorts felt that a sale price of 50 percent of revenues was a benchmark because Kay's highest earnings were only $0.88 per share and cash flow (negative) and book (irrelevant for retail) were not important. That put the buy-out at $17, so the stock was a short around that level.

In March, year-end earnings came out down 98 percent from the previous year, with revenues up only 2 percent. "Bloated inventories and cash short," said the *Wall Street Journal*.[9] The stock languished, a victim of a dead takeover market.

A denouement of sorts was reached July 2, 1990, when Ratners Group, a British jewelry chain, made an offer: to buy Kay for stock worth $17 a share to Kay holders if the bondholders agreed to revised terms. The speculators who bought at the top for a quick profit ended up breaking even if they held their shares. The shorts who stayed short bought at $14.50 after the announcement, so they made a little. The shorts concluded from the buy-out announcement frenzy that short speculation on "for sale" candidates was a less risky business than risk arbitrage—particularly if you could stand the news announcements and upward lurches.

◆ *Morrison Knudsen*

William Agee's company, Morrison Knudsen, got a lot of press in 1995 when the earnings hit a brick wall. Board members were surprised: The *Wall Street Journal* noted that they said "their chief beef was that Mr. Agee had not warned them about the perilous state of the balance sheet."[10] A quick jog through the 1993 Annual Report should have told any board member at the peak of the stock price that Agee was mortgaging the future for the quarterly earnings quest.

Bill Agee joined Morrison Knudsen in 1988 after the company had had a couple of losing years that suggested the hefty dividend of $1.48 a share might not be prudent. He took the company back to profitability in 1989 with fully diluted earnings of $2.82 from continuing operations. Earnings in 1990 were a little better at $2.85, but long-term debt jumped to $194 million from around $12 million. A glance at the income statement showed that "other income" was the growth engine of the earnings—almost $22 million, up from $7 million in 1989. So the business of the company way back in 1990 appeared to be interest and dividends, not railroad cars and construction.

The 1991 Annual Report had smiling Bill in a bright red-and-tan pullover heralding the new era for Morrison Knudsen. "Paved the way . . . for the decade of the 1990s to be truly record-breaking," he said.[11] He was right. Earnings had slipped a little to $2.59 ($36 million out of $58 million came from "other"), but the balance sheet showed more cash, with receivables down and debt even with the previous year. Maybe Bill had constructed a smooth pavement for accelerating company fortunes.

Bill was still smiling in 1992, with a more soothing blue sweater and much talk of "a reliable framework for the future."[12] The stockholders letter hardly showed that 1992 had been a bit of a stumble on the highway to higher earnings: Operating income was down significantly. That wonderful growth vehicle "other income" was in decline compared to the previous year, but still the pillar of profits—$23.7 million of operating income of $24.4 million. That was the year of the beginning of massive deterioration in the balance sheet. Cash flow would have been barely positive, except for the increase in short-term liabilities. Cash was down, total debt was up, and inventories and receivables were both climbing. The stock split two-for-one in May 1992.

The 1993 Annual Report probably hit the stands in March 1994 when the stock was close to $30 (see Figure 8.4). Bill's toothy grin was gone, and he wore peach and talked about a "banner year" and how the company was "poised, ready for the 21st century."[13] By that time, it was all over but the public display.

The annual, past and current, showed that a substantial portion of pretax came from nonoperating revenues again. The income statement (Table 8.4) showed that $10.6 million came from a gain on sale and $25.8 million from other income, net. Further disclosure (Table 8.5) showed that, if operating expenses like receivable sale losses and miscellaneous expenses were deducted, "other" categories accounted

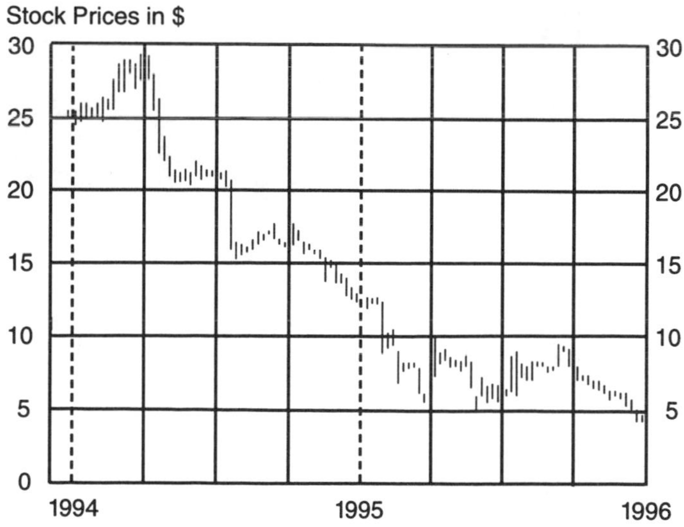

Figure 8.4 Morrison Knudsen, February 1994–December 1996. Chart from MetaStock by Equis International, Inc.

Table 8.4 Morrison Knudsen's Income Statement (dollars in thousands, except share data)

	Year Ended December 31,		
	1993	*1992**	*1991*
Revenue	$2,722,543	$2,284,931	$2,024,791
Cost of revenue	(2,646,081)	(2,233,624)	(1,942,877)
Operating income	76,462	51,307	81,914
General and administrative expenses	(37,358)	(38,160)	(48,813)
Research and development expenses	(3,701)	—	—
Gain on subsidiary sale of stock	10,602	—	—
Interest expense	(3,277)	(12,307)	(16,156)
Equity in net earnings (loss) and interest earned from unconsolidated affiliates	(5,757)	(133)	5,545
Other income, net	25,827	23,676	35,964
Income before income taxes, minority interests, extraordinary charge, and cumulative effect of accounting change	62,798	24,383	58,454
Income tax expense	(26,459)	(10,813)	(22,998)
Minority interests in net earnings of subsidiaries	(572)	(134)	—

Income before extraordinary charge and cumulative effect of accounting change	35,767	13,436	35,456
Extraordinary charge from write-off of unamortized debt issue, cost, net of tax	—	(3,096)	—
Cumulative effect of accounting change for postretirement health care costs, net of tax	—	(17,403)	—
Net income (loss)	$ 35,767	$ (7,063)	$ 35,456
Earnings (loss) per common share			
Income before extraordinary charge and cumulative effect of accounting change	$ 1.15	$ .44	$ 1.24
Extraordinary charge	—	(.10)	—
Cumulative effect of accounting change	—	(.57)	—
Net income (loss)	$ 1.15	$ (.23)	$ 1.24
Common shares used to compute earnings (loss) per share	30,991,169	30,410,585	28,544,432
Dividends per share	$ .80	$ .80	$ .74

*Restated to conform to 1993 financial statement presentation.

Table 8.5 Other Income (Expense) Net

Other income (expense) items are as follows:

	Year Ended December 31,		
	1993	*1992*	*1991*
Interest	$10,694	$ 6,222	$ 8,050
Dividends	2,733	10,860	9,371
Gains on sales of marketable securities, net	22,402	22,648	13,546
Provisions for unrealized losses on marketable securities	(1,000)	(3,549)	—
Foreign currency transaction loss	—	(1,651)	—
Loss for terminating a nonconstruction joint venture	—	(1,475)	—
Loss on receivable sales	(3,578)	(3,184)	(516)
Underwriting expenses, net	(1,480)	(2,807)	(1,316)
Miscellaneous expenses, net	(3,944)	(3,388)	(345)
Gain on sale of corporate assets	—	—	7,174
Other income, net	$25,827	$23,676	$35,964

for 70 percent of pretax in 1993. Income before tax was up nicely over the previous year, but, without the nonoperating profits, the company could hardly support the postsplit dividend of $0.80.

At the same time, cash was disappearing: Negative $64 million from operating activities and the footnotes said that total rentals had gone from $23 million in 1989 to $39 million in 1993, suggesting sale leasebacks to generate cash. The asset side of the balance sheet also had inventories up 69 percent, with sales only up 19 percent and costs and earning in excess of billings on uncompleted contracts up to $185 million from $127 million in the previous year. Morrison Knudsen's 1993 financials certainly did not look healthy.

The stock started dropping in 1994, and Agee announced operating losses and huge write-downs for the year-end 1994. It took the Board until early 1995 to respond to hints that there were potholes in Bill's highway. An anonymous letter came in November 1993 that suggested Bill was selling assets and investing the cash to create the vision of health. The Board agreed that Agee would exit in January, and the bankers sped the process with notification that the company was close to default.

Nine of the ten on the Board of Directors had been around since 1990 to watch the show. While the financials could have been more specific, a rookie analyst could certainly tell that the business was not what it appeared and that selling assets and investing the proceeds in financial markets was not a great long-term strategy, that nothing was getting fixed with Agee's sleight of hand but the appearance of earnings in the very short run. The stock traded at $1, and the company filed for bankruptcy.

Notes

1. James Grant, "The Annotated Harcourt," *Grant's Interest Rate Observer*, 5 October 1987, 5-10.
2. Greg Johnson, *Los Angeles Times*, 30 September 1988, 2.
3. Joseph C. Frazzano, "Weekly Research Review," Oppenheimer & Co., Inc., 6 December 1988, 6.
4. Thomas Hayes, *New York Times*, 14 August 1989.
5. Michael W. Derchin, "Research Abstracts." Drexel, Burnham, Lambert, 23 August 1988, 8054.
6. Ibid., 16 February 1989, 2077.
7. Personal communication, June 28, 1990.
8. Robert McAdoo, "Daily Action Notes," Oppenheimer & Co., Inc., October 1989, 3.
9. Vindu P. Goel, *Wall Street Journal*, 19 March 1990.
10. Joan E. Rigdon and Joann S. Lublin, "Call to Duty: Why Morrison Board Fired Agee," *Wall Street Journal*, 13 February 1995, B4.
11. Morrison Knudsen Corporation, 1991 Annual Report, 3.
12. Morrison Knudsen Corporation, 1992 Annual Report, 2.
13. Morrison Knudsen Corporation, 1993 Annual Report, i.

9

Industry Obsolescence: Theme Stocks

When a major, industry-wrenching change occurs, money can be made by taking a position in a group of stocks clustered around a theme. Massive industry change can be triggered by macroeconomic events, by a specific product revolution, or by the death of a fad.

When oil prices plummeted, any company associated with Texas wealth was ripe for selling. The Texas banks, in particular, were worthy candidates that reflected optimistic economic scenarios and pricing for months after the oil price drops. The Arizona real estate decline and the underregulated savings-and-loan (S&L) abuses represented two other opportunities to short an industry-wide phenomenon.

Industry obsolescence can also be the flip side of Wall Street's concept stock—a product change can sink a group of companies. When a tech toy, for example, becomes passe (like CB radios) or when a product is in less demand (higher oil prices sent recreational vehicle sales into a fishtail), any stock associated with those products is fair game for a collapse. Use a shotgun, not a rifle, for a sector bet.

Donald Trump's saga is an example of both phenomena. The real estate environment changed and the perception of Atlantic City as a high-growth gambling environment faded, so that bankers became concerned about a cash flow that had always been negative. A shotgun short of any of Trump's bonds would have yielded a reasonable return.

All it takes is an eye for trends because Wall Street turns like the

Queen Elizabeth II: There is a whole lot of time to get firmly positioned before the first wave of downdraft, followed by the tell-me-it-ain't-so bounce, sinks the stocks. Wall Street is much quicker to hype a new fad than to discard the old.

◆ *The Arizona Land Race*

Sometime in early 1988, visitors to Arizona started coming back with odd tales. It looked overbuilt. The crane count was still spectacularly high, despite the growing vacancy rate and slowing growth. The absence of zoning restrictions meant that every fast-buck developer in the United States was in there pouring concrete—and getting construction bank loans.

Because the Texas debacle was recent enough for even Wall Street's memory, the shorts salivated. In Texas, the inevitable bust had followed the not-so-eternal boom, and real estate collapses compounded oil price collapses to sink all the banks that had lent cheerfully and aggressively to anyone with a hankering to build.

Texas taught investors that when a region and its economy are built on growth, a slowing rate of change in the growth engine can pull the whole structure to the ground. A dropping real estate market takes the economy with it, including commercial loans and basic bank business. Even sacred single-family-mortgage default rates can escalate. It is not just construction lending that creates cannon fodder for bank regulators.

Banks are classic short candidates because the lending cycle is only as long as the credit experience of the current crop of bankers. Wall Street analysts forget the inevitable cycle and fail to extrapolate the lessons of Texas to Arizona and then to New England. The Arizona banking debacle was a classic example of a boom turned to bust and how to profit by the reversal.

When a sector is isolated as a potential war zone, the first step is to find lists of associated stocks. In the Arizona case, a local newspaper could provide lists of regional stocks—banks and S&Ls were easy to spot. Local gossip can be particularly useful because in-town developers usually know who is the aggressive lender in the area, whether balloon payments are common, and who has got the least conservative appraisal practices. A first-hand look at construction billboards lauding lender and developer alike can be another quick source of names. Western Savings (Chapter 6) was already well known, so sellers started looking under rocks for similar real estate plays. Three showed up: American Continental and Sun State Savings, both S&Ls, and Valley National, a commercial bank.

◆ *American Continental: What's All the Ruckus About?*

American Continental (AMCC), the big holding company for both Lincoln Savings and a land development company, had financial statements that made fine reading, even before Charles Keating started spending more time in Washington at hearings. Betting on a real estate downturn means short the companies with big real estate exposure. AMCC was almost all real estate and not much equity by the end of 1987.

Short sellers were confused by the ruckus in 1990 over Charles Keating and his S&L, Lincoln Savings. Anybody could have seen in 1988, even without an X-ray, what the skeleton looked like, plus or minus a few tumors. The short sellers' perspective on AMCC should be reassuring to investors who felt that the Securities and Exchange

Table 9.1 American Continental Corp., Short Interest

1988	*Number of Shares Short*	*1989*	*Number of Shares Short*
July	635,554	January	888,459
August	677,242	February	827,776
September	730,614	March	832,189
October	922,225	April	867,920
November	1,073,273	May	831,429
December	874,049	June	Not published

Commission (SEC) left stockholders without a blanket in a blizzard. The 10K and the annual report for the year ended December 31, 1987, were the documents that short sellers read first. The facts were clear, although some of the details would be missing for years. Perhaps the disclosure was not all-encompassing, but the numbers gave a good clue.

A Real Estate Company or an S&L?

AMCC was a Phoenix-based holding company that had been principally engaged in real estate until the acquisition of Lincoln Savings for $51 million in 1984. Prior to the acquisition, Lincoln's main activity was single-family-mortgage lending; AMCC realigned Lincoln's policy to emphasize mortgage loans exceeding $1 million. After the acquisition, AMCC phased out its own home-building activities but still worked in the areas of land development, syndication, sale, and management. In 1987, 86 percent of pretax income came from financial services, most of which was Lincoln.

Because Lincoln was a hefty percentage of revenues and assets for AMCC, the short sellers first needed to determine how much of the income came from basic S&L business and how much from nonrecurring, real-estate-related business.

Parent AMCC had consolidated earnings before preferred dividends of $19.3 million in 1987. Lincoln's net earnings were $41 million in 1987, so the parent was certainly dependent on the child for sustenance.

Lincoln's summary of operations (Table 9.2) showed net interest income, the major component of old-style S&L earnings, of $16.1 million. The notes mentioned that this was after capitalization of $65 million in interest expense, but including $14 million of additional interest related to loan profit participations. The 10K went on to explain that "at December 31, 1987, Lincoln Savings' interest-bearing liabilities exceeded its interest earning assets by $1,086,000,000."[1] Lincoln Savings also owned $622 million in corporate bonds, "substantially all of which securities are rated less than investment grade," that

Table 9.2 Lincoln Savings' Income Summary (dollars in thousands)

	Year Ended December 31,		
	1987	*1986*	*1985*
Interest income	$292,113	$269,356	$235,103
Interest expense	275,979	268,838	231,964
Net interest income	16,134	518	3,139
Net gains on sale of investment securities, loans, and mortgage-backed certificates and distributions from unconsolidated affiliates	89,657	131,407	120,129
Other income, net[1]	92,569	79,689	55,977
General, administrative, and other expenses	135,210	129,925	78,895
Earnings before income taxes and cumulative effect of a change in accounting for income taxes	63,150	81,689	100,350
Income taxes	25,205	32,731	20,500
Earnings before cumulative effect of a change in accounting for income taxes	37,945	48,958	79,850
Cumulative effect of a change in accounting for income taxes	3,075	—	—
Net earnings	$ 41,020	$ 48,958	$ 79,850

[1]"Other income" includes real estate gains of $78,708,000, $73,924,000 and $47,567,000 for the periods ended, December 31, 1987, 1986, and 1985, respectively. See "Business—Real Estate Activities." Source: American Continental Corporation, Form 10K, 31 December 1987.

added dramatically to interest income.[2] So net interest income did not come from the traditional spread between deposits for CDs and lending to single-family mortgagees.

Where did the bulk of earnings come from? Net gains on sale of securities, loans, mortgage-backed certificates, and distributions from unconsolidated affiliates accounted for $89.6 million. Other income (including real estate gains of $78.7 million) was $92.6 million. And 1987 was not an aberration; in fact, net interest income was higher as a percentage of net income than in previous years. AMCC, therefore, was not a mom-and-pop lender.

Shorts' next look was at Lincoln's balance sheet (total assets of the consolidated parent were $5 billion with shareholder equity, including preferred, of $137 million) to see how stable and liquid the assets were in the event of the expected real estate crash (Table 9.3). Stockholders' equity was $221 million. Goodwill was $106 million, real estate was $827, and other assets were $531 million (including $60 million in investments in unconsolidated subs). So by deducting intangibles, shaving real estate by 10 percent, and arbitrarily scratching out the subs, the balance comes in at negative $28 million.

Table 9.3 Lincoln Savings' Balance Sheet (dollars in thousands)

	As of December 31,		
	1987	*1986*	*1985*
Cash and cash equivalents	$ 242,612	$ 358,681	$ 843,607
Investment securities—equity	157,699	96,249	90,879
Investment securities—debt	1,298,190	1,193,453	426,750
Loans receivable and mortgage-backed securities[1]	1,585,820	902,021	929,519
Real estate	827,272	777,165	553,696
Other assets[2]	530,622	466,974	258,653
Excess of cost over net assets acquired	106,252	109,184	108,654
Total assets	$4,748,467	$3,903,727	$3,211,758
Savings deposits	$3,374,531	$2,821,375	$2,406,958
Borrowings	813,784	629,890	570,173
Other liabilites	338,775	259,438	89,047
Stockholder's equity	221,377	193,024	145,580
Total liabilities and stockholder's equity	$4,748,467	$3,903,727	$3,211,758

[1]"Loans receivable and mortgage-backed securities" include mortgage-backed securities of $472,461,000, $67,135,000, and $58,364,000 for the years ended December 31, 1987, 1986, and 1985, respectively.

[2]"Other assets" include $60,525,000 in 1987, $69,996,000 in 1986, and $105,895,000 in 1985 of investments in unconsolidated affiliates, representing the Company's interests in certain companies accounted for under the cost and equity methods. See Note (A) to the Consolidated Financial Statements.

Source: American Continental Corporation, Form 10K, 31 December 1987.

A winner—and that is without increases in nonperforming assets or without deducting for the problems in the $622 million junk-bond portfolio. Regulators were not as fond of negative net worth as leveraged buy-out (LBO) impresarios, even back in 1988.

For a little more detail, short sellers went to the loan portfolio to see how much was loaned for construction: $225.8 million for construction in 1987, up from $138 million in 1986. Acquisition and development lending was a monumental $760.6 million, up from $482.7 million. Conventional mortgages were a piddling $179 million, versus $250.5 million in 1986: no plain, ordinary, single-family lender here, just like they said in the 10K.

AMCC's other line of business was real estate, which contributed $221 million in revenues and $3.6 million in pretax earnings in 1987. The Phoenician, a glitzy luxury resort hotel, was under construction and rumored to be running over budget. The ratio of earnings to fixed charges, including all noncash charges and capitalized interest (another $65 million), was 1.18 coverage for 1987. So the parent was equally exposed to real estate.

Insiders Sell Stock—To AMCC

The related-party transactions in the back of the 10K gave a flavor for management. The company and the Employee Stock Ownership Plan (ESOP) purchased 1,141,878 and 1,014,561 shares from 1985 to 1987 from Chairman Keating and from the directors, officers, and others for an aggregate of $10,742,000 and $8,000,000, respectively—beats paying commissions. In May 1986, the chairman purchased from a subsidiary a limited partnership interest for $3.45 million. The list of purchases and sales of partnership interests went on from there. Corporate salaries were spectacular: Keating made $1,954,914 in 1987, plus use of the aircraft and other facilities. His son and three sons-in-law worked for him. Charles, the son, earned $863,494, and Robert Wurzelbacher (a son-in-law), $647,129.

In spring 1988, Lincoln did the famous $200 million bond deal that supposedly flipped CD holders into veritably worthless AMCC paper that had no recourse to Lincoln. Shorts chuckled over the offering document, amazed that it had a market. The bond prospectus recapped in lurid detail the short case: low interest-rate spread, no recourse to subs, big junk-bond portfolio, profitability dependent on nonrecurring earnings, risky real estate loans, real estate operations, substantially all activities conducted through the subs (to which there was no recourse), ongoing Federal Home Loan Bank Board (FHLBB) and SEC investigations, and no market for the new securities. How could anyone buy with a document like that?

So it required only an hour to read AMCC's financial documents and reach a judgment on the condition of the company and short it the first half of 1988. That was the easy part.

Short Squeeze

The hard part was staying short the stock in the supposed soon-to-be frontal attack by Keating to squeeze short sellers silly. Rumors flew about buy-ins and harassment of stock lenders by AMCC to stop lending stock. On December 26, 1988, *Forbes* detailed the tactics of the squeeze: Keating had a two-pronged program.[3] First, the bank would lend to the stock's owners to take them off margin at their brokerage houses so the stock could not be loaned to short sellers by the brokers. Second, stockholders requested delivery of 1.5 million shares housed at two brokerage offices, thereby reducing the float to around 2 million shares, with a short position of 1 million. Furthermore, they hired a proxy-soliciting firm to ask shareholders to have stock delivered out of margin accounts. AMCC's stated purpose was to convince the marketplace that trading was illiquid.

As early as September 1987, *National Mortgage News* came out with the first story on the Keating Five, and, in the fall of 1988, the regulatory concerns came to the fore again. Squeeze or no, Keating was being circled.

Remaining short sellers were rewarded for tenacity with a classic warning bell, as the 8K announced a change in corporate accountants. Arthur Young had quit because of disagreements on timing of capital gains and declined to be associated with any financial statements after December 31, 1987—an admirable showing during a time when accountants appeared to be somnolent. But a lot of good it did short sellers: The stock failed to drop.

Losses mounted, equity declined, and Charles Keating kept on blaming the regulators for his problems. Cash deficit for the first nine months of 1988 was $100 million. The SEC was investigating AMCC's accounting.

In December 1988, *Barron's* article "Phoenix Descending" came out, with its detailed work on the real estate market and the related lenders.[4] Naturally, AMCC was featured, along with Sun State, Western, and Valley.

The price of AMCC did not really break until February 1989, and, by the first of March, it was around $3 (see Figure 9.1). A proposed savior for Lincoln fell through, and the Justice Department was investigating a couple of the officers for fraud. In late April, the stock was trading in fractions. By then, the regulators had seized the bank, reported to be one of the two most costly bail-outs, and Charles Keating was just starting his long saga in Washington.

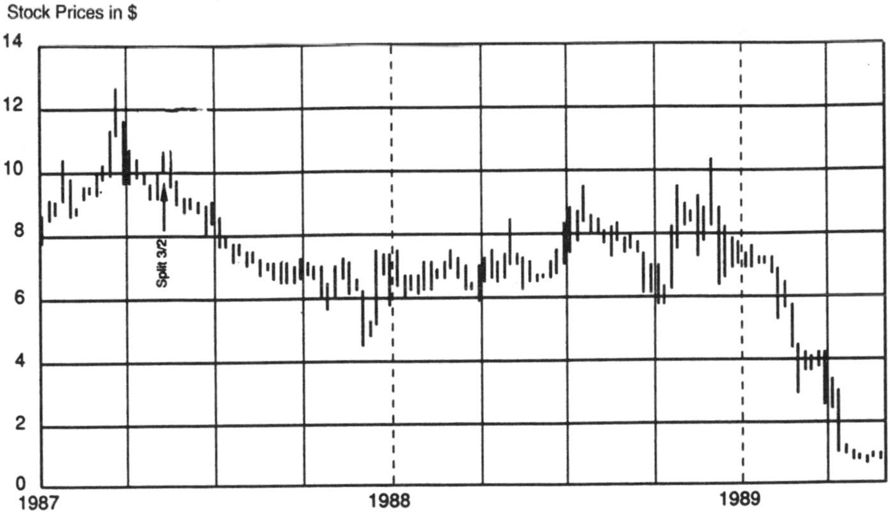

Figure 9.1 American Continental Corp., January 1, 1987–May 31, 1989

◆ *Sun State Savings Acquired on Margin*

"Phoenix Descending," to borrow *Barron's* headline, was a nice combination of levity and brevity for the short sellers. Sun State was classic stuff, and anybody who could borrow it had fun.

Sun State Savings and Loan Association (SSSL) commenced operations in 1980. By December 1987, it was a full-blown real estate lending-and-developing S&L in the best Arizona tradition. Stockholders' equity was $7.90 a share, with 5.85 million shares outstanding and earnings per share of $1.10 for the year.

The financial statements were a little gamey. Acquisition, development, and unimproved land loans totaled 33 percent of the loan portfolio at $218 million. Construction loans were another $89 million. Nonaccruing loans were $17 million, with allowances for loan-loss reserves of $2.4 million. Investments in real estate were $29 million and in joint ventures, $50 million. The joint-venture program put up all the capital on undeveloped land and bore all the losses, while the partner provided expertise in planning, zoning, and developing to offer to a third-party developer. And that was with equity of $42.8 million and foreclosures climbing from $7.4 million in 1986 to $28.4 million in 1987. Sun State looked poised to go off the high board into a waterless pool.

Buy-Out on Margin

But that was before the amazing Maniatis or, to be more precise, after Maniatis's first 13D filing but before he decided to buy the whole thing. David Maniatis and family filed a 13D on April 14, 1987, on 19.27 percent of common stock. On January 21, 1988, Sun State filed a complaint against the Maniatis Group alleging misleading information. SSSL said Maniatis had been denied the right to purchase more than 15 percent by the superintendent of Arizona banks, that this was not disclosed, and that, besides, the position was not just for investment, as the 13D said.

So Maniatis filed an amendment attaching the denial by the su-

Table 9.4 Sun State Savings & Loan, Short Interest

1988	*Number of Shares Short*	*1989*	*Number of Shares Short*
July	171,662	January	952,268
August	188,372	February	1,030,137
September	101,910	March	1,182,150
October	315,359	April	934,277
November	916,638	May	664,630
December	912,561	June	Not published

perintendent dated October 20, 1987. The superintendent's letter made some provocative points. It said that "the financial condition of the applicant is such as may jeopardize the financial stability of the Association," and that the "overall moral character or integrity of David P. Maniatis indicates it would not be in the interest of the depositors, beneficiaries, creditors or shareholders . . . to permit [him] to control the Association."[5] Harsh—and that from Charles Keating's own state.

The action escalated in the fall, which is when the shorts got intrigued. SSSL received an unsolicited acquisition proposal from Maniatis at $11 a share on October 21, 1988. His group owned 1.4 million shares that they had bought on 50 percent margin through their broker, Blunt, Ellis & Loewi.

Earnings Continue to Drop, But Not the Buy-Out Bid

On October 25, 1988, SSSL announced the quarter's loss, bringing the total loss for nine months to $2.6 million. Nonperformers and those joint ventures appeared to hurt earnings. The head guy said "No problem." He added that the big lenders in town had cut back on loans because of area real estate problems. SSSL had taken advantage of that departure by increasing its loan originations by 30 percent![6]

SSSL turned down the Maniatis offer as too vague, despite Blunt, Ellis & Loewi's letter that they could finance it. A spokesperson also said in *The Business Journal* on November 7, 1988, that Maniatis's margin purchase of Sun State stock at an average price of $9 was the reason he made the offer, an attempt to move the price up. Maniatis responded that "his margin calls were irrelevant."[7]

Indefatigable Maniatis came back in December 1988 with another alternative transaction, accompanied by "an unusually qualified highly confident letter from Blunt and Ellis."[8] That was unusual, it seems, because it contained no details for financing—maybe they planned more margin calls.

On January 20, 1989, SSSL announced a problem quarter, with an aftertax loss from $6 million to $16 million. The accountants were not able to be precise yet. The FHLBB, in fact, had sent SSSL a letter telling them to restrict growth and reduce the risk profile. Maniatis mulled another offer. Is this, you ask, a Monty Python skit? Why is this man bidding repeatedly for disappearing assets?

The stock traded from $6 to $7 in the first quarter of 1989, presumably supported by the offer on the table. And then, in the second half of March, it rolled over to $2 (see Figure 9.2). Around March 31, 1989, the company became more explicit about the issues that concerned the

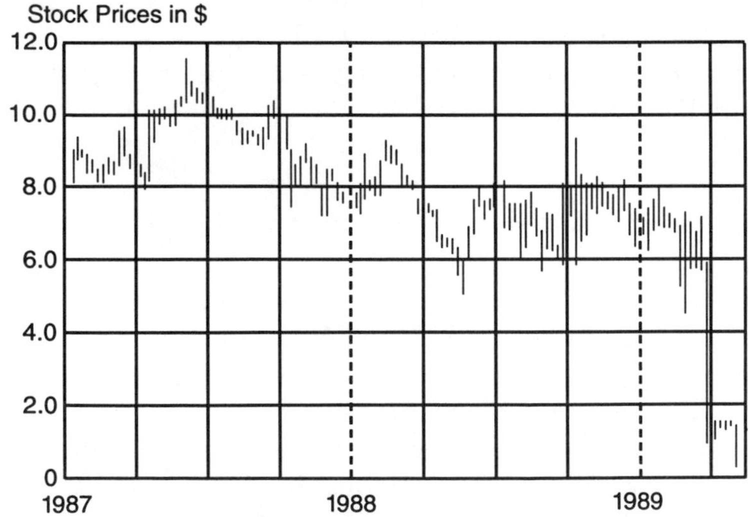

Figure 9.2 Sun State Savings & Loan, January 1, 1987–June 30, 1989. Chart from MetaStock by Equis International, Inc.

auditors: real estate appraisals, accounting matters involving below-market interest rates, loan loss reserves. It seemed clear, said the company, that "we will fall short of meeting the current 3 percent minimum regulatory capital requirement."[9] So the board decided to meet with Maniatis—perhaps the superintendent no longer had moral and financial problems in the face of the growing avalanche—but to no avail.

The loan problems continued until capital was decimated, and, on June 16, 1989, both Western Savings and Loan and Sun State Savings were seized by the regulators.

◆ *Valley National: Uncharacteristic Wall Street Battle*

The big commercial bank in the Phoenix area was Valley National Corporation, something of a Wall Street darling. Unlike the other sector bets in Arizona, it had broad institutional ownership and an analyst at almost every house on the Street. The shorts barged in without thinking too much about supply and demand, the effect on the stock price, and the duration of the position. Short interaction with professional analysts had been minimal in the years prior to 1988 (before HBJ and Texas Air). The bank analysts on the Street, meanwhile, were not aware that a few short sellers were independently foaming at the mouth over Arizona. So Valley was unique.

First, the financials. The year-end 1987 Annual showed stockholders' equity of $580 million. Total nonperforming assets was $294.7, with total loans past due 90 days and accruing interest of $34.3 million. The bulk of nonperformers were real estate—no surprise there. Allowance for credit losses was $195 million. The Valley picture, then, did not look great, but it did not look like AMCC and Western, either.

The number that engrossed the short sellers was loans for construction and development—$1.264 billion, out of a domestic loan portfolio of around $8 billion. If Phoenix was really blowing up, nonperformers would explode as well. That was spring 1988, with the stock around $24.

A Little Media Attention Sparks Discussion

Grant's Interest Rate Observer chronicled the Valley story in the April 15, 1988, issue, noting that its ratio of total real estate to equity was in the top 25 in a ragged real estate environment.[10] *Forbes* wrote up Valley in the May 30, 1988, issue, a blurb that commented on the real estate problems and the price perspective—lower, was the conclusion.[11] The stock price, however, failed to recognize the rising voices and pointed fingers.

The battle escalated from there because that was the first clue Wall Street had that there was a marked difference of opinion on the value of Valley. Several analysts shifted estimates and ratings and reassessed the Phoenix economy. It was rare in 1988 for bank analysts to consider the real estate environment in a particular geographical area in their view of a bank's loan portfolio. Remember, real estate prices had moved only up since 1974 (except in Texas, and that was a fluke). They mostly looked at the numbers and listened to the bank officials. Arizona was a good warmup for New England.

Charles Peabody at Kidder, Peabody was the first big-name bank analyst to depart from groupthink with a resounding sell in October

Table 9.5 Valley National Corporation, Short Interest

1988	*Number of Shares Short*	*1989*	*Number of Shares Short*
January	2,535	January	1,922,930
February	33,811	February	2,148,008
March	Not published	March	1,890,543
April	24,673	April	2,088,248
May	118,616	May	2,584,052
June	148,727	June	3,445,731
July	218,514	July	3,689,062
August	153,080	August	3,562,404
September	202,519	September	3,682,334
October	247,378	October	3,671,649
November	595,548	November	3,648,937
December	1,114,252	December	4,713,386

1988. He went from a two to a four rating (from buy to sell), in itself unusual for Wall Street because everything is always half steps and slow motion to avoid conflict. Management, he said, was not dealing with the problem, and he felt that, instead of taking a proactive restructuring stance, they nibbled and hedged. His conclusion was to sell.

Management came to town the end of October for a dog-and-pony show at the New York Society of Security Analysts. They made the Street a bit more nervous because they did not address the real estate debacle until the question-and-answer session, when they reassured the audience that reserves were adequate. They did talk about cutting costs and margin improvements, but everyone naturally wanted to know the details of the life-threatening injury, not just the cosmetic work.

So late winter 1988-1989 turned into a bit of a shoving match between analysts: "Are reserves enough?" "Aren't." "Stock's cheap." "Not either." Everyone pulled out a battery of statistics and devised various ways of looking at deterioration and turns in real estate. They calculated different formulas for the effect on earnings and the appropriate level of reserves, if reserves were appropriate. As nonperformers climbed, half the analysts lost their nerve and went to "hold" until a trend was discernable.

The short sellers sat back and watched. Real estate always takes a while to work out because it is not marked to market every day. The stock moved up; the stock moved down.

Turmoil Intensifies

And then around January 1989, things started to get bad. The short sellers had been chatty among themselves on Valley, contrary to their usual restraint and paranoia. The chatter snowballed. Inexperienced nouveau short sellers shorted Valley, and that did two things. First, the supply of stock evaporated, so buy-ins started occurring randomly, and no stock was available to borrow to short on run-ups. Second, the nouveau shorts did not have conviction or experience, so every time the stock flurried, they panicked and ran it up some more by buying. A rabid short hater could not have strategized more effectively.

Tom Brown at Smith, Barney had just come off a huge score the year before on BankAmerica. He was (and is) acknowledged by institutions to be one of the top bank analysts. He had had Valley rated a buy since June 1988, but, come January 1989, he picked it as his stock of the year. Phoenix, he thought was old news. The *Barron's* article was late to the party, he argued; 1986 was the right year for the Arizona crash, and the environment was improving. "I believe," he said, that "Valley's real estate related nonperforming assets will peak here in the fourth quarter and decline throughout 1989, and there will be no need for a special loan-loss provision to boost the reserve."[12] He continued to say that the short sellers "have driven the stock down and they're the ones that are going to help drive it higher in 1989."[13] And the stock responded by moving to $27 from $24.

Charles Peabody answered his rival's recommendation and commented on Valley's fourth-quarter-earnings announcement on January 18, 1989. Real estate nonperforming assets (NPAs) were up from $292.7 million to $319.1 million, with loan-loss reserve declining from $187.3 million to $178.8 million. The ratio of total reserves to NPAs went from 47.3 to 39.7 percent. A four rating was justified, he concluded. "Unattractive," agreed Paine Webber's Sandra Flannigan.[14] "Excellent investment opportunity," said Tom Brown. "Fourth-quarter EPS on target."[15]

So Valley acted like it was possessed by poltergeists. Price action had no connection to announcements, or to any discernable reality. On one preholiday afternoon, the company reannounced a previously announced asset sale, and the stock spiked a couple of points. Nobody was around to tell anybody what to think or do, so the few nonanalytical sorts staring at the Quotrons spooked the action. The options took on a life of their own, with trading shifting to puts which exhibited a high implied volatility for the far out cycles. It was nuts. And it reminded old, grizzled, short veterans why they never talked to anyone: all those incompetent shorts got involved and jerked the price around.

The Effect of Real Estate on Banks

The argument on Valley, which seemed to last for years, centered around one very big point. How much damage can a wretched real estate environment do to a bank? Most of the young analysts could not remember the 1974 real estate downturn and subsequent bank collapse, so they had no benchmark. The real estate pros knew that when it came, it lasted—three to four years minimum to clear out the overhang, with banks trading as low as 40 percent of book. And furthermore, no one rang a bell at the bottom. The stocks just started sneaking back up, but it took more than a quarter's earnings to prod the prices off the lows.

So the shorts felt comfortable that all the Wall Street spreadsheets on banks reserves, core earnings, and rate of change on nonperformers would not—could not—condense mayhem into one quick number. They just watched.

They knew that buying a bank stock or an S&L stock was like buying a blind pool. Buyers never knew what they had, so the macroenvironment had better be right. This point was reinforced repeatedly in the Valley debate. For example, one analyst of large repute said, "Valley has no strip-shopping-center loans." Another equally renowned prognosticator said, "Valley has 9 percent of total loans in strip shopping centers." The shorts said, "Who cares? It ain't the point, guys."

A fair number of analysts decided after a year of bad quarters that things had to get better soon. So they marshalled their courage and rerecommended the stock. And the push-pull would start all over again. First Boston joined Smith, Barney; both thought the stock price fully reflected the difficulties. Charles Peabody continued to recommend short sale of the stock. The *Wall Street Journal* "Heard on the Street" column and the *New York Times* recapped the conflict on February 21, 1989. Roger Lowenstein at the *Journal* quoted Brown and Peabody, who threw the special language of banks around like mantras. Peabody repeated that the domestic loan-loss reserve ratio to nonperforming loans was only 47 percent, compared to an industry average of 80 percent with more traumas on the way. Brown said nonperformers would come down and the reserves would look adequate. Valley backed Brown; Eliot Rosen, investor relations for Valley, said, "Tom Brown has been out here to kick the tires three times in the past year. He has done his homework. Charles Peabody's report isn't very insightful. It's the type of thing you could do from press releases."[16]

Valley officials finally took off their gloves and punched back after a round of what they felt was specific misinformation in late April 1989. Valley was exposed to Maniatis (of SSSL margin fame) with a $14.5 million loan on one of his real estate partnerships, Peabody said, and he linked Valley to AMCC, as well. Valley officials demanded a retraction, stating, "The information is absolutely wrong."[17] "Remember," they should have said, "it is a blind pool." The company executives reminded analysts one more time to keep their honest opinions to themselves. "Dummy up and take notes" was the message. Come out and visit, and we will give you the right story.

The second quarter was a loss of $90 million to clean up everything and was somewhat uneventful.

Earnings Announcement Clears Controversy

Everyone was surprised in October 1989, and no one was more surprised than Tom Brown. The company announced yet another big loss of $72.2 million for the third quarter and suspended the dividend. Nonperformers were $523.2 million. The stock dropped, or more accurately, plunged to $13.50 and then wallowed for months (see Figure 9.3).

Rumors continued to drift. In the silliest sequence (but not uncommon), the Dow tape showed first-quarter 1990 earnings at $0.62 versus $0.62 late on Maundy Thursday afternoon. The stock moved up a couple of points in euphoria. Few had noted that they were the wrong earnings—those for Valley of New Jersey. The stock moved down the next Tuesday when the real numbers came through at $0.03 versus $0.96.

By that time, bank analysts also had New England and the East coast to think about. Phoenix had been overshadowed by more cur-

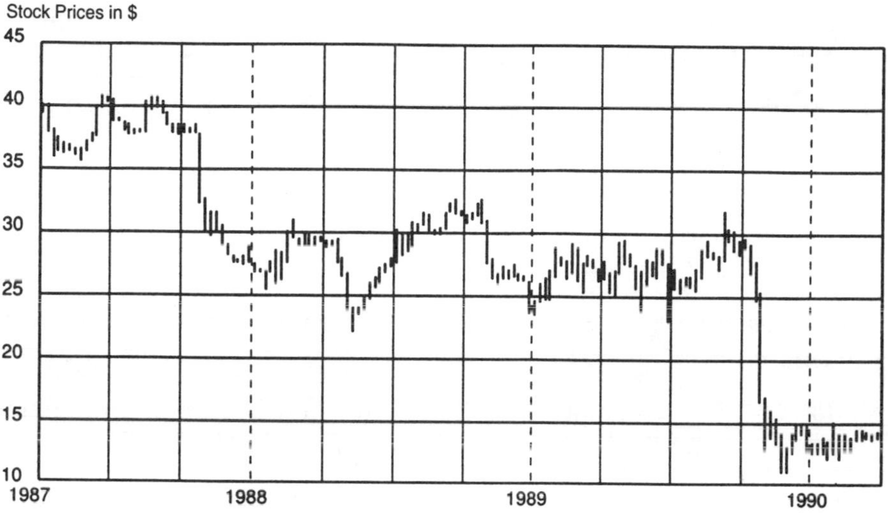

Figure 9.3 Valley National Corp., April 1, 1987–March 31, 1990

rent controversies. When no one really cares anymore, it is usually time to buy long or to at least cover shorts. In the years following the Arizona-bank downturn, shorts swarmed after the examiners as they rapped knuckles across the country in the liquidity purge of the 1990s.

Banks, with their arcane and specialized terminology, are boring to analyze, much like insurance companies. As a group, banks are perceived as sacred, inviolate, protected by the government and the many insurance programs. They are, in fact, highly leveraged corporations. When equity is only 5 percent of assets, it does not take much to nibble through the base. So banks can be profitable and predictable on both sides, particularly if stockholders or stock sellers count cranes in their own backyards to determine how frenetic the pace of real estate expansion really is relative to the perceived economic growth in town.

◆ Notes

1. AMCC Corporation, Form 10K, 31 December 1987, 4.
2. Ibid., 13.

3. Allan Sloan and John H. Taylor, "Mr. Keating, Meet Mr. Short," *Forbes*, 26 December 1988, 35-36.
4. Jonathan R. Laing, "Phoenix Descending," *Barron's*, 19 December 1988, 8.
5. Letter of the superintendent dated 20 October 1987, attached to Maniatis Group Amendment no. 13 to the Schedule 13D, Sun State Savings & Loan Association, Form 10K, 31 December 1987, 39.
6. Sun State Savings & Loan Association, press release, 25 October 1988.
7. Pat O'Brien, "Maniatis Determined to Gain Control of Sun State Saving," *The Business Journal*, 7 November 1988.
8. Sun State Savings & Loan Association, press release, 8 December 1988.
9. Ibid., 31 March 1989.
10. "Real Estate Lenders," *Grant's Interest Rate Observer*, 15 April 1988, 9.
11. "Down in the Valley," *Forbes*, 30 May 1988, 330.
12. Tom Brown, Smith Barney, 3 January 1989, n.p.
13. Ibid.
14. Sandra Flannigan, Paine Webber, 18 January 1989, n.p.
15. Tom Brown, "Valley National Corporation," Smith Barney research, 30 January 1989, 2.
16. Eliot Rosen in Roger Lowenstein, "Heard on the Street," *Wall Street Journal*, 21 February 1989, C2.
17. Valley National Corporation, press release, 26 April 1989.

10
All of the Above: Crazy Eddie

Sophisticated bubbles, Wall Street icons, and greed bring the strains of previous chapters together in a short for the all-star list—Crazy Eddie, Inc. (see also Chapter 1). First, the financials were a dream, with debt and inventories increasing steadily. Next, Wall Street hype pushed the bubble higher and higher. Finally, the level of obvious sleaze and greed was particularly gratifying to short sellers when the bubble burst. And all of it was there for the reading in the June 1986 convertible prospectus, long before the precipitous decline in the stock price began in October 1986—and not a short squeeze or buy-in in the whole saga.

An Identifiable Story Stock

In June 1986, Crazy Eddie owned 24 retail consumer electronics stores in the New York metropolitan area. The television advertisements made the company visible to every analyst and portfolio manager in the area: Even people who had not been in the store knew Crazy Eddie, the store, because of Crazy Eddie, the actor, hawking the merchandise and prices on TV. Name recognition also helped the stock price: It moved from $4.50 in the second half of 1984 to $37.50 in the second quarter of 1986. By then, 15 analysts covered the stock, and it was 41 percent institutionally owned.

The company caught the attention of the shorts primarily because of valuation. Crazy Eddie earned $0.96 per share for March 2, 1986, year-end, so the stock was trading at 39 times earnings. With approximately 15.5 million shares outstanding, the capitalization was $580 million, or $24 million per store (that is around two times revenues). Crazy Eddie rented the stores, so no underlying real estate inflated the valuation. Each store averaged $13 million a year in sales, with aftertax net of 5 percent. And this was for a company selling a highly competitive commodity product in the most competitive market in the United States. To put this in perspective, Kentucky Fried Chicken sold their stores about the same time for around $700,000 per store and 1.4 times revenues.

So the stock seemed a little overpriced, but so did many stocks in the summer of 1986. Clearly, the Street analysts were counting on growth. And that was when the prospectus began to fill in the blanks where the valuation exercise left off. First, it showed same-store sales growth of 10 percent for the quarter ended June 1, 1986—not spectacular, which meant the growth had to be coming from new stores. The financials supported the feeling that top-line revenue growth was the key to the company. Then, the reader's eye drifted to the character of the men who would direct the ambitious store-opening program.

◆ *A Private Family Bank or an Electronics Chain?*

The real pith to the Crazy Eddie story was the insiders. The prospectus was particularly rich with detail; nobody could make this one up. Where to start?

The organizational chart was made up solidly of Antars or Antars-in-law. Crazy Eddie Antar himself (yes, there was a real person named Eddie) was at the helm: 38 years old and another Sam Walton, according to his fans. Cousin Sam E. Antar was controller and was soon to become chief financial officer at 29. Brother Mitchell was executive vice president of marketing. Uncle Eddy was treasurer. Cousin Mort Gindi was vice president of store development. Another cousin, Solomon Antar, was senior vice president and general counsel. Two members of top management, however, were not Antars.

Next, Sam and Eddie Antar had sold stock worth approximately $71.5 million by the June 1986 convertible prospectus date. Cumulative six-year net income for the company was only $24.2 million. The Antars believed in being compensated for their genius; stockholders could wait for price appreciation.

The prospectus repeatedly referred to new employment contract terms for chairman of the board, president, and chief operating officer Eddie Antar to be decided at the annual meeting. He was currently paid $300,000, and an increase had been postponed until then.

The stock option plan appeared to be generous, but, again, a new plan with options for a total of 1 million shares might be approved at the upcoming annual meeting.

Crazy Eddie had a stock appreciation right (SAR) plan initiated in July 1986 in keeping with the family-directed largesse in the prospectus. The company gave the recipients cash, large amounts of it, periodically if the stock price appreciated. For example, the insiders had SARs for 264,200 options at an average price of $8.29. The stock sold for around $40. The plan gave the options holder $31.71 in cash. The market for the stock did not have to take the hit, and Securities and Exchange Commission (SEC) Form 144 was not filed. At one point, there were 605,000 options outstanding at an option price of $34; for every $1 in stock appreciation, the shareholders were billed for $605,000 in additional payment to their executives in a hit to the next quarter's earnings. A total of 2 million shares were reserved for issuance in the 1987 annual.

The Money Purchase Pension plan also contributed 25 percent of W-2 compensation for each eligible participant. This unusual fringe allowed Eddie to extricate an additional $267,001 from the company.

◆ *Does a Medical School Count as Vertical Integration?*

The "Certain Transactions" section of the prospectus was particularly entertaining, less complex than Jiffy Lube but with a reckless abandon rarely found in a Wall Street darling. First, the company leased a couple of stores from family members—not too bad. Next, Benel Distributors, a corporation owned by a brother-in-law and sister, had numerous odd dealings back and forth with Crazy Eddie, including inventory sales, leases, and joint advertising expenses.

The best section by an ample magnitude, however, was "Transactions with other related companies." Prior to the initial public offering (IPO), Crazy did business with or made loans to a number of family-owned entities, including Acousti-phase, which manufactured speakers; Disc-0-Mat, which sold prerecorded cassettes; S&M Discount, which sold unnamed home entertainment; and—the most compelling—the University of St. Lucia School of Medicine, Ltd., and Educators International. The Antar family operated its own Caribbean island medical school and a medical school recruiting company, Educators. This was right out of "Doonesbury." How could you not short a retail electronics company that operates a medical school?

In addition, prior to the May 1984 IPO, the company made interest-free loans to Eddie, Sam, and other family members; the company was unable to determine the exact amount. The company also guaranteed borrowings by Shoe Time, another Sam company, which filed for bankruptcy. Crazy Eddie had all the trappings of a personal bank for the Antar family—or, perhaps, personal mint.

Wall Street Hysteria and Home Shopping

So, why did Wall Street embrace this company with slobbering euphoria? Analysts liked the industry. It looked good. It had momentum. Videocassette recorder (VCR) sales had accelerated in 1984 and 1985, up 86 and 56 percent, respectively. TV and video were 53 percent of Crazy's sales. Wall Street straightline projected VCR growth with their collective spreadsheets. Popular wisdom said that every VCR owner would trade up; every home would own many—and would replace them frequently. Weird. Compact disk (CD) players were just hitting the stores, and, clearly, people would buy a lot of them at high prices—no competition, just blissfully high margins forever.

Analysts particularly liked the company's way of doing business, the company strategy. Prices for electronics in Crazy Eddie stores were not actually that low, comparatively speaking. Customers were supposed to bargain, to argue, to negotiate a cheap price, and Crazy Eddie would comply. But most people do not like to haggle for hard goods, so Crazy Eddie stores had a reputation for low prices without the financial burden of consistent price competitiveness. Analysts liked the feel of pulling the wool over the consumer's eyes—ironic, as events turned out, because Eddie Antar was ultimately more successful at conning smart Wall Street analysts than street-smart New Yorkers.

Drexel, Salomon, Morgan Stanley, First Manhattan, and Wertheim loved the stock. Wertheim was a particularly rabid promoter. The reports read like a Crazy Eddie TV advertisement: "We judge the results no less than outstanding, especially given the company's known conservative accounting practices. . . . Eddie Antar relishes beating earnings estimates, and we see no reason to deny him this pleasure if the company continues to perform exceptionally well."[1] Is this a stock or a fetish?

The Drexel analyst, Barry Bryant, was equally ebullient: "By 1990, we believe Crazy Eddie can achieve $1 billion in sales and be the dominant consumer electronics retailer on the Northeastern Seaboard . . . a better buying opportunity, in our view, may not appear in the future."[2] By the summer, Bryant's January report was badly outdated: He had projected annual increase of shares outstanding at 8 percent, and the company had already surpassed his five-year 1990 number with the new shares issued plus the convertible and stock options. He kept raising his earnings-per-share estimate nonetheless.

The financials became more interesting over the summer. Because Crazy Eddie was in a commodity business and aftertax margins were only 5 percent, it needed to turn inventory quickly to generate a high enough rate of return to support the stock price. However, inventory turns were dropping. Inventory was building. And the inventory accounting system was manual. Amazing! Clerks wrote tickets by hand at night, and the company figured out what the stores had, what had been sold, and what to order in a couple of days. Eddie made a point of saying computer systems cannot run a retail business. The Street analysts applauded his gutsy retail acumen.

◆ *The Plot Develops*

Eddie Antar was not content with a 39 multiple—he went for the brass ring.

Placid shorts sat with their positions like pigs in mud and waited for the stock to work back down. One Friday afternoon in late July, they were shocked off their collective Quotrons by a cattle prod; the stock started moving fast and big, the kind of move that shrieks of buy-out or cure for cancer, up five points to $40. Many phone calls and many calculator punches later (times revenue, times cash flow, times earnings), the cause was identified. Crazy Eddie Antar was going in for home shopping. He bought a transponder, whatever that is, and announced at an Atlanta trade show the wave of the electronic retail future. "Icing on the cake," the bull analysts yelped. "Gained a jump on competitors," they cried. The shorts sighed and settled in for the second home-shopping siege of the summer.

Analysts were quick to evaluate euphorically the impact of the new shopping service. The Drexel analyst, Barry Bryant, had a comment out by Monday, with a long report soon after, that moved the price target from $50 to $55, following that old analysts' adage that if the price moves, change the target and earnings estimate accordingly. He said home shopping would contribute $0.20 to earnings in 1987. He arrived at this number after serious thought: He assumed that Crazy would do "half the sales volume at half the profitability achieved by Home Shopping Network in its first six months of national broadcasting."[3] He also mentioned in his report that Crazy said the main market for the new show was 1.5 million satellite-dish owners. He neglected to point out, however, that each and every dish owner would have to buy $43.33 of merchandise a year to hit his $65 million revenue target.

The Goldman Sachs analyst, Gary Balter, was insightful enough to comment that the home-shopping announcement would primarily affect the stock price and multiple (and not the earnings) because of Wall Street's current assessment of home-shopping stocks. He did not recommend sale, however.[4]

Salomon analyst, Bruce Missett, pounded the table: "High-demand product line, powerful buying organization, strong balance sheet."[5] He got the number of shares wrong, too, and planned for well-controlled expenses, apparently not giving credence to Eddie's lust for personal wealth or the family appetite for salaries and stock options.

In September 1986, senior Wall Street retail analyst Walter Loeb at Morgan Stanley jumped on the bandwagon with a rousing purchase recommendation: "I strongly recommend purchase . . . satellite-television home-shopping network planned for introduction later this year could catapult the Firm into national prominence." New products, he continued, a bunch of new electronic products would propel sales up 35 percent a year for five years. Jewelry, too, he said; they're test marketing jewelry.[6]

Crazy was relatively quiet through the early fall. The stock split, and earnings were announced in October for the second quarter. The press release said that same-store sales were up 15 percent for the second quarter and net income was up 57 percent on a net sales increase of 41 percent. The stock traded down, although the number was on track. Analysts explained that stockholders were used to earnings above Street consensus and that the target number was below the unusually high expectations of some owners. That was the beginning.

In the middle of October 1986, Eddie Antar told institutional investors that the third quarter might be slightly lower than some Street estimates. The stock dropped 15 percent to a post-two-for-one split price of $15.25. Analysts compliantly followed the leader and lowered estimates "slightly": $0.02 for the quarter, none for the year for Barry Bryant. (Mysteriously Barry's new home-shopping-induced price target of $27.50 was back down to $25.) Nobody was too concerned, except perhaps the stockholders. Analysts collectively said that expense increases result from developing a major new business and that competition in New York creates price erosion, slowing same-store sales due to already extraordinary volume in stores. No problem! Buy now!

stock price is the opportunity of a lifetime. The shorts nodded and loaded up.

The 10Q for the second quarter, when it came out in October, showed that inventories were up 147 percent, with sales up 42 percent. General expenses were up. Interest expense was up. More important, but nobody noticed, incentive stock options and nonqualified options for 735,360 shares had been issued to management in August 1986—more shares means lower earnings per share, but nobody cared. Another odd point was that the press release said "Identical store sales increased 15 percent for the second quarter and 13 percent for the first half," but the 10Q said "5% comparable store increase" for the three-month period and 12.8 percent for the first half—strange disparity. Analysts apparently read press material, not financials.

A word is in order here about the Crazy Eddie press agent, Ed Colloton of the Colloton Group. He was the best: smooth, enthusiastic, helpful. He knew all the analysts on the Street and was always available with the latest word from Eddie Antar. He made it easy to be an analyst. Wall Street analysts just wrote down what Ed Colloton told them and did not bother with all that messy financial stuff. Then they could revel in the sales charm of Eddie Antar himself and feel comfortable that everything was okay.

Meanwhile, Bloomingdale's left the electronics market in New York—too much competition. Lafayette Radio had exited in March. Trader Horn was up for sale. "Opportunity for savvy specialists, such as Crazy Eddie," said First Manhattan.[7]

The dissonant clues continued. In November 1986, Crazy Eddie Antar sold 1.5 million shares—for tax reasons—at $13.875. In December, he gave 500,000 shares away, reducing his position to 2.9 million shares.

On December 23, 1986, Crazy Eddie, the company, announced the repurchase of 3 million shares. "Reflects the board's confidence that the stock is undervalued," said Walter Loeb at Morgan Stanley."[8] He made, however, no comment on key executive Eddie's opinion of the stock's valuation when he put his feet solidly behind his company outlook with the early December stock sale.

◆ The Big Break

On January 5, 1987, the stock dropped $1.375 on big volume, 1.3 million shares, to $9.875 (see Figure 10.1). Crazy Eddie announced after the close that same-store sales decreased 9 percent during December 1986. On January 9, the company announced that Eddie Antar had resigned, effective immediately, for personal reasons. Rumors had been circulating since December that he was terminally ill. Same-store sales for the quarter were up 5 percent, and the company would repurchase an additional 2 million shares. Earnings of $0.12, up from $0.09, were also released.

A call to helpful Ed Colloton yielded the information that he was no longer working for Crazy Eddie. Crazy Eddie was now without key player Eddie Antar and street mouthpiece Ed Colloton. Wall Street was a little concerned, but not panicky. "Hold," said Morgan Stanley. "We expect these very capable executives (Mitchell, 30, and Sam, 29, Antar) to follow diligently in the chief executive's footsteps and continue the Company's expansion."[9]

Here is where shorts made their first big mistake. Some of them

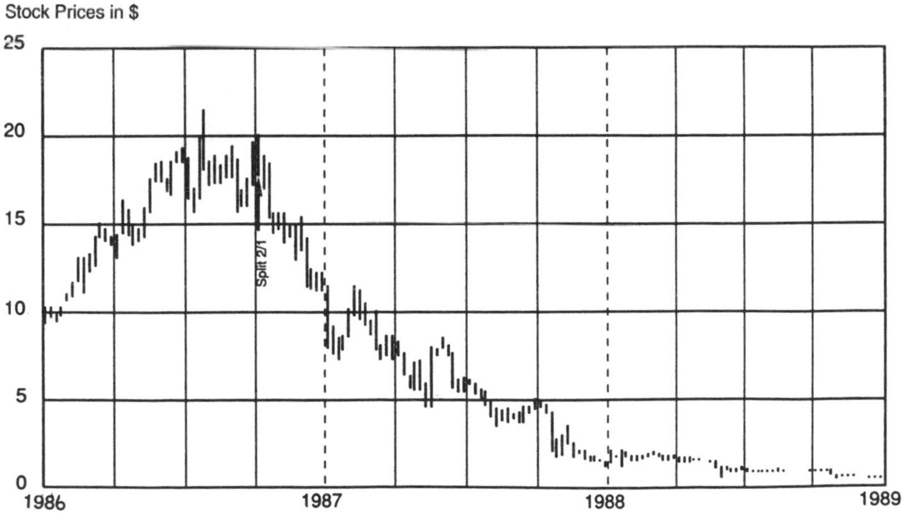

Figure 10.1 Crazy Eddie, Inc., January 1, 1986–December 31, 1989

covered positions: Short interest went from 460,686 in December 1986 to 227,720 in January 1987. Eddie had quit and sold. The 10Q was due out any day with more puzzle pieces. Evidence was mounting that the Crazy Eddie situation was much worse than previously imagined, and $20 to $10 is only half a collapse.

The 10Q came out in the middle of January. The 10Q is probably a short seller's favorite document; it tells whether the short is right or wrong, whether to cover, hold, or short more. The Crazy Eddie 10Q was a nice example. First, one of the main clues for the initial position was inventories: up 134 percent year over year (to take out seasonality), with sales for the nine months up 42 percent. To say it another way, inventory turns continued to drop—from 4.3 times last year to 2.9 times. The situation looked worse. Total debt was $178 million, with equity of $92 million. The proposed share buyback, up to 5 million shares authorized, would increase the debt further. Gross margins were down 1.6 percent from the previous quarter. The company also continued in its role as employee banker with new loans of $275,000 to employee Edmond Levy. Despite short-term investments of $100 million, $22.7 million in commercial paper (used for working capital) was outstanding, suggesting restrictions on the cash balances. Short more, the financials screamed.

Business did not get better. On March 10, 1987, the new management lineup announced that same-store sales were down 19 percent for the quarter, with sales up 22 percent—a far cry from analysts' aspirations for 50 percent-plus growth. Management offered solutions: Crazy would now sell appliances, like refrigerators, and jewelry; but best of all, Crazy would install operating systems, including point-of-sale systems. In other words, Crazy was getting a computer to track sales and inventories.

Earnings for the fourth quarter were announced on April 28, 1987—$0.02 versus $0.26, with gross margins down again, from 25.9 to 22.8 percent in a year, in a business with slim aftertax margins. The stock price continued to edge down.

In May, Eddie came back to save the day. He made a $7-a-share bid for the company, only to be topped by Elias Zinn of Entertainment Marketing with an $8 offer. Both bids were subject to a definitive agreement and other contingencies. The stock popped up over $8 on takeover talk.

In June, the SEC announced an inquiry. The 10K revealed that Chemical Bank had cut off its $52 million line of credit. The 10K also had five pages of legal proceedings that included an action filed by the New York State attorney general for selling air conditioners that did not meet state standards. It also noted that Sam the elder had resigned from the board on March 17, 1987. The company loaned Sam the younger $100,000 in May. The old family lending practices proved habit-forming.

The 1987 10K continued the encouraging trends that the shorts had uncovered in the previous year's prospectus. Eddie's salary had been doubled in September 1986 to $600,000, and he had continued to collect it, despite his resignation in January. Shareholder suits proliferated. Benel Distributors, the brother-in-law's tape distribution company that Crazy had considered buying, filed for bankruptcy.

Then in August, Eddie dropped his takeover bid after suggesting that his group might have trouble financing it. The stock traded down to $3.50, and Eddie was rumored, again, to be a recluse, seriously ill. Wall Street did not offer opinions or jump in to buy cheap stock.

In November 1987, the shorts got moral satisfaction; escalating inventories of the previous year were finally explained. New management said that they were missing $45 million in inventory. Elias Zinn, with his winning bid, took over on the first of November and closed the stores to count inventory: His audit showed $75 million rather than $126.7 million in goods. The loss grew to a $65 million shortfall, and Peat, Marwick, the auditors, were named in a complaint. (How do accountants really count inventories?)

As the financial puzzle continued to clear, the company charged that Eddie had falsified inventory and profit reports, created phantom inventory, and destroyed the records in a coverup in order "to artificially inflate the net worth of the company" and the value of the stock. (So that is why they did not have a computer system, you say.) Eddie also inflated same-store sales figures by including wholesale sales with lower margins in revenue figures.

Eddie looted the company, sold stock on insider information

(someone had to know about those bogus inventories), and took Wall Street for one big-time joy ride.

The company finally filed for bankruptcy in June 1989. Eddie was on the lam with many unhappy ex-participants trying to repatriate his winnings (alleged $60 million) from miscellaneous foreign caches. He surrendered to U.S. marshals in February 1990.

Crazy Eddie Antar taught investors that sleaze is sleaze and does not change. For those who read the proxy and the "certain transactions" section of the 10K or the prospectus and who followed the insider sales, an irrefutable profile appeared. It was not necessary to meet the man in order to understand his priorities.

◆ *Notes*

1. Robert J. Schweich, "Specialty Retailing Notes," Wertheim & Co., Inc., 9 July 1986, 1.
2. Barry Bryant, "Crazy Eddie," Drexel, Burnham, Lambert, 24 January 1986, 1.
3. Barry Bryant, "Crazy Eddie" Research Abstracts, Drexel, Burnham, Lambert, 29 July 1986, 5466.
4. Gary Balter, "Crazy Eddie," Goldman Sachs Research, 28 July 1986.
5. Bruce M. Missett, "Crazy Eddie, Inc., New Venture Adds to Company Prospects," Salomon Brothers, Inc., 5 August 1986, 1.
6. Walter F. Loeb, "Crazy Eddie," Retail Purchase Recommendation, Morgan Stanley, 18 September 1986, 1.
7. Cathleen W. Mackey, "Crazy Eddie," First Manhattan Co. Research, 24 October 1986, 3.
8. Walter F. Loeb, "Crazy Eddie" Research Comment, Morgan Stanley, 12 January 1987, 28.
9. Ibid.

Part Three

History and General Lessons

11
Shortcomings

Short sellers are a little different from most institutional managers because they spend a fair amount of time and energy analyzing their mistakes—probably because errors are terrifying and costly or because their egos make it particularly tough to admit defeat. Hindsight, by definition, is valuable when trying to understand mistakes. The short seller's post-price run-up exercise is to determine where the clues failed, why the price levitated, and why a normally accurate trail sign was misleading.

Three Short Sins

Sloth

The first and biggest reason for failure in stock selection on either the short side or the long side is *too little work*. Particularly treacherous on the short side, the absence of a carefully reasoned case can have painful consequences. Because short sellers, by their nature, cannot blame mistakes on analysts or friends or even assistants, analytical sloth is cause for the short equivalent of a hair shirt and mental flagellation.

Usually, sloth is prompted by shorting someone else's idea. If, in moments of greed for new ideas, short sellers short stocks without the normal painstaking file-building, spreadsheet-accumulating, brain-crunching work, the stocks will *always* go up quickly and scare the hell out of chastised short sellers. But they cannot admit, then, that they did not do the work, that they shorted without cause (an extreme violation of short principles, making them no better than longs). So they cover. As one hedge fund manager says, "Shorting's easy. You short a stock, watch it double, cover in panic, then wait for the inevitable bankruptcy"—like being short Texas Air or HBJ and covering when they spiked, if someone else had done the work.

Pride

The second major sin is *hubris*. Shorts have prima donna problems, like the rest of megabuck-earning Wall Street. But with investment bankers and mutual fund managers, it is other people's money. When shorts get the big head, their own pocketbooks and pride get clipped resoundingly. Short sellers normally revel in two-sided arguments; they like to be disagreed with and they generally listen. When they do not, the lapse is noteworthy. Success, of course, is the cause of the glitch. Always being right hurts in the long run.

Hubris is manifest in two primary analytical errors: (1) the sudden use of rigid formulas and (2) the short sale of good companies. The rigid-formula problem arises when short sellers start acting like Wall Street analysts and apply the same formula or spreadsheet or valuation methodology to a group of stocks without thinking. If they have seen six S&Ls go under with the same profile, it is easy to short the seventh without worry. And that is the one that will bite: Something might have changed—like the real estate environment or the government—but they quit paying attention because the formula worked before. Merabank (Pinnacle West's S&L) was a disaster, as ugly as any in Arizona. The shorts shorted Pinnacle West but underestimated the marginal stupidity of the government and its propensity to bail out anything that looked like it had anything to do with taxpayers or a regulated industry. The shorts started thinking things were rational, and Pinnacle lost them money on the positions, then made them pay again out of their taxpaying pocket. The irony was not lost.

The second hubris error is the good-company mistake. Most professionals have this one branded in fire someplace on their body; most amateurs do not realize that it is why they do not like to short stocks anymore. Both Julian Robertson and Jim Chanos identified this phenomenon as the major short error. Shorting a good company is always risky. A good company is a company with smart management who pay attention to business trends and customers and who have financial statements reflecting that unlikely blend. If the stock is sold short simply because of valuation, the market immediately shows how high the earnings multiple can go. Buy index puts, instead; a valuation short is no different than a market bet. If the stock is shorted because of perceived temporary problems and because of excessive valuation, good management can fix the problems fast.

Jim Chanos talked about shorting Federal Express. He said Federal Express was overvalued relative to earnings expectations. The company had temporary problems with both Zapmail and new competitors that were causing operating margin problems. The company told him these were solvable. "I do not know whether it was overconfidence, hubris, or what, but I did not believe them," he commented.[1] When they reported the quarter, it was a turnaround, and the stock ran up 40 percent.

Most exceptional short sellers are investors, not short-term traders. On occasion, they might make profitable trades based on temporary imbalances in the financial statements. But on the whole, even if they know the company cold, it is impossible to be prescient about the timing. When they make those bets, they do it with the knowledge that they are departing from fundamental wisdom; and, if the bet does not work quickly, it is smart to exit. Novices, fools, and retail brokers sell short for quick trades.

Timing

Timing, the third major sin, is an error of judgment for which short sellers have no solution. It is what turns a profitable and monumental bankruptcy into a 2 percent annualized return because the seller was too visionary. The timing error is another one that scares novices into permanent T-bills. Because professional short sellers earn interest on short balances, they get paid to wait; most individuals do not have the luxury. The timing problem is the single biggest argument against individuals' selling short—it throws off the risk/return relationships and suggests that individuals should use the discipline for selling or not owning stocks rather than for selling short.

The first reason for bad timing is underestimating the insanity of the public, a problem that took many short sellers out in the 1990s bull market. Optimism in the face of defeat is a custom of the country, as short sellers of Harrier, Crazy Eddie, and numerous other companies will attest. Investor ebullience can keep a stock price up for years in spite of no earnings, even no product. CopyTele is generally acknowledged to be the Rasputin of stocks. Despite the lack of product (a purported flat computer screen) and its faithful promise of appearance at every annual meeting, the stock trades routinely from $9 to $12 and back again. New drug companies never decline in price: Who knows what the outlook is, but it might be fantastic.

The second reason for the timing problem is the ability of investment bankers to sell another round of financing despite a seriously flawed corporate business plan. Continued flows of financing can keep a dead company on a respirator for years. Integrated Resources certainly outlived its corporate mission; the untimely survival was promoted by bankers and investors who bought the paper without reading the financials.

Unfortunately, in some instances, the lag time between the discovery of the fatal flaw and the demise of the company results in a change in the macroenvironment that bails out the troubled short-sale candidate. McBear mentioned Capital Cities and Fannie Mae as examples. The interest-rate turn saved Fannie Mae from bad operating results. With Capital Cities, some of the companies' other lines of revenue strengthened and saved the basic business, which was losing money.

In the same vein, some short sales fail because the seller underestimated the ability of a leveraged company to grow its way out of the problem—to grow top line faster than the debt capitalization, for example. In the 1980s, when short sellers were first titillated by the leveraged-buy-out (LBO) balance sheet, they failed to realize how long debt takes to sink a company when the business environment is good. Short sellers respond to the problem in several ways. Michael Murphy, a short seller and newsletter writer, covers automatically after a 25 percent price run-up and waits to short again. Murphy feels that if the price moves that far, something is wrong, either the timing or the analysis, and that short sellers err the same way longs do—they cut the profits and let the losses run. Other managers wait until a stock cracks to short initially, after the first drop when the earnings and price momentum have slowed. Joe DiMenna never shorts a stock with great relative strength, such as Home Shopping on the rise.

Almost every short position lasts too long for sellers. Once they solve the puzzle, they feel that everyone should. Another prescriptive to the timing error is to add to short positions fearlessly when the crack finally comes. If conviction keeps you in the stocks when they spike in the face of rumors, conviction should require additional investment when HBJ sells Shamu for too little money or when Eddie Antar sells his stock.

◆ *And a Multitude of Small Follies*

Commodity Cycles

Trade cocoa if you want to, but do not double the risk unintentionally. If a stock you are thinking of shorting is affected by commodity prices, track the underlying commodity price. If you are short a chicken stock, make sure you understand the chicken cycle, the impact of a drought or an ice storm, and corn prices. It is easier to find fundamental balance-sheet flaws than to trade grain prices, unless you work on the Chicago Board of Trade.

Sometimes, however, the presence of a large inventory of a commodity on a balance sheet can be a good clue that the company is either speculating rather than attending to business or has lost control of inventories. Jan Bell Marketing was a hot Wall Street pick at Christmas 1989: The First Boston analyst picked it as growth stock of the year and Goldman, Sachs brought it public earlier. Inventories, including raw materials inventories, rose 152 percent, with sales up only 40 percent, for the first nine months. The company management implied that the increases were due to smart buying on diamonds and gold, and the Street applauded.

A month later, Jan Bell surprised Wall Street with lost contracts and lower-than-expected sales and earnings. The business of the company was selling gold jewelry, not speculating on gold prices (with the cost of carry eating into very competitive margins). Banks that speculate on securities, stocks, or junk bonds are another example, as are utilities with real estate development. But make sure the bet is on the company, not the commodity.

Technology Stocks

Many shorts avoid technology stocks like the plague because the normal trail signs do not usually apply. Normal inventory-change ratios do not work: Technology inventories rise when a new product is in the works. Insiders own volumes of stock and sell often and without apparent regard for company condition. Receivables are strange beasts, with so many payment terms that the occasional swells do not consistently tell of collection problems. Margins can contract and expand with product cycles and the pricing curve. The anomaly of technology is certainly consistent on the long side because few analysts have consistent credibility on the stocks. Technology stocks caused major fissures in short portfolios in the 1990s: America Online, U.S. Robotics, and Iomega were all stocks that caused great pain when shorts failed to heed their own maxim of avoidance.

Squeezes

Short squeezes could be considered a market phenomenon rather than a short error, but they are, in fact, a self-inflicted wound. The float of a stock is of paramount importance for a short position. As in the case of American Continental, sometimes the return is worth the risk.

To review from Chapter 1, brokerage houses can lend out stock that is in margin accounts or available for lending from institutions who charge a fee to the brokerage house for the loan. Each short sale must be backed by the loan of stock from one of these places. If the stock is no longer available to lend, a buy-in can occur. (As Joe Feshbach says, "If you want to whine and complain about buy-ins, you're in the wrong business.")

If a company gets hostile or aggressive toward short sellers, it can do two things: Write stockholders and ask them to take stock out of margin accounts and either put it into cash accounts or have it sent to them; or ask major institutional owners not to lend their stock. Indirectly, the company can also reduce the float by buying in stock for the company or the company retirement accounts or by placing large blocks in friendly hands. Some companies also use diversionary tactics like odd cash dividends and strange new shares of preferred or Class Z stock. Or the company can employ the most vicious defense: improve revenues and earnings.

Short-slamming tactics do not work well for a company with a large float and a heavy Wall Street following. However, they are effective for small companies. The equation for the short seller is simply risk and return. If the stock has good potential for disappearing forever, short sellers can withstand the vagaries of squeeze problems for the possibility of a high return. If the company has significant but not fatal problems, most sophisticated sellers will not stay short the stock; therefore, a concerted effort to purge shorts works for those companies.

Total Systems (TSYS) is a good example. The company launched a short attack on June 29, 1988, when they sent a letter to shareholders describing abuses of naked short selling (selling a stock without borrowing it) and the consequences to the stock price. The company management thought naked short selling could be squashed if shareholders ordered out their shares:

> If there are traders holding substantial naked short positions in TSYS stock for their own account, they are interested in keeping

> the price of your stock down rather than allowing it to rise. It is also certain that the shareholders of TSYS by acting together can put a stop to this practice. If all TSYS shareholders will simply call their broker and "order out" their shares. . . .[2]

The float was small, and the institutional and large individual holders were friends of the company. Total Systems had a product, earnings, and revenues. So short sellers quietly departed on dips, despite the erroneous information in management's letter. (Naked short sellers by definition do not borrow stock, so ordering out stock does not have any effect.)

General Development was said to have attempted the same strategy in February 1990. It was a race that short sellers won by a couple of lengths when bankruptcy courts embraced General Development before the executives could squeeze the opposition.

Any history of squeezes in the 1980s includes Chase Medical as a cornerstone. The Chase started with Alan Abelson in a December 12, 1988, *Barron's* column panning the stock.[3] The company had 2.6 million shares outstanding, with less than a 1.3 million-share float. The stock price was $10, and the short interest went up to 137,852 shares in December, versus 25,319 for the prior month. A corner ensued that would have thrilled Jay Gould, classic turn-of-the-century stuff.

The stock price had doubled on huge volume since August, despite declining company prospects. Then, right before the New Year's holiday, the AMEX stopped the stock, announced that a brokerage firm had accumulated much of the float, and reopened the stock after 1 P.M. with the price down $2 on the day. The shorts who whined about stock manipulation were pleased that trading was finally going in their favor, although it was too small a stock to spark much serious short interest.

Next, the brokerage firm Moore & Shley, Cameron & Co., announced that, in fact, they had acquired more than 10 percent of shares outstanding to satisfy Reg T calls and that firm and customers combined owned 1.5 million shares. But, of the 2.6 million shares outstanding, insiders owned 1.2 million (subsequently changed to

1.3 million). Soon people noticed that 1.5 plus 1.2 equals more than 2.6.

In effect, Moore & Shley had cornered the available supply of the stock and more. Short sellers could not all have stock to borrow, so some had to cover, and the only owners were Moore & Shley and insiders who could, and presumably would, charge any price for Chase stock. Short squeeze. The stock was duly stopped again, at $13 this time, by the AMEX and the SEC, pending an investigation.

Time passed—months, in fact. Earnings came out that showed revenues of $400,000 for the quarter after a write-down with a loss of $1.47 million. The AMEX delisted the stock.

And then, on August 10, 1989, the stock started trading in the pink sheets from $4 to $6.50, and the shorts were pleased to get out alive although roughed up pretty badly. "Imagine a mugging in progress," said Floyd Norris in his September 8, 1989, column in the *New York Times*. "Just as the mugger is about to get away with the victim's wallet, the cops arrive and arrest the mugger. Then, as the victim is thinking how wonderful the police are, they hand some of the money in the wallet to the next person to walk down the street."[4] That is a short squeeze.

Buy-Outs

Buy-outs were the scourge of the 1980s short market. All short sellers, no matter how sophisticated, have felt the cattle prod of stopped-stock-with-takeover-pending announcements in their portfolios. At the beginning of the leveraged-buy-out (LBO) cyclone, sober shorts did not understand the ridiculous multiple that investment bankers would pay for an acquisition. By the middle of the cyclone, most understood the analysis better than the bankers—HBJ, Kay Jewelers, and other wins are testimony to their acumen.

The jury is still out on many of the acquisitions. Most shorts feel buy-out losses were not caused by mistakes but by deal-crazed bankers paying outrageous prices for cyclical companies with dubious earnings or assets. The process certainly tightened up methodology: LBOs were responsible for sharpened pencils on asset value and real cash flow.

Raw Fear

Short selling is the proper province of roller coaster afficionados. It works best for people who thrive on raw fear or masochism. Because most short sellers are inconsistent, even in their neurotic need for terror, most will panic at some point and cover a well-thought-out, rational position in fright. Everybody bolts sometime. Generally, it is a market phenomenon. In the late summers of 1987 and 1989, most shorts had lost hope that the market would ever be rational again. It went on forever. They just sat and waited for bankruptcies (in the summer of 1987 at least several occurred; not so in 1989).

When you cannot stand the pain anymore, buy something. It might make you feel better in the very short run. Or, even better, short more; if it scares you to death, it is probably the right move. The pain always continues for much longer than the pleasure. That is what makes short sellers different, and that is why the oldest living all-short professional seller is only 52 years old. The rest of them retired rich when they could not stand the thought of one more cycle of screaming enthusiasm and irrational, always optimistic security pricing.

Pigheadedness

If something changes, cover. It is not you against them: It is you against you.

Complexity

Many short sellers fall in love with their own analysis, particularly if it is extremely complex. If they can convince themselves that no one else understands a stock, they have closed their minds. Or if they have spent a zillion hours on a company, they feel they must have an opinion and buy or sell the stock. It is a little like reading Proust: After finishing the last volume, a reader has to like him.

Crowds

Crowds in a stock are a new phenomenon. Too many nouveau shorts are the bane of the pros' positions. Inexperience makes a stock volatile, and it scares potential buyers away when the short seller is trying to initiate a position. A bunch of scared short sellers can create more pain and aggravation for the pros than the game is worth. Like having horses in a burning barn, it is easier to deal with the crisis without all the stamping and whinnying.

◆ *And Last of All*

Direct from Joe Feshbach is the statement, "The mistake is always shorting the company that's not that bad." He used the examples of New England Critical Care, Systems Software Associates, and L. A. Gear. The analyst has to be convinced that the core business will be overwhelmed by the problem and not just hiccup. "The biggest mistakes we've made are where we've seen a company that is overstating earnings but where the internal engine of the business is still strong."[5]

Companies can manage earnings in many ways—by reducing the reserves for doubtful accounts, by booking earnings aggressively and expenses slowly, and by not writing off bad assets. All these signs are easy for a trained analyst to detect. But if the revenues grow by quantum leaps, the manipulation will continue to be only an intellectual point of interest, not a trigger for shorting. You can hide disgusting accounting practices with growth for a very long time.

Short sellers might add to Joe Feshbach's good company maxim: The greatest mistake of all was being short during the strongest and longest bull market of the century.

Notes

1. James Chanos in an interview, 4 May 1990.
2. James H. Blanchard and Richard W. Ussery, Letter to Shareholders of Total System Service, Inc., 29 June 1988, 2.
3. Alan Abelson, "Up and Down Wall Street," *Barron's*, 12 December 1988, 39.
4. Floyd Norris, "Market Place," *New York Times*, 8 September 1989, D6.
5. Joseph Feshbach in an interview, 1 June 1990.

12
History and Controversy

Short selling is as old as the commodity markets. Whenever a centralized market for goods has existed, business people have hedged their risk and speculated on prices. Short sellers usually go unnoticed until a financial disaster occurs. Then, historically, they have become newsworthy as ruined investors look for a scapegoat for their misery.

History

Holland

Short sales became common in the earliest organized markets—the Amsterdam exchanges. Around 1610, joint stock companies were created to fund new ventures, such as the Dutch East India Company, for exploration and trade in the New World. A speculative frenzy arose in the shares of that company and others like it on the Amsterdam Bourse in an early version of the South Sea Bubble. As the bubble of the market excess burst, the securities of the Dutch East India Company fell, and the directors of the company launched attacks on short sellers for causing the declines. In response to this drop in the stock price, they wrote a memorandum to the government in 1610 stating that "bear attacks, which generally assume the form of short selling, have caused and continue to cause immeasurable damage to innocent stockholders, among whom one will find many widows and orphans."[1]

The agents of the Amsterdam Bourse responded, "The decline in the price of the corporation's shares has been caused by unsatisfactory business conditions, and even prevailing levels appear too high, as a careful analysis will doubtless reveal. Furthermore, *many highly reputable stockholders would gladly surrender their shares to the directors if they could be assured of a reasonable return on their investment. If speculation were prohibited, prices would be much lower . . ..* " (emphasis mine)[2] In February 1610, the Bourse passed a law prohibiting short selling, which was subsequently disregarded and later repealed.

The Dutch failed to learn the lesson of manias, and, shortly after the incident on the Bourse, Tulipmania swept the country. The Tulip Bubble from 1634 to 1637 in Holland was a frenzy of buying and selling of future delivery of tulip bulbs. The furor gained momentum until many more bulbs were traded than existed. When the bubble burst, the courts and magistrates declared some contracts void and attempted to get buyers and sellers to negotiate their differences because no one, short or long, seemed to want to take or give delivery of the bulbs.

A tax was levied on profits from short sales in January 1689 in response to another speculative cycle. It was later repealed, but the author of the law was accused of knowing more about the corpus juris than commerce.[3]

Great Britain

The South Sea Bubble in Great Britain in 1720 saw the same phenomenon repeated. South Seas Company shares surged from 325 to 1,200 pounds sterling as eager purchasers fought for the right to own a piece of the monopoly of trade in the South Seas. The shares finally fell to 86 pounds sterling, and a political scandal followed. Short sellers were again among the many scapegoats. Sir John Barnard, a political figure and opponent of Robert Walpole, introduced a bill enacted in 1734 that voided sales where the securities where not possessed by the seller. The courts, however, said the prohibition did not apply to foreign shares or shares in companies, only to British public stocks, so the law had no teeth at the outset. It was finally repealed in 1860, although, during its tenure, it was ignored as harmful and unenforceable.[4]

A wave of speculation in securities in the London market from 1863 to 1866 resulted in a bank stock panic in Great Britain in 1866, with the failure of the discount house Overend, Gurney. Several banks also failed during the panic, and the result was universal caution and credit shrinkage.[5] The collapse was attributed initially to short sellers because it was thought that short selling bank stock and the ensuing drop in stock price caused a drop in confidence and a run on deposits. Overend, Gurney had been converted from a partnership to a corporation, and short selling of the new security was also thought to have led to a run on that institution. Leeman's Act, to prohibit short sales of bank stocks, was passed by Parliament in 1867 and was soon disregarded by both businessmen and the courts.[6] Testimony in the Royal Commission in 1878 showed that the collapse was attributable to unsound banking practices and poor asset quality, rather than to short sales.

France

France's predecessor mishap to the South Sea Bubble, the Mississippi Bubble, under the leadership of Scotsman John Law, brought criticism of short selling after the crash. A royal decree in 1724 limited transactions to exchanges at which the securities were in the possession of the seller.

In the last days of the monarchy as well as during the beginning of the Revolution, the securities markets in France were chaotic. "The readiest scapegoat, as usual, was 'speculation' and the 'short seller.'"[7] The politicians demanded regulation, erroneously assuming that changing the rules of the market would provide economic stability. When the Paris Bourse was reestablished, it forbade short selling.

Napoleon shared the prejudice against short selling because he felt it dropped the prices of government securities and, therefore, interfered with the financing of his plans for expansion. He argued with his minister of finance, Mollien, that the practice was treasonous because short sellers wished government securities to collapse.

Restrictions were lightened in 1856, and, after the French Panic of 1882, they were lifted at the recommendation of a special commission appointed by the government to study term dealings and short sales after a curb market (the Coulisse, where futures transactions were permitted) was formed to compete with the Bourse.

United States: Pre-Twentieth Century

In 1812 in the United States, the New York legislature prohibited short selling after heavy speculation in paper money and bank shares during the outbreak of war with England. The stock exchange at that time was only a curb market with the primary securities bank and insurance company stock. The volume was small, the impact of the prohibition minuscule. Panics and speculation occurred frequently, particularly in canal and railroad stocks. During the 1857-to-1859 depression, the short-selling prohibition was repealed.

The American government also attempted to restrict short selling in the Gold Speculation Act of 1864. It was repealed 15 days later after aggravating the condition it was created to fix: Gold rose from $200 to nearly $300 in two weeks when the law was in effect.

Until the Securities and Exchange Commission (SEC) was appointed watchdog and the laws were changed after the 1929 crash, lockups, stock manipulation, short squeezes, and corners were frequent features of the securities markets, despite the vigilant eye of stock exchange officials. Before 1900, stock corners were routine, particularly in railroad stocks because the resources of the players frequently dwarfed the capitalization of the stocks. A *corner* was defined as a case in which short sellers were no longer able to borrow stock and were, therefore, compelled to buy it from the creator of the corner, who owned all available stock. Overextended short interest might result in a short squeeze and a subsequent rise in stock price; a short squeeze is not a corner, however, unless the available supply is held solely by one or two entities.

In 1868, Jay Gould and Jim Fisk raised capital for the Erie Railroad with a masterful "lock-up" of currency and the manipulation of Erie Railroad stock, skills that would later assist them in the Gold Ring manoeuvre of 1869. Kenneth Ackerman's history, *The Gold Ring*, relates how the two men flooded the market with new-issue stock, ballooning the capitalization from $34 million to $57 million (after previously issuing a $20 million convertible in England without telling the public, their directors, or stockholders). Then they started selling short massive amounts of stock. They simultaneously withdrew millions of dollars from the New York banking system, already seasonally low in funds in autumn because of the outflow of money for the grain harvest in the West, to create an artificial depression and liquidity crisis. Word leaked in the press that speculators had locked up currency; interest rates moved sharply higher, and markets were chaotic, with stocks dropping until Washington stepped in to release funds. Gould and Fisk covered their Erie shorts and led a bull charge to short squeeze Daniel Drew, a compatriot who reneged on their joint pact and eventually lost $1 million on his short position. Erie moved up 50 percent in 24 hours, and the two Erie executives got authorization to buy back shares for the company at $50 from their own personal holdings, which they had bought at $35 after covering their shorts.

Their attempt to squeeze gold shorts a year later was met with abysmal defeat when President Ulysses S. Grant stepped in to flood the market and drop prices.[8]

The New York Stock Exchange (NYSE) policy on listing small companies reduced the occurrence of corners in the twentieth century. Only one corner was reported after 1900—the Stutz Motor corner of 1920. Allan Ryan cornered the supply of Stutz on the NYSE, supposedly to protect the company from short sellers. The NYSE Governing Committee asked him to rectify the situation and provide an open market on the issue. He refused, the stock was delisted, and Ryan was expelled from the exchange amid accusations that the exchange was protecting short sellers.[9]

Germany

The German experience with short selling in 1896 was one of the more telling historical examples. The Germans attempted to abolish speculative trading, and particularly short selling, in both the stock and the commodity markets during a business depression.

In 1888, a corner in coffee occurred in Hamburg, followed by an abysmal drop in sugar prices in 1889 and a break in grain prices in 1891. The failure of several Berlin banks that had been speculating with deposits was the final straw, and politicians rallied for legislation to prohibit speculation.

A commission was formed to study the excesses. It recommended regulation, rather than prohibition, of speculation; for example, brokerage houses that failed after speculating were to be criminally prosecuted. The commission's somewhat temperate recommendations failed to pacify the agrarian party, which had been battered by plummeting prices.

The Reichstag responded to the outcry by passing a law, effective January 1, 1897, that prohibited the purchase and sale of grain and flour futures, mandated a public register of all "speculators," and prohibited term dealings for mining and industrial shares.

The law was an immediate disaster. The agrarians thought that a prohibition against short sales would cause the price of grain to rise. In fact, the market was thrown into chaos when the traders physically moved from the Bourse so they could continue to carry on the futures business. No central mechanism for pricing existed, so prices were lower and less stable. Similar problems arose in the securities markets, with markets moving to the larger exchanges in London and Amsterdam, thus draining German capital flows.

The law was finally repealed in 1909 for securities and in 1911 for commodities. The German exchange was weakened as a result of the prohibition of free trade, with securities transactions moving to the Berlin banks, which have retained the power in the twentieth century.[10]

United States: Twentieth Century

The twentieth-century history of short selling in the United States is more a history of people and companies than of government intervention. Several legendary investors are rumored to have accumulated fortunes through astute short selling. Jesse Livermore, Bernard Baruch, "Sell 'Em" Ben Smith, and Joseph Kennedy were a few of the active practitioners in the early twentieth century.

Jesse Livermore

Jesse Livermore got his start shorting stocks in the early twentieth century and became known as the "King of the Bears" on Wall Street. In 1906, he is reported to have made a killing shorting Union Pacific the day before the earthquake hit San Francisco. In 1907, he sold short without mercy in a market crash until J. P. Morgan asked him to quit or accept the consequences for a market collapse. His biographer reports that Livermore stopped selling only because he knew he would not realize his profits if brokerage houses folded. He emerged with $3 million, his national reputation made.[11] He was bankrupt by 1915 but not bowed. Borrowing money to speculate, he made it back and, with the profits, set up an irrevocable trust that would be his sole support in later years. After losing repeatedly on the short side in 1923 and 1924, he exited stocks for commodities. Returning to Wall Street before the Crash of 1929, he made a couple of million but lost it all when he went long too soon. He never attained his previous success, lived off his trust and, in 1940, shot himself in a New York hotel, the day after having his picture taken at the Stork Club.

Bernard Baruch

Bernard Baruch accumulated part of his fortune through selling short—although, according to biographer James Grant, he was not significantly short during the Crash.

Baruch tells of his first notable short sale, Brooklyn Rapid Transit, in *My Own Story*. He began to follow the stock promotions of ex-governor Roswell P. Flower, who was a corporate turnaround artist with a large following of eager stock purchasers. After successfully reversing the fate of several companies (Chicago Gas and the Chicago, Rock Island and Pacific), Flower took charge of Brooklyn Rapid Transit Company; as revenues increased, so went the stock price. The governor touted the stock, said the price would go to $75, then $125, which it did—from a starting level of $20 when he took charge. Baruch watched and noticed that "the company's statements were not as clear as such statements should be. I had a hunch that something was not quite right."[12] The stock had moved to $137 when a story circulated on the exchange that the governor was ill. It was denied in the press, but by night he was dead. The stock collapsed and was supported by pools, including Morgan, the Vanderbilts, and John D. Rockefeller. When it rallied to $115, the pools stepped out, and the price again stalled and then sank for several months. Baruch shorted it at par; it never sold at that price again, and he made $60,000. In the best tradition of contemporary short selling, Baruch studied the financials, correctly identified a Wall Street hype, and waited for a trigger to take action. He said, "My confidence began to return. "[13]

The next notable Baruch-short-sale episode shows him a master of supply and demand in the commodity market. In 1901, the Amalgamated Copper Company organizers attempted to corner the copper supply, and the stock moved to $130, with talk it would continue to $150 or $200. An acquaintance of Baruch's—Herman Sielcken, a coffee merchant—thought that the high price of the commodity was suppressing demand and that the market would shortly become glutted, despite Amalgamated's attempt. Baruch shorted the stock in the face of advice from mentor Thomas Ryan, and he kept shorting as rumors circulated that insiders were also selling.

He was attacked for wicked short selling that would "tear down a constructive enterprise."[14] Baruch responded in his autobiography,

> All this was nonsense, of course. If the Amalgamated had not overcapitalized and then blown the stock up, it never would have risen to such heights or descended to the depths it afterward did. What was dropping the copper shares was the irresistible force of economic gravitation seeking its proper level . . .. In the face of these attacks, I sat silent, knowing that if I was right, I would win.[15]

The market consensus on Amalgamated was that the dividend was sound, but the directors cut it one Friday. The stock price dropped to just above $100 Saturday, and Baruch anticipated closing the short on Monday after another probable decline. His mother intervened, inviting him for Yom Kippur—which, of course, meant seclusion. Instead of covering after a two-point drop on Monday, he returned to the exchange on Tuesday to find the stock still lower. He rode it to an eventual profit of $700,000.

In 1913, Baruch assisted with a privately printed pamphlet supporting short sales, titled *Short Sales and Manipulation of Securities*, to attempt to explain the technique to hostile observers. The pamphlet was a compendium of quotations and historical incidences of short selling, with the recurrent sentiment that short selling steadied markets and prices and was a reflection of the judgment of the seller about prices rather than a dishonest manipulation.

His outspoken short politics came under fire after the panic of December 1916. Baruch and many other Wall Street operators were accused of trading on advance information about diplomatic affairs concerning American neutrality in the First World War. Republican representative William S. Bennett stated on the floor of the House that Baruch was responsible for leaking the information to Wall Street and shorting 15,000 shares of U.S. Steel in advance of the December 21 market decline. Grant's biography recounted Baruch's distress over the charges and his ensuing congressional testimony. When responding to a question on abolition of short selling, Baruch answered:

> I believe that if you had a market without short selling, that when the break comes—of course, trees do not grow to heaven overnight—and when securities go up as we see them, and when they start to fall down there might be a crash that would engulf the whole structure, and there is also this, if I may add, that the short seller is the greatest critic of the optimist, who continuously calls the attention of the man who is long on securities or the individual who might become long, of the defects, you might say, of these securities, and you might in that way keep people from buying securities at extraordinary high prices.[16]

He had, in fact, shorted U.S. Steel, but early in December; and he had covered most of it on December 20 before the market panic. He was absolved.

September 1929 found Baruch in New York shorting Radio Corporation of America. He covered the Monday before Black Thursday. On November 15, he cabled Winston Churchill, "Financial storm definitely passed."[17] Grant estimated that, by the end of 1931, Baruch's net worth had shrunk from $22 million in 1929 to $16 million. Although master of the short-sale discipline, he missed the largest move in the history of the American markets.

Joseph Kennedy

Joseph Kennedy learned about short selling and security trading in the early 1920s while working at the Boston brokerage firm Hayden, Stone. He became adept at both sides of the market, managing a famous bull pool to defend Yellow Cab from bear raiders in 1924. It was rumored when the stock dropped precipitously a few months later that Kennedy had turned and led his own bear raid. His biographer David Koskoff suggested that the size of Kennedy's fortune was too small in the 1930s for him to have been a large short seller during 1929, although the press said he sold short $15 million during the panic.[18] When Franklin D. Roosevelt later appointed him head of the new Securities and Exchange Commission (SEC), it was popularly thought to be a case of the fox guarding the chicken coop. He proved to be a serendipitous choice for constructing rules and laws because he was familiar with all phases of manipulation and market abuse.

Ben Smith

Ben Smith was tagged as one of the villains of Wall Street because of his reputed gains during the Crash. He suffered losses on his long positions in the first wave, then reversed and became an outspoken bear. At some point after November 29, 1929, he was said to have rushed into the boardroom of the brokerage house where he had an office and shouted, "Sell 'em all! They're not worth anything!"—thus, his nickname, "Sell 'em" Ben Smith.

Albert Wiggin

The most appalling example of short selling was Albert H. Wiggin, the president of Chase Bank, "the most loved banker on Wall Street."[19] Wiggin, in addition to his duties at the bank, was also on the board of 59 other corporations. The majority of his wealth came from a group of family corporations, Shermar and Murlyn, and from three Canadian corporations that he also owned. He made prodigious amounts of money trading on insider information (legal in the 1920s) in his corporations and then used a loophole in the Canadian law to avoid capital gains taxes. As Ferdinand Pecora tells it in *Wall Street under Oath*, if Shermar sold stock short, Murlyn bought the stock and loaned it to Shermar to cover. Shermar would not realize the gain because the purchase had not been made by the corporation that shorted the stock.[20]

Wiggin starting selling Chase stock short on September 19, 1929, and continued "until he covered on December 11, 1929 (using, by the way, borrowed money from the Chase to buy the stock to cover), to the tune of making $4,008,538, on which he paid no taxes."[21]

Of the stock sold short, he was reputed to have sold some to the very pool of bankers (of which he was a member) that tried to support stock prices during the Crash with organized buying. He feathered his own nest at the expense of his colleagues and his employer.

The Union Industrial Bank Crowd

The most capricious incident of short selling during the 1920s bull market came from a speculative group of bankers in Flint, Michigan, at the Union Industrial Bank. Gordon Thomas and Max Morgan-Witts retell the sequence of events in *The Day the Bubble Burst*.[22] A group of employees, two stockholders and the president's son among them, embezzled bank funds as a group to speculate on the market in the late 1920s. At their weekly meeting in the bank boardroom, they tallied individual losses and perfected new methods of hiding the ebb of bank capital. They subverted money that customers sent to be loaned in the broker call money market in New York by wiring it out, then back in the next day without booking the return. The tellers also pocketed cash at the teller windows, and the group capitalized on teamwork in a faked note scheme in which they forged the necessary paperwork for bogus loans.

Problems ballooned because they were, individually and as a group, terrible investors. They sold short in 1928 and early 1929. After egregious losses, they uniformly cried "uncle" and went long in 1929 buying Radio Corporation of America at the tail end of Michael Meehan's famous pool, bagged yet again. They had a run of successes on the long side, wiping out half their debit balance by the middle of 1929, but the tide turned again in September. By the end of October, they had lost $3.592 million, and margin calls continued until one of the group confessed to the president, who called the chairman of the board, Charles Stewart Mott. Mott replaced the stolen money from his personal account. The embezzlers were prosecuted and sentenced to short prison terms in adjoining cells, doubtless opponents of short selling for life.

◆ *Witch Hunts and Regulation*

After a panic in the financial markets, politicians and business leaders institute panels and studies to place blame for the havoc that reigns when the bubble bursts. In the past, short sellers have been censored for deleterious activity. Incidents in Amsterdam, London, France, and Germany and the U.S. House investigation in 1916 were followed by similar discussions after the 1929 Crash. J. Edward Meeker, economist to the New York Stock Exchange, addressed many of the arguments against short sellers in his 1932 book, *Short Selling*.[23]

Meeker distills the arguments against short selling into several cogent points. Short sales, the critics said, established an inflated supply and caused price declines. Bear raids generate margin calls, loan liquidation, and the sale of securities by customers who are long. Margined stock should not be lent to short sellers without the express approval of the client because it may be contrary to the owner's interests.

In his defense of short selling, Meeker states that short selling stabilizes prices when no other buyers exist, reduces the risk of manipulation, deflates bubbles, and provides liquidity.

He reviews the history of the New York Stock Exchange (NYSE) regarding short selling in this century. In the 1919–1921 bear market, there was no evidence of shorting. In the 1921–1929 market, short sellers repeatedly lost money. In 1929, the volume of short sales was small and was judged of no importance in the overall drop. Total number of shares short on the NYSE was only 0.001524 percent on November 1, 1929. In 1931, short sales were again analyzed by the exchange, and it was determined that liquidations, not short sales, were responsible for the drops and that short selling steadied prices with buying.

Investigations concerning "bear raids" (organized depression of prices caused by a great volume of share sales) were also made from 1929 to 1931 by the NYSE. The exchange could find no evidence of conspiracy by unscrupulous bear operators. They found that short sales had been made after careful study of company prospects and business conditions. Large-volume sales were frequently the result of institutions' attempts to get similar prices on pools of managed accounts. Of the 50 or 60 large-block sales investigated, only one was a short sale, and that one was entered as an order to sell by scaling up on sale execution price so that the stock was not battered by the order.

In conclusion, Meeker said that "recent governmental attempts to regulate markets have shown their uneconomic character and their extreme danger to everyone. . . . The law of supply and demand cannot be contravened by laws artificially restricting marketing methods."[24] Or, in the words of Bernard Baruch, "No law can protect a man from his own errors. The main reason why money is lost in stock speculations is not because Wall Street is dishonest, but because so many people persist in thinking that you can make money without working for it and that the stock exchange is the place were this miracle can be performed."[25]

Ferdinand Pecora, counsel for the Senate Banking and Currency Committee that investigated Wall Street after the 1929 Crash, said that the impetus for the months of testimony that led to the Securities Act of 1933, the Securities Exchange Act of 1934, and the formation of the SEC was concern over alleged market activity by short sellers. Apparently, a concerned Republican senator, Frederic C. Walcott of Connecticut, received information that short sellers were planning a series of bear raids to discredit Herbert Hoover before the election that pitted Hoover against Roosevelt.[26] The committee investigation that ensued with Pecora at its head instead revealed that the old regime had used their collective power for personal gain and public detriment. The subsequent bills outlawed double dealing, deceptions, and manipulations by insiders in favor of full disclosure. So what began as a short-seller witch hunt ended in the laws that form the base of current markets.

In 1938, the SEC adopted Rule 10a-1, under the Exchange Act of 1934, the *tick rule*, which requires short sales on exchanges to be traded on plus ticks or zero-plus ticks. Congress previously, under Section 10(a), had granted the SEC the authority to regulate short sales on the national exchanges. The thrust of the law was to prevent short sellers from causing mercuric declines and accelerating an already declining market.

In 1986, the National Association of Securities Dealers (NASD) published the Pollack Report, a study of the need for additional regulation of short sales at NASDAQ. Irving Pollack's *Short Sale Regulation of NASDAQ Securities* is the most comprehensive source of information on short selling. The study concluded that most short selling was done by professionals (traders, market makers) to provide market liquidity and that there was no evidence of widespread abuse. It noted naked shorting, however, as a potential area for concern and suggested surveillance procedures. NASD implemented all the recommended actions as a result. It adopted a short-sale rule prohibiting short sales at or below the current inside bid when that bid is below the previous bid. Market-makers, option market-makers, and warrant market-makers trading are exempt when trading is connected to market-making activity.

The Pollack Report also supported the SEC's findings that allegations of ruinous short selling were overblown. Many complaints were unfounded (short positions did not exist), and a number of the companies later showed losses or had regulatory actions taken against them. The report commented: "While each situation was unique in important respects, it became clear that a valid basis existed for short selling in most of the selected securities. Given the benefit of hindsight, heavy short selling in these securities would have surprised no one."[27]

1989 House Subcommittee Hearing on Short Selling

After the 1987 crash, panels were again formed to study how the system failed and who pushed the stock market over the cliff. Congressman Doug Barnard Jr. from Georgia chaired a House Committee to review the effects of short sellers on small companies and the need for regulation in the markets. The witness list included executives from three over-the-counter (OTC) companies, the editor of *OTC Review*, the chairman of Berkeley Securities, and representatives from NASD, the OTC Association (NAOTC), the NYSE, the AMEX, and the SEC.

Barnard stated at the beginning of the hearings that the key questions were:

1. Does the market work for new, small companies to assist them in raising capital?
2. Do the differences in the exchanges make OTC stocks more vulnerable?
3. Is the SEC doing its job in regard to these issues?

Two ancillary abusive practices were also under investigation: naked shorting and rumor-mongering.

The editor of *OTC Review*, Robert J. Flaherty, summed up the concerns of the anti-short contingency: He felt short sellers needed more regulation and disclosure. He was supported by OTC companies, Carrington Labs, American City Business Journals, and IGI, Inc., all favorites of short sellers for the occasional absence of earnings. Flaherty agreed that legitimate short selling served a positive function in the marketplace—deflating bubbles of over-optimism and stabilizing markets. His main concern was bear raids by secret networks of short sellers.

The discussion centered around three issues: (1) lack of an uptick rule on the over-the-counter markets (because it was thought that it would be largely unenforceable), (2) naked short selling, and (3) disclosure of large short positions.

The NAOTC companies president, John Guion, presented his association's survey. Of 1,000 companies surveyed, 25 answered that they had been subjected to abusive practices by short sellers, and 13 companies said short selling had been accompanied by false rumors and negative information. Guion called for disclosure of short positions in excess of 5 percent of the stock shares.

The arguments were much the same as on the Amsterdam Bourse or during the Crash in Meeker's day. The AMEX, NASDAQ, and NYSE testified that current regulations were sufficient to control reputed abuses. The AMEX representative expressed the concern that disclosure of large short positions would lead to further price declines as investors sold in tandem with shorts—besides, a short position was not exactly a "controlling position" as the spirit of a 13D would imply. NASD testified that new rules had been implemented to further reduce incidents of naked short selling.

The SEC turned in a voluminous report, again mentioning the positive attributes of short selling—market liquidity and pricing efficiency—and reviewed the history of the regulatory process. Small companies countered that short selling, bear raids, and rumor mongering inhibited capital formation for start-up companies. A Mexican standoff resulted.

Ongoing Concerns

In 1996, a trio of possible abuses by short sellers was reported. Separate incidences pointed to the same concerns that investors have voiced over the centuries.

The SEC and the U.S. Attorney's office began an investigation to determine whether short sellers acted in concert to drive down the price of Organogenesis. The focus was specifically on Evan Sturza's letter, Sturza's *Medical Investment Letter*, but has larger ramifications for media dissemination of negative information. Organogensis shareholders believe that bursts of sales and the heavy option transactions that drove down the stock price were centered around publication dates of the newsletter. The investigation focus does not concern the spread of false information but collusion in connection with price action.[28] Because the media often queries short sellers for information for stories and because the bull market has created a bull market for financial press as well, the spread and impact of negative stories is greater and quicker than it has been in the past.

The second instance, Sensormatic, points to the difficulty of legal action. Sensormatic, a high flyer of the 1980s was seemingly targeted by short sellers who, according to company reports, harassed customers with aggressive calls and spread false reports about the health hazards of the companies antitheft devices. Short sellers were outspoken about the company's accounting abuses and inventory problems that later were recognized by Sensormatic. Frequently, part of the claims of short sellers turn out to be accurate, and the burden of proof of malice is on the company. So lawsuits are rare. In this instance, Sensormatic has taken no action, although some companies sue for slander.[29]

A much broader and more troubling investigation centers on the collapse of Hanover Sterling & Company and of Adler, Coleman Clearing Corporation. Diana B. Henriques detailed the case in a *New York Times* article on April 18, 1996.[30] Hanover Securities promoted a number of penny stocks that were sold short. Hanover continued to buy the stocks, despite price pressure from selling, until it ran through its capital and collapsed. The clearing agent for Hanover, Adler Coleman, collapsed as well in a domino affect, and the trustee for the Securities Investor Protection Corporation demanded that the shorts deliver the borrowed shares by buying stock at his prices, thus denying short sellers their profits. The trustee said the shorts were part of a conspiracy. The shorts said the trustee was creating an illegal "corner" on the market. The result is a criminal investigation that might change the rules of short selling.

An investor might conclude that nothing much has changed since 1689 and the days of tulip bulb transactions.

Notes

1. Quoted in James Edward Meeker, *Short Selling* (New York: Harper and Row, 1932), 205.
2. Quoted in Meeker, 206.
3. Ibid., 207.
4. Ibid., 107.
5. Clement Juglar and Decourcy W. Thom, *A Brief History of Panics and Their Periodical Occurrence in the United States* (New York: Putnam, 1916), 4.
6. Meeker, *Short Selling*, 107.
7. Ibid., 219.
8. See Kenneth Ackerman, *The Gold Ring* (New York: Harper and Row, 1989) for details on the Erie manipulation and the attempted gold short squeeze.
9. Meeker, *Short Selling*, 188-193.

10. Ibid., 224-231.
11. Tom Shachtman, *The Day America Crashed* (New York: G. P. Putnam's, 1979), 53.
12. Bernard M. Baruch, *My Own Story* (New York: Henry Holt, 1957), 125.
13. Ibid., 126.
14. Ibid., 129.
15. Ibid.
16. U.S. Congress, House of Representatives, Committee on Rules, Investigation Relating to Alleged Divulgence of President's Note to Belligerent Powers, 64th Cong., 2d Sess., Washington, D.C., January 1917, 173:212.
17. James Grant, *Bernard M. Baruch* (New York: Simon and Schuster, 1983), 241.
18. David E. Koskoff, *Joseph P. Kennedy: A Life and Times* (Englewood Cliffs, NJ: Prentice Hall, 1974), 41.
19. Shachtman, *The Day America Crashed*, 13.
20. Ferdinand Pecora, *Wall Street under Oath* (New York: Simon and Schuster, 1939), 131-161.
21. Shachtman, *The Day America Crashed*, 167.
22. See Gordon Thomas and Max Morgan-Witts, *The Day the Bubble Burst* (New York: Doubleday & Company, 1979), for a fuller description of the Union Industrial Bank embezzlement.
23. Meeker, *Short Selling*, 4-19.
24. Ibid., 18.
25. Baruch, *My Own Story*, 264.
26. Hillel Black, *The Watchdogs of Wall Street* (New York: Arno Press, 1975), 10.
27. Irving M. Pollack, *Short-sale Regulation of NASDAQ Securities* (Washington, D.C.: The National Association of Securities Dealers, Inc., 1986), 67.

28. Laura Johannes, "Newsletter Writer Sturza," *Wall Street Journal*, 19 April 1996, C1.
29. Robert Frank, "Hostile Short-Sellers Take on Sensormatic," *Wall Street Journal*, 18 April 1996, 1.
30. Diana B. Henriques, "And They All Came Tumbling Down," *New York Times*, 18 April 1996, D1.

13
Six Pillars of Fundamental Short Selling

General methods of fundamental analysis can be gleaned from the short sellers and used to advantage by analysts, portfolio managers, and other serious observers of the stock market. The anecdotal information from previous chapters can be condensed into a more orderly framework that is applicable to any stock, short or long.

The Short Seller's Random Walk for Ideas

Short sellers get ideas from many sources. Some of the best ideas come from the most obvious places—*Barron's*, the *Wall Street Journal*, *Forbes*. Frequently, the stocks drop immediately after a negative article and then pop back up. A good *Barron's* exposé used to make a great short a year later; it took that long for the termites to eat through the supports in a bull market. *Barron's* "Phoenix Descending" article was published in December 1988, and the stocks started dropping seriously in February 1989.

One more source is the short-interest data published in the *Wall Street Journal*. Frequently, middle-sized short positions (relative to the stock float) are good stocks to look at if the stock is not an arbitrage play (a buy-out or a common stock with a convertible). For example,

Jan Bell Marketing had short interest of 576,500 shares in December 1989, with a float of 13-plus million shares and a percentage price increase for the year of 107. A look at Jan Bell's financials showed the inventories out of line and the valuation lofty. The subsequent short sale resulted in a quick profit when the stock crashed in January 1990. A short interest of 300,000 to 500,000 shares means a professional short seller has already looked at the stock and shorted it. The short interest and the stock float are important: A short seller should make sure the short interest is not so high that a short squeeze can increase the risk relative to the return. In the stock market in the early 1990s, a short position in excess of 15 percent of the float seemed to have generated buy-ins.

Another productive source is experience. If observation or business sense suggests that Wall Street might be blindsided, sellers should proceed in their analysis. Worlds of Wonder, an excellent example, was dramatically inflated from the wondrous talking bear Teddy Ruxpin in the fall of 1987. When a second product, Laser Tag, excited analysts even more, the stock price stayed at ludicrous valuations. Any toy-shopping parent could tell that the stock was a short when the stores did not have the product before the key Christmas selling season. Production was not sufficient to fuel demand for a fad product with competition intensifying. Sure enough, Laser Tag could not pull in revenues to support manufacturing costs because the product was not in the stores—a hit turned into a colossal stumble. Toy-buying parents get important advance information on magnitude and availability of fads—consistently better than Wall Street scuttlebutt.

Reading the previous chapters should convince anyone that some industries are particularly conducive to financial manipulation. Franchises (Chapter 4) have extensive potential for financial stumbles; and once one franchise is analyzed, a group of them can easily be perused. A short seller should look for types of businesses that eat money—financial services (Chapters 6, 7, 9), and real estate (Chapter 9)—or companies with complex financial statements and blind pools of investments—the financial services sector is another solid choice in this category.

Once a company is targeted, it should be analyzed with skepticism and curiosity every time a new financial document is published. Although stock analysis is frequently an untidy business, these six pillars might provide structure for an open-ended task.

◆ 1. *The Pessimist's Guide to Financial Statements*

The financial statements are always the first step for any serious student of stocks. Appearance is reality, or that is how most analysts perceive financial statements. Short sellers, on the other hand, attempt to discover what is behind the numbers, what drives the company, what the business prognosis is. The best source books on how to read financials are Leopold Bernstein's *Financial Statement Analysis*, anything written by Abraham Briloff, and Thornton O'glove's *Quality of Earnings*. These short-sale guidelines do not presume to emulate an accounting textbook, but just mark some guideposts in the search for quality.

To begin the financial quest, a short seller should call the company and ask for the last six 10Qs; the last two 10Ks, proxies, and annuals; and any 8Ks (amendments to Ks and Qs). That gives two years of quarterly data, enough to compare trends on inventories, receivables, and margins, and three years of annual numbers. After studying these documents, the short seller might need to go back farther chronologically.

Before the entrails are pulled from the cadaver, it should be dissected, then reassembled with a clearer knowledge of how the company works. Reading the financials is, therefore, a multistep process.

Quality Control

The first look at the financials is with the intent of breaking the company into tiny pieces and checking to see if all those pieces are real. Is there anything funny about the numbers? The most useful part of the financials will be, of course, the footnotes. The other consistent keys are what is not there and what cannot be understood.

One should start with the last dated balance sheet, looking for bogus assets or assets for which the market value is less than the balance-sheet value. Examples are:

- Securities not marked to market.
- Real estate at inflated values.
- Inventories with obsolete products.
- Receivables that have been booked too aggressively.
- Receivables with loss provisions too low.
- Bad loans.
- Fuzzy, unbankable assets.

For example, ICH Corp. had an asset line of $101.6 million that read "the present value of future tax benefits."

Then accounts receivable and inventories should be tested by looking at the growth in receivables and inventories versus previous year and comparing that to the growth in sales and cost of goods. If the receivable growth is substantially greater than the growth in revenues, problems with earnings will be likely (unless, of course, an acquisition has reduced the numbers to noncomparable). (See National Education in Chapter 6.) The inventory indicator—growth in inventory versus growth in cost of goods—is the single most reliable sign that a manufacturer or retail company will stumble. That financial flag urged investors to sell U. S. Surgical, Cott Corp., L. A. Gear, Snapple, Royal Appliance, American Power Conversion, and Sofamor Danek in advance of dramatic stock price collapses. (See Cott and Snapple in Chapter 5.)

A frequent area of abuse is deferred charges. A company that pushes expenses into the future can experience an earnings reversal if revenues dry up. Examples of deferred charges are prepaid advertising and deferred commissions or sales charges. L. A. Gear had the most creative use of deferred charges in the February 28, 1989, 10Q: The company added to earnings—$0.20 with deferred advertising that had not been spent yet. That is a double negative for a positive.

Another category worthy of a jaundiced eye is goodwill and other intangible costs—potential clues that a company has overpaid for an acquisition or is failing to expense drilling costs or software development. Capitalizing routine expenses is another clue that a company is manipulating earnings. Capitalizing or deferring expenses like policy manuals and start-up costs might spread them over too long a period for the benefits of those expenses. Check the footnotes for exposition and see if the company discloses the schedule for expensing the policy manuals.

Accumulated depreciation is a sleeper balance sheet line that nobody much watches. If accumulated depreciation drops when gross Property, Plant, and Equipment rises, the company might have changed the average life assumption and run the reversal through the income statement or might have simply reduced the depreciation expense in subsequent quarters (see Autotote in Chapter 6).

Next, look at the liability side of the balance sheet. Are any of the descriptions odd or unrecognizable as types of liabilities? Are any of the liabilities approximated or present valued with assumptions made by management? Check the footnotes and the notes on financial conditions to see if the company has any off-balance-sheet liabilities, any debt guarantees, or recourse-factored receivables. Is short-term debt growing? Is long-term debt up?

The quality-detecting exercise for the income statement is primarily carried out in the verbiage that explains earnings. For now, note all lines of revenues that appear to be nonrecurring:

- Sale of equipment, land, and real estate.
- Sale of securities.
- Interest on securities or cash equivalents.
- Tax credits.
- Currency gains as a reduction in cost of goods sold.
- One-time credits from manufacturers.
- Reduction in provision for Doubtful Accounts.

- One-time license agreements.
- Change in accounting.

To dig this information out, flip to the footnotes to see the assumptions that the company uses to book revenues, then read the notes explaining earnings in the current period. Make a subjective decision on what percentage of the business is stable and repeatable. If a company has had consistently real revenues and suddenly hides a gain in an unlikely place—like J. Bildner's hidden cookie gain in Chapter 4—look harder.

Do not forget that old Wall Street favorite, earnings per share. Earnings per share is an interesting test of Wall Street's viewpoint. Are earnings per share up only because there are fewer shares out? Compare using fully diluted shares outstanding, not just undiluted average shares.

Fully diluted shares outstanding is close to the toughest calculation required on financial statements, and that is why it is so frequently wrong. Take number of shares off the front of the 10Q, add in convertibles shares if they are close to conversion or likely to be converted (but add back interest expense), then try to determine how many options are close to being exercised, not to mention warrants. Add those all up for fully diluted shares outstanding.

A Bunch of Ratios

Does the company appear to be trying to show a per share trend to pander to the needs of the Street? (This is certainly not reprehensible in a savage environment for steady predictable growth in that number, but a point to be noted.) Then massage the numbers. Start with the balance sheet and look at capitalization: long-term debt to equity, total debt to total capital, long-term debt to capital. Compare several years of balance sheets to see the trend in these ratios.

Then look at the return ratios: return on equity, return on assets, and return on invested assets, which is a particularly worthwhile calculation. Income before interest and taxes *divided by* equity *plus* all interest-paying debt gives several useful types of data. When calculated for a sequence of years, it tells the trend and volatility of returns over time. It also tells, by comparison, what the company does relative to other companies in the same industry and whether a company earns more than its average and marginal cost of debt, currently and historically.

Keep track of valuation ratios. If the stock runs up, it is nice to have immediate access to numbers that quantify insanity. *Price to earnings, price to book, price to revenue,* and *price to cash flow* are the four key indicators. If a takeover occurs in a similar company, these ratios let the analyst calculate quick comparables. Valuations ratios are relative to specific industries, however. Price to revenue is higher for retail than for manufacturing. Price to earnings reflects growth potential. Price to cash flow is a buy-out indicator.

A minimum list of ratios should include the following:

Checklist of Ratios

Capital Structure	*Return Ratios*	*Valuation Ratios*
Long-term debt to equity	Return on equity	Price to earnings
Total debt to total capital	Return on assets	Price to revenues
Total debt to equity	Return on invested assets	Price to book
		Price to operating cash flow

Then go to the income statement to common size the statement: Put everything in percentage of revenues to see if the percentage relationships are changing. Is research and development or advertising declining as a percentage of revenue? If so, is the company deferring or not spending to the detriment of later business? Compare the anomalies to the balance sheet. If sales, general, and administrative (S, G, and A) is declining as a percent, are prepaid expenses or other assets rising? Is depreciation flat while fixed assets increase? Compare pretax operating profits. What is the sequential trend, as well as the annual one? Does it make sense for the business? Look for deviations and trends.

Cash Flow Is King

The Statements of Cash Flow are always the toughest of financial documents. It is frequently difficult to determine what is a *necessary* cost from a business point of view. Each company is different. The Financial Accounting Standards Board Statement no. 95 changed the way companies report cash flow in July 1988. The three-part presentation of operating, investing, and financing flows has made the task easier. The quickest check is a look at the "Cash Flows from Financing" section. Does the company have to go to the markets repeatedly to keep afloat? Are short term and long-term debt ever-escalating? Is there a stock or convertible issue every year?

The next step for the Statements of Cash Flow is a back-of-the-envelope calculation on what the company actually spends (or takes in) to do business. Generally that calculation is some derivation of net income *plus* depreciation, amortization, and deferred taxes *minus* nonrecurring items (tax-adjusted, if possible) *plus or minus* changes in current assets (without cash, but broken out by lines to see what specifics are causing cash drain) *plus or minus* changes in other items perceived to be relevant (like some portion of capital expenditures).

That calculation edits the Statements of Cash Flow by adjusting the "Cash Flow from Operations" section. Make sure operating income is adjusted by what you see as nonrecurring. What has the company put in the "investing" section that is a necessary expense of doing business, like buying property for a real estate company or programming expense for a media production company? Adjust for free cash flow by subtracting necessary capital expenditures (if the company tells you; if not, guess) and dividends. Is that number positive or negative? Look at the Statements of Cash Flow versus previous years (then quarter by quarter, if necessary) to see if an expansion plan has made for a one-year anomaly or if the trend is appreciably worse. If it is a cyclical business, is the balance sheet strong enough to support needed cash infusions when operating flows dry up? Is the company in a financial position to meet the debt repayment schedule if the financing environment gets hostile to refinancing? Be sure to check PIKs (payment in kind), zero-coupon bonds, and other odd-ball instruments.

Reading the Sleep-Inducing Verbiage

Now for the hard part. The first financial run-through was simply a test of your accounting skills and your ability to follow the footnote trail and to understand accounting jargon. Read the 10K description of the business and the competition. See if you understand the financials in relation to that business plan.

Try to determine what drives the company, what the two or three most relevant numbers are. What is the most important number to watch to identify a developing problem? If it is a low-margin business, the key is probably revenues and inventory-turnover ratios. If it is a franchisor, it might be system sales or same-store sales. Does the financial structure make sense for the business? (Do not leverage a cyclical company too much, do not build inventories too high if there is potential product obsolescence.)

Think About It

Try to see the three financial statements (the balance sheet, the income statement, and the statements of cash flow) as a 3-D chess game to judge how they interact and to see what tugs and pulls on what.

Determining the key variables in the health of the company is the most complex part of analysis. That ability is almost a gift, not a learned skill. The people who do it easily have great success on the long side, as well as the short, because it gives them x-ray vision to see developing trends in a company using only the financial statements.

Backup and track the Qs and Ks over time in order—first to last—to see if anything changes for better or worse.

After that, read the Annual and see if what the officers say matches what you saw. Give it the buzz-word test. Every company communicates its vision of itself in recurring use of certain phrases: *Synergism* is a popular one for companies viewed by the Street as confusing. Literally count the pictures of babies: Too many babies in a drilling or defense company annual report suggests that executives either do not know their business or are trying to imply that the company sells something they do not own. (California Energy had its fair share of babies one year.) Watch for auditor turnover. It is the one signal that is truly indicative of trouble.

Think about what is not there, what you did not understand. Some popular items that are often *not* included are:

- Description of nonrecurring revenues.
- Information on explicit valuation procedures of odd assets.
- Clear disclosure of revenue-booking procedures.
- Composition of fuzzy liabilities.
- Breakout of blind-pool assets (like loans).
- Comprehensible breakout of divisions: revenues, income, assets.
- Description of effect of an acquisition on inventories and receivables.

The hardest part is determining what the relevant piece of information is—what runs or ruins the business. Experience as businessperson helps more than analyst acumen.

2. *In Search of Greed and Sleaze*

The second step is easy and fun. It gives short sellers confidence in their financial analysis. It is also the step most frequently omitted by Wall Street.

Useful Data

The Securities and Exchange Commission (SEC) requires companies to release all sorts of data about management and large stockholders. Among the most useful are:

- *Form 144.* Key officers are required to file a Form 144 with the SEC when they place a sell order for their company stock with a broker—in other words, on or before the date of sale of stock. Some insider sales are reported in *Barron's* and the *Wall Street Journal*. Several services, including *Vickers* and the *Insider's Report,* also publish the list.
- *Form 4.* Officers must also file a Form 4, which lists purchases and sales of stock 10 days after the last day of the month in which positions were increased or decreased. Form 4s lag the action by too much to be of use to a careful observer. They are, however, the only purchase-and-sale source, besides the proxy of management purchases.
- *13-D.* Any entity that buys a controlling position in a stock, 5 percent or more, must file a 13-D with the SEC within 10 days. These positions are usually publicized in the news, *Barron's, Vickers,* and the *Insider Report,* as well as in the proxy.
- *Proxies.* Each year, a company must file a proxy statement (the best of all data sources) with the SEC. The annual meeting is the trigger for publication. The purpose of the proxy is to tell stockholders what they may vote on at the meeting. It also reveals how much stock is owned by management, what their salaries and employment contracts are (including options, bonuses, and some perks), and the stockholders who own over 5 percent. The proxy tells who the accountants are, what the pending lawsuits are, and what other relationships and related transactions are pertinent. It is also one of the best sources of information about management philosophy.

Many money managers allow outside services to read proxies for their position stocks. These services vote the proxy issues for the manager, supposedly saving valuable time for portfolio managers. Shorts consider this an appalling custom: Would you let a person who does not know that management earns 30 percent of company net income vote a proxy for you? They view it as one more indication that institutional investors do not know which facts are important and where to find them.

Management contracts have become incredibly creative in recent years. Read the proxies in search of greed in corporate America. A lot of the finer details are not delineated in the SEC filings, but you get the flavor in the notes on "certain transactions."

Benchmark Proxies: Pantheon of Stars or Pigs at the Trough?

Southmark, a company resplendent in multiple companies and affiliates, mirrored its corporate confusion with the toughest proxy to date. It is impossible to quantify the benefits absorbed by the key players, but there are a lot of them.

Following are a few disclosures from the January 1988 proxy: Gene Phillips, chairman of the board, president, and director, was also director or chairman of the board of 11 other Southmark-affiliated companies. He had stock options on three of them, use of the company aircraft, and $860,608 in cash compensation. Phillips and William Friedman, vice chairman of the board, owned or controlled 23.45 percent of Southmark, as well as stock in most of the related companies. They pledged their Syntek Investment Properties shares and Syntek West shares to Southmark as security on loans of $8.5 million and a $1.5 million line of credit. The board authorized the loans so Phillips and Friedman would be able to meet any margin calls resulting from recent declines in the market price of the stock. The board felt that stock sales would depress the stock price and "distract" the sensitive execs.

Southmark loaned a lot of money to officers and officer partnerships: One loan in particular, to James Gilley, executive vice president, was nonrecourse, secured by the Southmark stock purchased with the proceeds. It collected interest at a rate equal to the rate of dividend payments of the stock that secured the loan—a pretty good deal, if the stock were worth anything.

Partnerships were extremely creative: 1601 Partners, for example, had 190 officers and employees of Southmark as limited partners for only a nominal contribution. Phillips and Friedman were the general partners. Southmark was generous enough to loan 1601 $13.8 million unsecured. As of June 30, 1987, $1 million in interest had accrued and no interest had been paid; Southmark wisely discontinued accruing interest for financial purposes. Phillips had taxable losses on his partnership interests in 1985 and 1986 of $1.22 million.

The proxy goes on and on with similar loans and partnerships and transactions. No one who read the proxy could have escaped the point. In a partial denouement, on April 19, 1990, the creditors' committee of Southmark asked a federal judge to allow it to sue the company's former top two executives to recover more than $83 million in assets.

L. A. Gear and **Bally Manufacturing** get the honors for one of the highest ratios of salary plus bonus to net income. In fiscal 1989, the two top fashion sports shoe kings at L. A. Gear made a combined $10.6 million, with company net income of $55.059 million. Presumably the stockholders did not care because the stock price went up 185 percent.

Bally stockholders were not quite as complacent in 1989. The Bally boys did not own much stock (3.2 percent in 1988, up to 4.1 percent in 1989, thanks to the generous incentive plan), but they paid themselves pretty well, relative to what stockholders have made in net income and stock-price appreciation. Cash compensation was $10 million total for the top 10 in 1989, with net income to common shareholders of $9.4 million. Richard Gillman, president of Bally's Park Place, Inc., got cash of $4 million. Donahue Wildman, president and CEO of Bally's Health got cash compensation in 1989 of $1.925 million. The stock price went from $22.125 to $15.125 in 1989, with earnings per share going from $1.12 to $0.35.

Pinnacle West's chairman of the board, Keith Turley, led the company into a major real estate expansion in Arizona at the top of the market. The company paid him $601,694 in 1988 (plus $530,962 in his later retirement) to take earnings from $233 million in 1986 to $4 million in 1988. He capped that record with a net loss of $551 million in 1989 and slashed the dividend, after giving one of the acquired subs, Merabank, to the taxpayers to bail out, despite its purchase by Pinnacle West under a "keep-well" agreement. One member of the Arizona Corporations Commission publicly termed Turley "a bozo." Some shareholders (Turley only owned 18,600 shares himself) might agree.

National Education had the most attractive severance package. Based on salary/bonus levels at the time of his departure, David Bright, chairman of the board and CEO, would have received severance payment of approximately $7.37 million. Alas, the departing officer is currently in litigation with the company over realization of his lovely parachute.

Medco Containment's Martin Wygod had the most creative bonus arrangement—his package included finder's fees and corporate finance fees. He received 1 percent of the consideration paid to the company for the sale of the company or any sub, or any piece of the business or the assets through merger, sale of assets, tender, sale of majority interest in the company, or liquidation. Just to cover all contingencies, he also got 1 percent of the number of shares or rights to purchase shares offered or distributed for shares of the stock in subs. What a great incentive to form and reform the company! Wygod received deferred compensation of $3.893 million on the consummation of the merger of Medco and Porex, which was not payable until termination of his employment, death, disability, or change in position. That payment was accelerated and received in 1989. No one should have been surprised when Marty sold Medco to Merck in the 1990s.

The year 1995 was one of excess for executive packages—largesse came in the straightforward form of option grants, salary, and bonus. **AT&T** paid chairman Robert E. Allen megabucks in 1995 after a lackluster year of company earnings. He got $5.2 million plus options worth almost $11 million.

Crazy Eddie and **Integrated Resources** share this author's regard as all-time favorites for scope and creativity of corporate perks. Chapters 7 and 10 detail the benefits for the Zises and Antars. The really big chunks of cash for both families came from sale of stock: Many shareholders were not as astute in their market timing.

The rule of thumb when you study a proxy is that if you have to read it three times, you have struck pay dirt. Try to determine if the company is run for the executives or the stockholders. (When the company is run for the stockholders, the executives are compensated with more stock options, not immediately convertible into cash, less salary, and fewer benefits.)

Checklist of Proxy Questions

Review the following questions when studying proxies.

Cash Compensation

1. Are executives paid exorbitant salaries? Look at cash compensation relative to company earnings.
2. Does the company pay big bonuses? What for? Is the bonus tied to extraordinary efforts, or is it just for doing the job? Is the bonus for increased sales, return on equity, or some other measure or combination of measures? (One biotech firm bonus was based on the success of a public stock offering.)
3. Does the company pay a percentage of pretax profits to the primary officers in the form of bonuses? Are they paid a percentage of revenues? Some bonuses are calculated on stock price appreciation.

Stock Options

4. Stock grants *versus* Stock options *versus* Stock Appreciation Rights (SARs)—SARs are the most generous for the executives, followed by grants. SARs give the grantee cash money, bankable immediately, with no stock-price suspense.
5. Does the company in any way pay for stock options?
6. Does the company pay a bonus for taxes on options?
7. Do the officers get any special deals if there is a stock/rights offering of company or a sub's stock?

8. What is the percentage of stock owned by the primary officers?

Parachutes

9. Does the company have an unusual severance pay contract, especially in case of merger or buy-out?
10. What are the terms of retirement contracts?
11. Are there extra perks such as large insurance policies, apartments, automobile use, plane use?

"Certain Transactions"—Arm's Length, No Doubt

12. Does the company permit the primary officers to engage in other activities, such as owning other businesses associated with the company? Does the company give favorable terms to the officers or give favorable contracts to businesses owned by officers?
13. Are many of the officers related to each other?
14. Does the company deal with any relatives of officers?
15. Does the company frequently loan money to the officers? If so, does the company charge interest?
16. If the company engages in limited partnerships, does it pay for the officers to become general partners or limited partners, or does it grant them bonuses for participation in partnerships (or just give them the tax losses)?

Miscellaneous

17. Are there a lot of lawsuits, and what is the liability?
18. What is the age range of the primary officers—all old or all young?

19. Who else owns the stock?
20. Check the board biographies. Is it a rubber-stamp, "good ol' boy" board or a working group? How independent is the board? (Quaker Oats pays board members $1,000 for each action taken by unanimous written consent.)

Some industries—entertainment and brokerage, for example—have higher salary/bonus plans. Even if the industry standards are relatively high, see if executives get bonuses for doing what they are paid to do before stockholders get paid. See what the top employees' total packages are relative to net income.

Stock ownership is a great incentive, but cash payment disguised as stock ownership does the shareholders no favor. Option plans can be so generous and expensive that stockholders get diluted and deluded through their own largesse. Stockholders approve the number of shares set aside, and the board sets the terms, vesting requirements, and payment conditions.

Proxies also tell you which executives have disappeared if you compare several years of documents. Sometimes, attrition is not well published, except by default.

One more word on proxies: Of late, a bit of a hubbub has been raised about institutions not reading and voting proxies. In particular, the Labor Department appears to be concerned about dereliction of duty regarding ERISA accounts and proxies—fiduciary responsibilities. A survey by the Labor Department found that 39 percent of the investment managers did not vote proxies and did not know who did. Corporate clients appeared to be equally fuzzy about assigning responsibility, but some executives are retaining the authority for themselves. Perhaps they should hire short sellers to read them!

◆ 3. *The Bigger Puzzle*

The third step is divided into two parts: research and store checks. The research segment starts in the library, whereas the store-check segment ends up watching the marketplace.

Research

Review the industry and the company's competitors and clients. The 10K should give you a good preview of how the company fits into its industry and the names of competitors, customers, and suppliers.

Start with the big picture and check the library and *Value Line* for industry information. Most public libraries have a copy of the *Standard & Poor's Industry Surveys* to synopsize industry fundamentals. Next, see what trade publications are available and if a government office tracks data. Several services, like Washington Researchers, provide comprehensive information gathering on any topic.

Masses of industry data are available, even without use of computer on-line searching facilities. For example, the *Poultry Times*, the U.S. Department of Agriculture economists, and state agriculture departments in poultry-producing states all supply volumes of information on chicken prices, including a hot line of daily trading data and projections of supply and demand.

Other publicly traded companies' financial statements can also provide a lot of data, so discover who else is in the business. Reading competitors' financials to compare margins, return on invested assets, growth rates, and inventory and receivable turns can give an analyst an idea of who is out of line and what looks different.

Store Checks

Back in the first step (Financial Statements), you decided what the business of the company was and what the trigger numbers were. Use that information for checking in the marketplace. If the key is store volume, visit a store and count customers, check average ticket size, talk to the store manager. If it is a hot new company with a to-die-for product, see if competitors have heard of the product yet. If it is an oil-change franchise, count cars at peak hours to see if franchisees are hitting break-even assumptions.

Do not base a conclusion on store checks alone; frequently one store or geographical area can be an outlyer in volume. Observing does give, however, the flavor of the business plan's execution.

◆ 4. *Who Owns It?*

The fourth step is following the trading patterns, volume in particular. Track the percentage of institutional ownership. (*Vickers On-Line Service* and *Spectrum* compile quarterly numbers and names of holders.) High institutional ownership and high Wall Street coverage can make for a quick collapse if something unexpected happens. Always follow the short-sale numbers to tell you when a squeeze might develop so that the relative impact on the portfolio can be monitored. Watch option volume and relative pricing to note takeover speculation. Continue to pay attention to 13Ds and 144s.

◆ 5. *Check the Water Temperature*

The fifth step is to accumulate any brokerage reports to provide the company-think and Wall Street's attitude. Sometimes brokerage reports will supply pertinent industry data. Frequently, the company will send you brokerage reports with the financial statements, if you ask (particularly if they are favorable, which they are bound to be).

As you read Wall Street reports, remember the job description of analysts: They are not paid to make waves or to disagree or to be on the cutting edge of stock analysis. Analysts are relative: They are supposed to do a little better than their peers and charm the institutional clients who vote on the *Institutional Investor* all-star list. The problem is that some misinformed clients expect analysts to read the financials, even if their bosses do not. Use analysts for indications of Street-think and as conduits of management information. It is not good guys versus bad guys, shorts versus analysts; the point is how effectively you use the information presented to you.

Check the library periodical indexes for all past media references to the company and ancillary topics—*Forbes* and *Barron's* do good, strong, analytical fact-finding. Nobody fires them if they make waves. Many indexes carry only two or three years of references, but make sure you have at least five because ancient history is relevant to corporate hanky panky or to the firm's cultural tradition of hanky panky.

6. *Pay Attention*

The sixth step is to keep paying attention: If you decide not to short a stock after the preliminary analysis, it might be a great idea next year. If you do short it now, watch it. Events move so slowly in the financial world that it is hard to maintain concentration.

First watch for earnings releases. Note when they are expected to be published and what Street expectations are. The date of the earnings release is also statistically relevant: The later they are, the worse the numbers. Many companies will fax the PR release, together with the income statement and balance sheet. Quick information is important. If it is a large, Street-covered stock, small investors are at a disadvantage because Street analysts get the faxes and phone calls first, little players sometimes not until days later.

Next, know when financials are expected out. The 10Qs and 10Ks are read slowly by Wall Street, so quick attention can yield important data—little players can make up for the delay on receipt of earnings-release information. Waiting for new financials is like waiting for Christmas. It is fun to see if you were right and how things are developing. Go first to the key numbers, then the cash flow statement, and finally the verbiage. Read the Qs carefully.

Keep watching—once a potential target, always a possibility. If you know a company well, you might recognize a trigger, like the Zises' selling their Integrated stock, or HBJ selling Shamu, or J. Bildner's closing stores or running over expected costs and out of money.

Do not be surly about admitting defeat. If you shorted the stock because the inventories were too high and the 10Q shows the company has corrected the problem, cover—NOW.

Do not cover just because of price movements; wait until the resolution of the scenario. If Integrated looks like death, wait till it is buried.

Short selling can be much like a cat waiting outside a mouse hole—the level of persistence, patience, and attentiveness is not for everyone, especially over sustained periods of time.

Concept Recap

The short sellers' credo can be summarized into several points:

1. Dissent is Okay.
2. The facts are somewhere, free for the digging.
3. Hard work is outmoded, so if you do a little, you will be far ahead. Analysts look at company PR rather than fundamentals and financials, and that provides opportunities and longer periods of market inefficiencies.
4. Computers confuse and build false confidence in portfolio managers, and that also provides opportunities.
5. Some accountants sanction almost everything, and that helps a lot, too.
6. Finally, Wall Street ices the inefficient cake with compulsive conformity. Everyone gets on the bandwagon and stays until the evidence is too compelling, then they all fall off with a jolt.

Conclusion

The key points to remember about selling, short selling, or simply not buying are several:

- Never assume that the same paradigm applies to all stocks. Each company and industry is different, so it is dumb to measure by the same scale if the yardstick is not relevant. If a company owns land at 1932 prices, do not worry about earnings or price/earnings. Think about the business and decide what the market wants you to pay for (cash flow, assets, earnings). Then, after thoughtful consideration of the prospects, value the company according to your own analysis.

- Do not genuflect in front of a business, an executive, or an analyst. Keep your distance and your objectivity. The stock market is about people disagreeing over stock prices. Short sellers are entitled to their opinions, as are executives and analysts. And so are you. Do not take it seriously; it is only money.
- A short seller is a skeptic with a constructive, optimistic bent. If you are appalled when an executive lies about earnings prospects, do not just sell the stock, consider shorting it.
- When the short interest peaks at a staggering percentage of total volume and the lemmings embrace pessimism, remember that the stories of short-sale candidates are lessons in the antithesis of good company characteristics. Buying low and selling high is the game, no matter what the order of the transaction.

Appendix

Margin Accounts and Short Selling

Short sellers of common stocks borrow stock from a brokerage house to sell in the organized markets. They are borrowing property, not money, and can short only through a margined account.

When a customer opens a margin account, an agreement must be signed. That form states that the customer is hypothecating (pledging) securities as collateral for a margin loan. Stocks deposited into a margin account are put into Street or nominee name, not client name. The broker can then rehypothecate a customer's securities, up to 140 percent of the debit balance, as collateral for further borrowings.

The current Federal Reserve requirement (Reg T, as it is known in the industry) is at 50 percent, meaning that a customer must initially put up 50 percent of the short-sale price in cash or 100 percent in fully paid securities.

For a short sale, the broker obtains the to-be-borrowed stock from one of two places: from other customer margin accounts (if there are sufficient hypothecated shares) or from another broker dealer.

After the customer makes the short sale, the brokerage house marks the position to market: that is to say, the broker uses the closing security prices to compute a gain or loss. The account is then credited or debited for the price change. Usually, this is done on a weekly basis, but if the market begins to fluctuate actively, mark to markets are figured daily. Since the turmoil of late 1987, some brokers have begun marking to market daily regardless of trading activity.

If the price has moved above the original value, the short seller is required by the brokerage house to put up more collateral. Using the example in Table 1.1 (page 15), if the price of the stock rises to $12,000, the equity would then be $3,000, and the account becomes restricted (technically, any account under the 50 percent equity level is considered restricted). Although the New York Stock Exchange (NYSE) requires a minimum maintenance level of 30 percent, most brokers issue maintenance calls when an account goes below the 35 percent equity level. In this example, the equity is now at only 25 percent. To comply with NYSE regulations, the short seller would need to deposit an additional $600, or an additional $1,200 in securities, to bring the account up to the 35 percent level. Unlike Reg T calls, which must be paid for within seven days, maintenance calls are due immediately. Most carry a deadline of 48 hours.

The NYSE and National Association of Securities Dealers (NASD) also have a set of special maintenance rules for "cheap stocks": Stocks selling between $0 and $2.50 require minimum equity of $2.50 per share; those selling between $2.50 and $5 require 100 percent of per-share value; and those selling above $5 require $5 per share or 30 percent of per-share value, whichever is greater.

If the price moves down, the seller has use of the excess funds. Using the preceding example, if the stock falls to $80, the $2,000 excess can be used for other shorts or purchases or can be deposited in a money market account.

Index